Frank the Pilot

Amazing revelations of what a professional pilot sees, thinks and feels

By
Frank J. Donohue

Not-Y, Virginia Beach

Frank does an amazing job of placing the reader, pilot or non-pilot, right there in the captain's seat. As a professional pilot, when I read Frank's book, I began to feel the increased heart rate and sweaty palms each time he describes a scenario. Great book and thank you for so perfectly telling these stories about "flying the line."

—Robert Fogelsanger, FedEx B-777 First Officer, CFI/II

I always enjoyed most when Frank built up suspense—would he pass the test, would he land safely? Were the wheels really down? Perhaps the most gut-wrenching scenes were when he was landing in inclement weather. However, I actually enjoyed all of it, even the non-dramatic moments. For some reason, I was really caught up in the conversation between the plane and the tower. It was as if someone was pulling the curtain back and exposing the Wizard of Oz.

—Steven W Rodgers,
"Revolutionary Gentleman," rock opera, Washington, D.C., Writer, Composer, Lyricist

To us aviators, **Frank the Pilot** *speaks our language. To the general public, it gracefully translates the aviation lingo into an idiom which not only makes you understand the world of flying, but also helps you comprehend the reasoning behind pilots' decisions. People often see the glamorous image of a pilot, depicted in a Hollywoodish way.* **Frank the Pilot** *goes above and beyond the surface and reveals how much scrutiny and hard work pilots have to go through, so that they can fly you, your loved ones, and your packages. If you ever asked yourself, "What does it take to become a professional pilot," or even if you are starting your career in aviation,* **Frank the Pilot** *welcomes you into the cockpit, like in the good ole days. A marvelous book for everyone who ever looked up to the skies and wondered why.*

—Captain Joey Uliana, Pilot, Aviation Safety Officer, Author

Read **Frank the Pilot** *for the love of flying. New and aspiring pilots will enjoy the excitement and thrills and learn from the "experience" of the writer. This is a how-to guide to a career in flying outside of the military. As you read* **Frank the Pilot***, you will learn from the experiences of* others—one of the greatest teaching tools for pilots of all ages. As a former military pilot, airline pilot, and current charter pilot, I have learned you won't live long enough to make all the mistakes yourself, or survive them; so, the best way to avoid mistakes, or know how to handle them when you get there, is to learn from others. Frank Donohue provides critical learning in a fun and enjoyable format. Pilots and non-pilots will enjoy the humor, thrill, and excitement of his phenomenal career. Frank provides a great look at a life of flying—from the high notes to the low times, but always with the love of flying all pilots share. Pilots will see themselves in many of the same situations, while young aspiring pilots will dream these stories. Every reader will enjoy the thrill.

—Bob Harvey, Colonel, USAF (retired) F-16 Squadron Commander, Airbus320 Captain, Author

Thirty-six years.

From the moment Frank started his very first flight, he knew it would be a wild ride. Almost four decades later, he experienced more than most commercial pilots ever would. This book is his story, a way to share with readers what it was like flying some of the world's most advanced aviation machinery, but it didn't all go to plan.

Whether it was a thunderstorm, mechanical malfunction, plane crash, smoke in the cockpit, landing gear issues, or even a sleeping incident, Frank had to learn how to navigate these and many other situations that crisscrossed his professional career.

Join Frank as he starts, endures, overcomes, and exits his flying adventures, learning many lessons that can be applied to anyone's life to see things through when turbulence rocks their otherwise calm flight path.

Start reading **Frank the Pilot***, and discover your next favorite memoir.*

—Ryan Luz's Blurb, Author of multiple fantasy novels

It started with a love for travel and became the adventure of a lifetime.

Frank spent his youth marveling in everything from bikes to boats, anything that could get him where he needed to go. Eventually his eyes turned skyward and the first dream of being a pilot entered his head.

From there it was full speed ahead. Frank joins the Air Force and, while in England, takes his first flying lesson and becomes hooked.

Frank's adventures in flying are detailed with such passion and energy from his first solo flight to his very last takeoff and landing. At times harrowing, others relaxing, Frank soars above the earth in a decades spanning career that sees him in emergencies, bad weather, bad passengers, and behind the stick of the world's largest plane.

The wear and tear of being a professional pilot draw readers in and never let go. Frank the Pilot is the true story of how one man lived his dreams and took advantage of every opportunity to do the one thing he was made for. Emotional and riveting, sit back and strap in as you take the skies with Frank.

—Christian Freed Retired combat veteran, science fiction and military fantasy author of nearly 30 novels

I'm a pilot with broad experience in several flying "disciplines:" 20+ years in Naval Aircraft Carrier operations around the world, 22 years of Commercial Airline Boeing 767 International flying, and many years ongoing of general aviation flying/ownership of my own single engine Bonanza. For me, **Frank the Pilot** *is an enjoyable walk down memory lane, rekindling old adventures, and challenging me to put myself in his seat—and wonder what I might do differently (if anything). For those who only dream about or long to be a pilot, it should be a very interesting ride alongside a true professional, and a teaser for what life as a pilot offers to any and all who wish to leave the mundane world behind—AND FLY!*

—Ralph R. Costanzo, Commander, USN (Ret.) B767 Captain, UPS Airlines

Frank has written this book to share with you a great love story. The correlation between love and flying is undeniable to the pilot. Frank has captured the excitement of those first solo flights. The building of experience and comfort that comes from growing with a friend. The ups and downs of his flying experience and finishing a great career. Reading this book puts you in the cockpit with Frank to experience that love, that relationship.

—Jeff Parker, B777 First Office FedEx, CFI, A&P, Van's RV8 builder, Cessna C195 Owner

Copyright Notice

Copyright © 2022 By Francis John Donohue, Jr.

All rights reserved.

Published by Not-Y, Virginia Beach, VA

First Edition

ISBN-978-0-9894678-8-9 (Print)
ISBN-978-0-9894678-9-6 (eBook)

Library of Congress Control number: 2022920436

Book Cover Design by ebooklaunch.com" on your book's copyright page

Portions of this work previously appeared, in a different form, as "School and Schooled"

Although the author and publisher have made every effort to ensure that the information in this book was correct at press time, the author and publisher do not assume and hereby disclaim any liability to any party for any loss, damage, or disruption caused by errors or omissions, whether such errors or omissions result from negligence, accident, or any other cause.

www.frankjdonohue.com

Dedication

I dedicate this book to all pilots, aviation lovers, Francis and Jared.

Contents

Foreword 1

Introduction: What a professional pilot sees, thinks and feels 5

Chapter 1: After High School
Always remember ... and you'll never forget. 7

Chapter 2: First Flight (USAF) England
Doing better than most but not as good as some. 10

Chapter 3: First Solo
Cool big-time pilot with a massive ego. 23

Chapter 4: Private Pilot License
Slice the big pie into small pieces. 31

Chapter 5: A Pilot in Development
The pilot license is a license to learn. 40

Chapter 6: The Things Pilots Will Do to Build Flight Time
Trust your instruments. 51

Chapter 7: California
Beautiful. 62

Chapter 8: ERAU
Fifty-four college credits in one year. 70

Chapter 9: First Pilot Job
Forty college student solo flights. 79

Chapter 10: Banner-Towing
First pilot emergency. 91

Chapter 11: Transamerican Airways
Building flight time. 100

Chapter 12: Midnite Express
Career-ending emergency. 105

Chapter 13: Southeast Airlines
Five pilot jobs in two years. 127

Chapter 14: Flying Tigers
Pilot goal in six years. 145

Chapter 15: Around the World in Ten Days
The sun rose and set during the flight. 155

Chapter 16: The Whale B-747
The largest airplane in the world. 164

Chapter 17: Memorable Flights
When you get up there, don't forget to land. 176

Chapter 18: First Jet
*We make our money above planet Earth
and it is serious business.* 186

Chapter 19: Captain's Responsibilities
That's why the captain gets paid the big bucks. 206

Chapter 20: Pilot's Life and Keeping Their Jobs
Keeping is harder than getting. 216

Chapter 21: Flying the Big Metal
Wind shear can kill you. 234

Chapter 22: Come Fly with Me, Flight 1340
Frank the pilot in action. 251

Chapter 23: Flight
Fifi landed the plane. 270

Chapter 24: FedEx Frank
Time becomes more valuable than money. 282

BONUS 289
Acknowledgments 291
Bibliography 292
About The Author 296
Author's Note 297

Foreword

Every professional pilot has a long string of true tales to tell, and too often we keep the best ones to ourselves. As a result, the non-professional pilots and the folks who are simply airplane buffs are stuck with the TV and Hollywood version of career pilots where every one of us is either a womanizing alcoholic with deep emotional problems or a flamboyant and dangerous maverick. In fact, the best way to insult a professional pilot is to call him a maverick.

Yet, we sometimes do our part to solidify that image in the general public, just for laughs. Once, while heading back to work after a two-day break spent visiting my parents in my hometown, I was catching the jump seat out of the local airport. It was an early morning departure, and I was sitting in the coffee shop with my folks, when out of the corner of my eye, I saw the crew for our flight arriving. Soon it would be time to go and fill out the paperwork, head up the jetway and meet the captain to request his jump seat. He approved me and told me to meet the lead flight attendant and ask for one of her seats in the back. The unwritten rule is to be respectful to the captain, and be sweet and charming to the lead, thus you'll get a good seat. So, I was told to just have a seat in first, because the load was extremely light. Parking my pilot's bag in the overhead, I took the window seat and stashed my cap under the seat in front of me while I dove into commuting pilots' reading material. A late, first-class passenger hustled in and plopped into the seat beside me. Since we were in first class, a flight attendant came strolling in with a tray of coffees and soft drinks for the half-dozen people seated in our section. I heard a familiar voice ask the businessman next to me,

"Would you like a coffee or juice?"

Looking up, I saw that the flight attendant was a good friend of mine from my high school years! She was beautiful, friendly and a real motormouth... I'm talkin' no filter, folks!

"Pixie!" I half shouted her nickname in surprise.

"Wes!" She replied as she served the businessman his apple juice. "How come you didn't say 'Hi' before we boarded?"

"I didn't know you were on this flight," I replied casually.

"Didn't you see us coming in?"

"I saw the crew, but I didn't recognize you."

Which didn't make much sense to her since we'd known one another for years, all the way back to when her fiancé was the goaltender for my hockey team 20 years earlier.

"Well," she quipped, cocking her hip to one side, "do I look that different in my clothes?"

The businessman did an actual spit-take.

Now what Pixie meant to say was "do I look that different in my street clothes," as opposed to her airline uniform. Of course, the businessman never caught that.

"No, no, no," I replied, trying to cover, "I was sitting with my mom and dad and just saw you guys out of the corner of my eye."

"Okay," she replied sweetly. "After the captain turns off the seat-belt sign, come to the back. I wanna introduce you to the rest of the girls."

I replied that I would do exactly that, and she went about completing the service. As we climbed above 10,000 feet, the seat-belt sign went off and I put away my reading, grabbed my cap, put it on, stood up, and excused myself to the businessman.

"It must be nice being a pilot," he muttered softly as I passed into the aisle.

Now, I just could not let that opportunity slip by.

"Sir," I said quietly, "you'd never believe it."

I spent the rest of the flight in the back riding in the flight attendant jump seat and talking with Pixie and the other FAs. When we landed, she went her way, and I went to the next leg of my commute as I asked her to say "Hello" to her husband and hug her kids for me. Years later, I told her hubby the whole story and he laughed. I guess I'd done my part to shore-up that misimpression that the whole outside world has about professional pilots and aviation.

In this book, you'll read just one professional pilot's story, and yet, he does an amazing job of pulling the curtain back and letting you see the true nuts and bolts of what we actually do. Indeed, a lot of the misconceptions and myths will be busted as you witness how it all works. This is not an "action-packed drama" but rather it is an honest example of how we work. The feelings are real, from the high points to the deep personal depression of the low points of this profession.

Often, I've heard people say, "Pilot! Gee, that must be very exciting!"

"No," I always respond. "We don't like it when it gets exciting, because that's when things are really bad. We like it boring, because boring equates to going home and having a good night's sleep."

For other professional pilots reading this book, you'll very often relate to similar situations in your own career. There are times when the author gave me more than one shiver and more than a few laughs.

For the non-professional pilots, you will see in these pages the world in which you may be aspiring to enter. Yes, this is what it's really like. As a member of the 3-furloughs club, I can tell you that getting that ATP in your pocket, does not mean that you have it made. This is a job, it's work… okay… it has a great view, but it's still work. It is one of the few jobs where doing it with perfection every time is considered the norm. Turning these pages, you will see that.

To the aviation buffs out there, we see you and your cameras at the fence off the approach end of the active runway. We know you're there. Reading this book, you may be a bit surprised at what comprises the world of aviation. There is no "Maverick" in professional commercial aviation. Those types don't get this far. Today's pilots are male and female, and consist of all sorts of races and backgrounds. From those who grew up as a poor resident in a trailer park to those who come from a long line of airline aviators, we are all here for the same reason as you are when you line up along the fence and take pictures. We love aviation and we have it in our souls. I'm sure that reading this book will give you the insight and thrill that it gave me.

Open these pages and take the adventure. It may be just one pilot's story, but it is a true depiction of us all. No Hollywood script writer would come up with a version of aviation that is as authentic.

Wes Oleszewski

Airline Captain/Corporate Pilot retired

Introduction

Mary complained to the passenger next to her, "We were supposed to land in Dallas. Why are we going to Houston? How am I going to get to my mother's house from Houston? I don't understand. What goes on up there? Who are these guys? What kind of a pilot is up there?" This book will open your eyes to why pilots do things they do, and will put to rest many of your questions about what goes on in the cockpit.

Enjoy delving into the mind of an experienced airline pilot. The multiple interesting pilot stories will transport you and evoke emotion by revealing who was involved and what, when, where and why it happened. Most importantly, how did it affect Frank the pilot and how might it affect your next flight?

Frank the Pilot puts the reader right in the cockpit to experience everything from the author's point of view. You will sit in Frank's pilot seat and experience what he was thinking and feeling inflight.

This is a story about a kid who left Long Island at age 18 with only a high school diploma and a driver's license, returned at age 26 with college degrees and a pilot's license, and flew around the world. This book is also about how an airline pilot is made. This story will hopefully inspire you to pursue your dream career. Many of the lessons of how Frank becomes a pilot can help you in your pursuit of your ultimate career goal.

Separation from family and outside social groups, along with disrupted sleep and irregular work hours, can cause some pilots to suffer from mental health problems. Malaysia Airlines flight 370, Germanwings flight 9525 and China Eastern Airlines flight 5735 plane crashes were all likely caused deliberately by pilots with mental health issues. Most flights occur without incident, mainly because pilots are meticulous in following procedures, but when something goes wrong, pilots must have the mental flexibility to troubleshoot and react in real time. There is a tremendous amount of thinking going on in the cockpit, especially when things are not normal.

Pilots have a unique skill set. When equipment malfunctions occur or when the visibility is near zero, it takes a certain toughness and point of view to keep things together and maintain control. The autopilot cannot be relied on to do it all.

Flying remains the safest form of transportation in the USA. Part of that safety record is credited to the training of the pilots—and the lessons we were taught about preparation, execution, troubleshooting and paying attention to details. These are all valuable lessons for everyone—even if you never desire to pilot a plane of any size. As an added bonus for you, I have provided the gouge—valuable information for pilots and non-pilots.

The author's qualifications include holding the Airline Transport Pilot license, Flight Instructor license, Advanced and Instrument Ground Instructor licenses, Flight Engineer License, Aircraft Dispatcher license, Remote Pilot Certificate, Bachelor's of Aeronautical Science degree and over 36 years of flying experience. Pilots are an elite group of professionals.

You may struggle with fears and misunderstandings of what happens in the cockpit. Who are those pilots, and how did they get to fly those planes? What goes on in the cockpit? What is the human nature of pilot errors? How does the pilot's job affect the passengers? How do pilot mistakes affect passenger safety? How could wind, fog, thunderstorms and wind shear affect my flight and my possible survival to my destination? I will give you these answers from my experiences.

You need to read this book to discover what is in the mind of a pilot—one who may have your fate in their hands.

Come on up, close the door and take a seat up here in the cockpit. Buckle up and put on the headphones. Let's power up the jet and go for a ride. I am sure you will enjoy these stories, as you fly along with Frank the pilot.

1

AFTER HIGH SCHOOL

Always remember ... and you'll never forget.

A machine is an apparatus using or applying mechanical power and having several parts, each with a specific function and together performing a particular task. A transport machine carries people or goods from one place to another. My first experience with operating a transport machine was when I learned to ride a bicycle at the young, adventurous age of five. This machine required leg power, a little arm and hand movement, and the use of my eyes and ears, as well as some strength and brain-motor skills. The bike operator learns balance, steering, pedaling, braking, changing gears and safety. Biking seemed five times more efficient than walking. These 14-inch wheels enabled me to travel the length of several houses and, with supervision, even a little further. WOW! I traveled all the way around the block!

At age 13 I received a Schwinn 10-speed bicycle for Christmas. This transport machine allowed me to visit friends, go to school and sporting events, and have my own newspaper route. David McCullough wrote, "Bring up the subject of shapes of handlebars or types of pedals on early 'safety bicycles' and Orville's whole face lights up." In 1893 Wilbur and Orville Wright opened their own small bicycle business.[1] Orville Wright loved bicycles. I loved bicycles too. This new transport machine ignited a travel bug within me and I wanted to go places.

When I was 16, my grandfather gave my brother and me a 14-foot boat with a 10 hp engine. This is a different type of transport machine that operates on the water. This machine requires oil and gas, along with my body movements and sensory skills to operate, and an increase in brain motor skills with a greater emphasis on safety. Among these concerns is that a boat propeller can easily slice right through a human body.

At age 16, I obtained my New York state driver's license. At 17, with two years of hard-earned money, I purchased my first car—a 1972 mezzanine blue Chevelle Malibu with a black hardtop. This was the most sophisticated transport machine that I ever had to operate. A driver's license, an automobile safety inspection and auto insurance were required to operate this machine. I had to take a written test and a practical driving test to get that driver's license. My car had to pass a safety inspection. Most of you are aware of all that's involved with driving a motor vehicle; there are many privileges and responsibilities.

So, at age 17 I had a car and a boat and was sitting on top of the world. I drove that car everywhere—to school, to work, to concerts at Madison Square Garden in New York City, to the great Long Island beaches. I even drove that car during a snowstorm to a Rock concert in Rochester, New York.

After high school, I left Long Island and did a little traveling around the beautiful USA. I traveled, worked and lived in various places in Texas, Oklahoma, Missouri and California. From San Francisco, I flew on a Pan Am Boeing B-747 aircraft to John F. Kennedy International Airport on Long Island.

The Boeing B-747 wide-body jumbo jet was the largest and heaviest aircraft in the world for many decades. The B-747 earned the title, "the queen of the skies." Three flight crewmembers were required to operate the aircraft—a captain, a first officer and a second officer. The B-747 could fly at a speed of over 500 knots (575 miles per hour), a distance of over 7,000 nautical miles (8,000 statute miles) and as high as 45,000 feet, or eight and a half miles above planet Earth. Inside the plane there were ten seats per row separated by two aisles with a huge storage bin above the seats. There were several subsections of seating. Specially dressed beautiful pretty air hostesses with attractive smiles helped direct me to my seat. They smelled alluring.

During this flight I was in awe of how this humongous air machine was transporting more than 400 people over 3,000 miles through three times zones in about five hours. These questions were swimming around in my head: *What makes this amazing machine stay up in the air and how does it operate? Who gets to drive this massive machine? How do you start the plane? What kind of steering wheel and pedals does this sophisticated* machine have? How many pilots are needed to fly this plane? Do you need a special driver's license to drive it? Surely driving airplanes is way better than driving cars to travel to places. Where else can this humongous air machine go?* Traveling had entered my blood, and surely this fantastic machine must be the way to travel to exotic locations.

Curiosity about flying had been instilled in me at this time. The wonders of flying were suppressed deeply within me. At 18 this was probably the first time I had an interest in flying, nothing serious, and I put those thoughts aside in the back of my memory. Little did I know at the time that such long-distance flights might one day become routine—and that my view out of the airplane would be from a completely different perspective.

After spending a week at home, I entered the United States Air Force (USAF) in December of 1979. I will always remember and never forget that at age 18 I left home with a high school diploma, a driver's license and some traveling experience. My thinking was, *The USAF with bases all over the world will open the gates for me to extend my travel adventures.*

I did some training in San Antonio and Wichita Falls, Texas, traveled around a bit in Texas and Mississippi and returned back to Long Island for short stay before heading to England. After a one-week stay, my parents drove me to McGuire Air Force Base in New Jersey where the USAF flew me to the Royal Air Force base in Lakenheath, England, for my first assignment.

Once again, I started wondering about pilots and flying as this Lockheed C-141 Starlifter air machine jetted me across the Atlantic Ocean on my way to a foreign country. I thought to myself, *Those pilots seem to get to go to a lot of interesting places. Do pilots have time to explore the places they fly to? Are these pilots the same pilots that flew me on the B-747 across the USA? Is it more challenging to fly a jet airplane across the Atlantic Ocean then across the USA? Are there parachutes and life boats for everyone aboard?* The C-141 is not as big as the B-747. *Are bigger planes safer than smaller planes? Who do I know that could provide answers to the many questions I have about flying?* Google did not exist until 1998, and there was no history of anyone in my family who was associated in any capacity with aviation.

2

FIRST FLIGHT (USAF) ENGLAND

Doing better than most but not as good as some.

I arrived in England in May of 1980. This was the first foreign country that I had ever been to. I was assigned to Royal Air Force Lakenheath, the 48th fighter wing, located in East Anglia in Suffolk County, about 70 miles northeast of London and 25 miles east of Cambridge.

In 1980, the base had a few squadrons of F-111 aircraft, which were installed with the Pave Tact System, enabling it to deliver weapons around the clock from both high and low altitudes. The F=111 was a two-pilot, multi-purpose tactical fighter-bomber aircraft with variable-sweep wings, which allowed the pilot to fly from slow speeds to speeds up to Mach 1.2 at a sea level and Mach 2.5 at 60,000 feet. The wings could sweep from 16 degrees full forward to 72 degrees full aft. The jet included afterburner turbofan engines, each capable of producing 25,000 pounds of thrust. The aircraft could carry a variety of conventional and nuclear weapons[2] and were quite different from the B-747 and the C-141 that I rode on. *How different are these special pilots that fly these sophisticated military jet fighters?* I wondered.

Donald Realget was the first real friend I made in England. He is a laid back, cool guy from California. Imagine a New Yorker like me becoming great friends with a Californian. Don could pass as Clark Kent's double. His attractive smile is side-armed with a right cheek dimple. Usually, he is dressed in *Gentlemen's Quarter's* man-of-the-year clothes with two-toned gray cowboy boots. We traveled together to London in his 1969 orange, black-striped Camaro. Londoners gazed in admiration at the American-built iconic ground transport machine. When I rode with Don, I felt almost as cool as him. I felt I was *doing better than most, but not as good as some.* Don did not meet women; women met him. He possesses that rare, female-attraction magnet, a valuable special gift human males sort after. Don is the cool god; he had become my idol.

After only a few months, I was fortunate to relocate from the base to a civilian flat in the town of Bury St. Edmunds. My first Air Force best friend, Don and I leased a flat located on the third floor of an old building on Guildhall Street, smack in the middle of the town. Bury St. Edmunds is located in the middle of East Anglia, about 17 miles east of RAF Lakenheath. The town included many other historical buildings like the Abbey Gate, the Cathedral Church of St. James, St. Mary's Church, Athenaeum Angle Hill, the Corn Exchange, a good market square and plenty of great pubs.[3] Although the pubs kept strange hours, I savored the non-traditional, non-American lager beer, stout beer, porter beer, bitter beer, black-and-tan beer and cider. At One Bull Inn I learned that the girls were known in the UK as "birds" or "lassies."

The language took some getting used to and so did the food, though I grew to enjoy some of the dishes such as Cottage Pie or Shepherd's Pie, Bangers and Mash, Black Pudding (made from dried pigs' blood and fat), Yorkshire Pudding, Fish and Chips and tea. I learned the difference between tea (a cup of tea) and tea (mini-sandwiches).

In England, people seemed much friendlier than Americans. The British were always willing to give a ride to an American GI hitchhiking, which I did often. After hitchhiking around England for several months, I acquired a two-wheeled ground transport machine—a Japanese-made Suzuki 250TS Motorcycle. This motorcycle transportation machine enabled me to travel to many new English destinations. *I was doing better than most, but not as good as some.*

During that first year living in England, I was just having fun traveling around, meeting Brits and accustoming myself to the English culture. At 21 I had no direction in life, and maybe subconsciously I was searching for some direction in life. In that first year I had been to my first air show and was around airplanes all the time. Between Mildenhall Airbase and Lakenheath Airbase, located only five miles apart, there were planes coming and going all the time. But I just gazed at those amazing jet airplanes wondering, *Where are those pilots going now?*

First flight

On April 10, 1981, pilot friend Jeff Guysyou invited me to Lakenheath Aero Club just to check it out. Jeff and I were assigned together at basic training in San Antonio, Texas, and again here at Lakenheath, England. Jeff was from Long Island, as I was, and we had similar culture and accents; we easily became friends. Jeff is 5'11" with brown hair, brown eyes and always projects a glowing smile whenever a conversation about flying is in the air. We were in the same squadron during Basic Training, during which time Jeff was always talking about flying and working toward getting his private pilot's license. He wanted to be an airline pilot, and his persistent, inner drive guided his day-to-day actions. Jeff was my "go to" guy to get answers to my numerous questions about flying. At Jeff's invitation, I eagerly checked out the aero club. Unbeknown to me, that day would be a life-changing experience.

The aero club consisted of a small, prefab, camouflaged building with two office rooms, a flight planning room, an administrator, a chief pilot, a Federal Aviation Administer (FAA), a Designated Pilot Examiner (DPE), two flight instructors and, of course, the airplanes themselves—a Cessna C-150, C-152 and C-172. At the aero club I was introduced to Simon Dreyfus, an FAA-certified flight instructor. Simon, an Englishman, obtained his commercial and flight instructors license in the USA because it was more economical to train there then in England. Simon stood at 5'6" with a full head of light brown hair. He wore jeans, a long, white, button-down shirt with a black tie and really cool Ray-Ban aviator shades. Instructor Simon was so knowledgeable about every aspect of aeronautics, I presumed he knew everything about flying. To me, he was the pilot god. His jovial English accent with his ever-present smirk generated good feelings. He was alluring to listen to, and fun to hang out with.

All of this flying chatter seemed very cool to me, and I had no idea what to expect when flight instructor Simon Dreyfus said, "Would you like to go flying?" Not knowing anything about flying an airplane or what was involved, I said, "Sure, that sounds cool." Throttle, mixture, yoke, altitude indicator, heading, airspeed, altitude, even the most basic components of the cockpit and flying I had never heard of, but I said, "Sure, that sounds cool." The thrill of going flying muddled my thinking. *What am I getting into and how will the next few hours change my life?*

The Cessna C-150 was a two-seater. Designed in the 1950s, it was capable of acrobatics. It had a four-piston, 100-horsepower continental engine driving a two-blade fixed prop. It was 22 feet long with a wingspan of 33 feet. The entire plane was not much bigger than my Cheville car, and the plane's cockpit was smaller than a Cheville's interior. The airplane weighed about 1,000 pounds, and the max takeoff gross weight was around 1,500 pounds. The airplane had the basic instruments of VHF radio, transponder, altitude indicator, altimeter, airspeed indicator and a compass. The C-150 could fly to an altitude of about 12,500 feet, a distance of around 500 nautical miles (575 statute miles) and a speed of just over 100 knots (120 mph). Over 23,800 C-150 aircraft were built, making it the seventh most-produced civilian aircraft.[4] Simon, a god-like pilot I had known for all of one hour, was going to take me flying in aircraft number N96621.

As we approached the C-150 airplane, Simon said, "Just follow me and listen." Simon performed the exterior and interior preflight safety check step by step, telling me what he was doing. Initially, I thought there might have been something wrong with this airplane because of all the scrutiny given to the condition of the plane by the instructor. You should have seen him; he checked the tires, the engine oil, the wing, the tail and everything, both exterior and interior. Later I would discover this is normal. He directed me to sit in the left seat of the cockpit, and he proceeded to read the checklist. Pilots are required by federal law to use the checklist as a safety measure to prevent missing an important step in their procedures in operating an airplane.

He pushed a few buttons, turned on the airplane and did a few more preflight procedure checks. He turned on the radio to listen to ATIS, an automatic terminal information service that provides the local aviation weather and other pertinent flight information. He grabbed a small, handheld radio microphone and spoke to the air traffic controller. He seemed to be requesting permission to fly. It seemed very strange to me at the time that my FAA-certified flight instructor needed permission to fly. As he read through more checklist items, he started to move levers. I curiously listened and watched him start the air transportation machine. As the two-blade propeller started turning, the engine began to roar. As the airplane sprung to life, it started to rumble a bit and I was assuming (or hoping) that this was normal.

The aircraft yoke may seem similar to the car's steering wheel, but when taxing an airplane on the ground you don't use this yoke to steer. Simon directed me to put my hands and feet on the controls and follow him. I put my hands on the yoke and my feet on the rudder pedals, which are located just above the floor of the cockpit. My feet followed his feet movements, which directed the airplane left and right while taxing. Little did I know that these rudder pedals also assist yoke movements in turning the airplane while inflight, up there, in the sky.

The parking brake and foot brakes were released. We were slowly moving now; we were taxing from the aero club to the runway—the same 9,000-foot runway that the F-111 fighter-bomber jets use. Small planes are permitted to use the same runway as big planes. It seems that pilots need permission to do a lot of things. The instructor requested and received permission from the control tower for us to taxi to the runway, taxi onto the runway and to take off. Go fly. WOW! Time to fly!

We taxied onto the runway; he moved some controls and the airplane accelerated. The airplane was moving faster and faster down the runway, and then Simon pulled back on the yolk and we started to fly. The C-150 lifted us off the ground. We were now in the air flying, WOW!

In a New York minute we had already climbed 2,000 feet. I was able to see the entire Lakenheath airbase, the F-111 jets, the military buildings, cars and even people. This was mind-blowing and felt really cool, like a god looking down on planet Earth. As we entered the flight training practice area, I was amazed that I was looking down at the beautiful British countryside while actually flying in an airplane. As we zoomed past a few puffy white cumulus clouds, I viewed horses, cows, sheep, streams, farmhouses ... even a lady vigorously commanding a bicycle on a mission like Elmira Gulch in *the Wizard of Oz* with Toto in the back basket. I could not believe it when, shortly thereafter, the flight instructor gave me the controls and allowed me to steer—to start maneuvering the airplane.

Simon instructed me in the proper use of my hands and feet to manipulate the controls and the throttle to fly the plane. During the flight he covered the four basic fundamentals of flying: turns, climbs, descents and straight-and-level flight. He covered the effects of the controls on flight. Still being wowed at 3,000 feet in the air, I did not comprehend much of what he was telling me. The initial fantastic feelings from absorbing the views of planet Earth and sky overwhelmed my bodily sensors, preventing me from learning most of what was being taught to me that day.

Flying an airplane a few thousand feet above planet Earth is so awesome, especially when I could maneuver the airplane. The introductory discovery flight seemed to fly by (Ha! Ha!). Before I knew it, we were heading back to land at Lakenheath.

The throttle was reduced to idle, and the yoke was pushed forward to initiate our decent. During descents, the cockpit window view is better than the level flight view. During descents, the cockpit window attached to the plane is lowered at an angle, allowing the pilots to observe more of wonderful planet Earth and all things, both natural and manmade.

On this first landing, the instructor explained to me what we were going to do and that he was going to be landing the plane, as it was the hardest part of flying.

We entered the traffic pattern at mid-point downwind, turned onto base, then turned to final and positioned the aircraft to land. These are the three sides of the four-sided box pattern pilots fly at airports. After landing we taxied back to the aero club, and Simon asked me, "Well, what do you think?"

"Yeah, that was very cool," I said.

This introductory flight lasted only 1.2 hours, but the flight made a lasting impression on me. This first flight to me was not so much a lesson as it was a "wow" experience, thrilling me with the magic of flying. During that first flight most of my total focus and excitement were on the aeronautical environment and not on trying to learn how to fly the plane. The small amount of time I spent attempting to do so, also made lasting impression on me. This new feeling was brewing in me, the feeling that *I was doing better than most, but not as good as some.* Simon and I agreed to fly again the next day.

Pilots take care of pilots. Throughout this book I will give you the little secrets, the tricks of the trade, the inside scoop, the skinny ... or what pilots call "**The gouge.**" Pilots help other pilots with "The gouge." There is good gouge and bad gouge, and I will attempt to give you the good one.

The Gouge. If you know beforehand that you want to learn to fly and be a pilot, I would recommend that you do some homework before climbing into the left seat for the first time. Get familiar with the basic flight controls and instruments; you won't be quite as overwhelmed, and you'll save yourself some money on instruction time. Learning the basics of the flight controls is also helpful for your first lesson. What does the yoke do? The rudder? Which direction on the throttle gives you more power? What is trim and how is it used? A review of the instruments and primary flight display is also helpful. Where can I see my speed? Where is the altimeter that tells me how high I am? Where is the heading indicator that tells me where I am going? But don't worry—not knowing anything about flying and being overwhelmed during the first flight experience, like I was that first time, is also a fantastic introductory flight memory.

Second Flight—First Flight Lesson

The second flight for me was more like the first flight lesson, because during that first flight I was occupied with absorbing the awe-inspiring experience. It was entertainment. On this second flight, lasting 1.5 hours, I was actually learning how to fly. Sometimes you have to get that "wow" factor out of your system before you can settle down and actually learning anything.

This flight lesson included the preflight. Pilots use checklists during several segments of flight, such as preflight, pre-start, taxi, before takeoff and cruise. It has been so successful for so many years that today, doctors use checklists for surgery to avoid mistakes.

This lesson also included straight-and-level flight, the use of trim, turns at various degrees of bank angle, climbs and descents, and orientation. The best part of this flight was the landing. The instructor allowed me to have my hands on the controls so I could feel what he was doing and we could land together, in a manner of speaking, as he walked me through what was happening. Landing is the transition from a plane flying to point-of-ground contact. Learning to land an airplane properly is the hardest part of flying.

The Gouge. There's a lot to cover in the first lesson, but it's mainly aimed at getting you acquainted with the aircraft, procedures and basic maneuvers. Be sure to study beforehand the lesson plan for the flight lesson.

Try to understand the basics before the details. Define and memorize important terms. Some things just will not click until you see it in flight. After each flight, take notes, review the notes and practice chair flying what you had just learned. Don't worry about how much you have to learn. All student pilots learn at different rates and comprehend certain pilot skills quicker than others.

The pilot decision

It was on day three, flight lesson two, that I realized how hard it was going to be to learn how to fly an airplane. Learning and performing flight maneuvers within certain limits like maintaining altitude plus or minus 100 feet, maintaining airspeed plus or minus 10 knots and maintaining heading plus or minus 10 degrees is challenging. Trying to master attitude control, trim control and cross-check awareness (ATC) seemed next to impossible.

Pilots utilize many checklists and abbreviations. ATC is one of those abbreviations. ATC stands for Attitude, Trim and Cross-Check.

What is the aircraft's attitude? Whereas, a plane's *altitude* is its distance from the ground, its *attitude* is the angle between the plane's longitudinal axis and the Earth's horizon, also known as the flight path vector. Is the plane's attitude in a climb, a descent, a turn, a climbing turn, a climbing descent or in a straight-and-level flight? The pilot looks outside to obtain this visual data, and there is an altitude indicator instrument located within the cockpit to back up what the pilot sees outside. Trim is for adjustment. Make adjustments to the flight controls and power controls to command the plane to climb, descend, turn, make a climbing turn, a climbing descent or straight-and-level flight. There is a trim wheel control that adjusts the aerodynamic forces on the control surfaces that helps the plane maintain a set altitude without pilot input control. The trim wheel relieves pilot hand pressure on the yoke. The idea is to make small changes to the planes altitude and make small trim adjustments accordingly. Cross-check is for scanning all the visual and instrument data to confirm the plane is in the desired attitude. Is the plane doing what you want it to do? If the plane is not doing what you want it to do, then make the necessary adjustments, trim the plane and cross-check the results.

Cross-check the attitude and everything again, the heading, airspeed and altitude, and so forth. Make adjustments, re-trim and cross-check, over and over again. There was this feeling of being overwhelmed just trying to maintain straight-and-level flight while maintaining airspeed and heading too. Just when I thought I might have mastered flying straight-and-level, Simon overloaded me with the task to navigate and communicate. Not only would I have to learn to fly the plane, I would have to know where I was going and communicate on the radio. The pilot abbreviation ANC means to Aviate, Navigate and Communicate. In priority order, first fly the plane (Aviate), then know where the plane is going (Navigate) and finally talk (Communicate) on the radio to the air traffic controllers. Self-doubt came over me in waves. *Am I really capable of doing this? Am I able to learn these skills, and can I be a pilot one day?*

On this flight, instructor Simon also demonstrated a loop, positive G force and negative G force, and then we headed back to the airport. G force is a measure of acceleration. This third flight (and second flight lesson) lasted 1.6 hours and provided a glimpse into the many challenges I must face in order to fly. *Did I want to and could I meet those challenges,* I asked myself. As I was walking from the aero club to a friend's dormitory room, I was pondering questions on whether I should enter this new endeavor. *Is this the direction in my life that I should follow? Flying is really cool, but is this what I want to do? How much is this going to cost and how will I pay for it?*

In my friend's dorm room, we watched via television the very first Columbia space shuttle launch. When someone asks me when I knew I wanted to be a pilot, I say, "That's easy. April 12, 1981." On this date, after completing my third flight, I watched astronauts Robert Crichton and John Young strap themselves into their seats on the Columbia space shuttle (Space Transportation System STS-1) and blast off into space.

The Columbia space shuttle was the world's first manned, reusable rocket launcher—100 tons of US space technology. This was the first time NASA had put man on an untested launcher. For hours, engineers had been pumping hundreds of thousands of gallons of liquid hydrogen and oxygen into Columbia's fuel tanks. When combined, the two elements would generate more than 1 million pounds of thrust. Two huge, solid-fuel boosters containing a highly explosive mixture of aluminum powder and perchlorate oxidizer, if all went well, would provide supplemental thrust.

Seconds before liftoff, the shuttle's turbo pumps (each powerful enough to empty a swimming pool in 20 seconds) started to force hydrogen and oxygen into the spacecraft's three main engines, where the two elements combined with unbridled ferocity. (I know this now because I would later write a college term paper about the shuttle.) In seconds, the temperature in the engines soared to 6000º C. (10,832 F.). Superheated steam generated by the explosive combination of hydrogen and oxygen caused an eruption at the base of the spaceship, and within 90 seconds, the spaceship's computer signaled the two solid rocket boosters to launch the space shuttle into space. America had successfully launched the first reusable spaceship.[5]

There I was, an American living in a foreign country for over a year, a year that had shaped my love for the British and their culture, gazed at American astronauts blasting off into space. Absorbing this stunning historical event rekindled my love and patriotism toward my country, the USA. The words of the Star-Spangled Banner oozed into my thoughts. I was proudly fixated on that thrilling sight and my country's accomplishment. Those motivational emotions overruled my logical deductive reasoning—*I am going to be a pilot!* I decided right on the spot. (Did you know that 80% of pilots are the first-born children? I was no exception! Thank you for having me first, Mother).

Viewing that very first Columbia space shuttle launch infected me. Making a decision to be a pilot led to … aviation addiction. I finally had direction in my life—I was going to be a pilot. Eventually, I became addicted to flying. Riding a bicycle, operating a boat and driving a car were great experiences of operating different forms of transportation machines, but flying an airplane was much, much cooler and more challenging. Unlike earthly transportation machines that operate on planet Earth, airplanes move about three axes above planet Earth. Planes move about a lateral axis (left and right), a vertical axis (up and down) and a roll axis (rotate around left and right). This new transportation machine fascinated me and I wanted to control it, or, in pilot terms, *command* it. Planes have a thrust force, a drag force, a lift force and a weight force, and I wanted to command these forces to control the plane's flight path. I could only imagine, as a commander of an airplane, all the interesting destinations I could travel to around the world!

This decision to become a pilot provided direction in my life, and I needed to take action. At the time I did not even know what type of pilot I wanted to be, but I knew I needed to take action. I had to get a student pilot license and a third-class medical certificate. I needed to buy a flight logbook, clip kneeboard, sunglasses (I wish I could afford the real cool shades Simon wore), aeronautical charts, pilot's operating handbook and other pilot flight books. With this new direction in life, I was taking a big chance investing in myself.

The Gouge. Learning to fly is like a big complicated pie—each slice, the mastery of another skill. Eventually, the student masters all the pieces of the pie and puts them together, enabling the student to be a pilot.

On April 13th I joined the RAF Lakenheath Aero Club, and on the back of my membership card was this poem:

Safety First, and Live

In days gone by, I proved my worth
By zooming low across the earth,
I buzzed the farms, the mountain ridges,
I flew beneath the river bridges,
I looped and spun, I snapped and rolled,
I took all dares for years untold,
I pressed my luck quite near the line,
But not for need—just thrills; that's fine
I tried most stunts, though it's been said
I never tried to use my head,
So, here's a toast—to you and me!
But you drink both, I'm dead, you see.

—Anon

Self-awareness within and about me grew. I was doing better than most but not as good as some.

Cessna C-150 verses Tesla 3

1 length by 5 widths

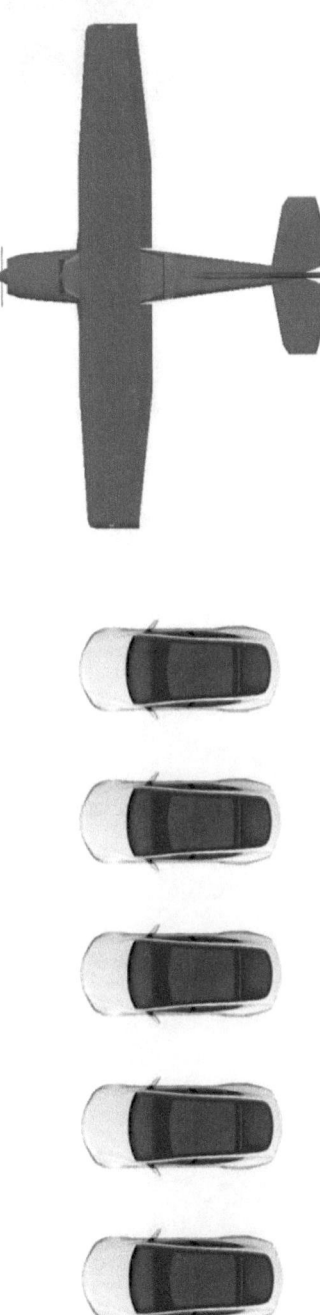

3

FIRST SOLO

Cool big-time pilot with a massive ego.

On June 7, 1981 in a C-150, tail number N961L, at EGULL (Lakenheath), CFI Simon Drefus and I taxied to the aero club after finishing a flight lesson. Simon signed my logbook and student pilot certificate authorizing me to fly solo—to fly by myself without an instructor onboard. Simon exited the airplane and said, "You're a good pilot, you're confident and you are ready to fly solo. I will see you back here after your flight."

"Thank you," I said.

In accordance with federal law, in order for a certified flight instructor to permit a student to fly solo, the student must demonstrate to federal aviation standards multiple maneuvers to include takeoffs and landings, traffic patterns, stall entries and recoveries, emergency procedures, go-arounds and more. Simon's signature on the paperwork was written proof that I was qualified to fly solo, and his departing words boosted my confidence: "You're a good pilot, you're confident and you are ready to fly solo." Like Dad giving me the keys to the car for the first time, I could not wait to get in the driver's seat.

Now almost completely at ease and yet excited, I taxied to Lakenheath's runway 6. Surprisingly, I felt no fear. The taxi segment was a nonevent, like driving a car. I was still on planet Earth. It was late in the afternoon, as I luxuriated in the golden radiance of the sun, low on the horizon. It seemed to overpower everything around me on the airfield. As I taxied parallel to the runway 6, still about a quarter-mile from the threshold, I watched an F-111 jet land. Its movable delta-shaped wings were extended forward, resembling a traditional jet airplane. The waning sun flashed its reflection on the fuselage a few times. This highly technological, sophisticated fighter jet effortlessly touched down on the same runway on which I was about to take off. The image was awe-inspiring and encompassed everything beautiful about flying. This made me proud to be a neophyte pilot and boosted my self-confidence, though another boost was hardly needed.

Let's see ... *the Before Start checklist complete, Before Taxi Checklist complete, and the Before Takeoff checklist complete.*

"Lakenheath tower, N961L is ready for takeoff," I radioed to the air traffic control tower.

"N961L, you are cleared for takeoff runway 6, at 2,000 feet turn left heading 300 degrees,"

came the authorization.

I responded, "Roger, N961L is cleared for takeoff runway 6, at 2,000 feet turn left to a heading 300 degrees."

Pilots always repeat ATC clearances back to the transmitter, mainly to ensure that the pilot received the correct clearance instructions and will comply with the clearance. If the ATC transmitter receives a readback that is different from his initial transmission, he will correct the pilot. It is prudent to write down long, complicated clearances before transmitting the read back. No one wants to fly the wrong clearance into a mountain or into another aircraft. It is to everyone's benefit to fly as safely as possible.

I was cleared to blast off and proceeded to line up with the runway centerline. I paused for a brief second or three to make a few last-minute cockpit checks and then set the throttle to full takeoff position. After scanning a few instruments, I turned my eyes to the runway. The engine erupted with excitement, the airspeed increased, 40 knots, 50, 55, 60, one last rudder and aileron adjustment, and then I pulled back on the yoke and received the precious privilege gift of flight. This is it! I lifted off planet Earth; I was airborne, flying the C-150 all by myself. The one thing I recall was that I was not awestruck with the outside cockpit views as I was on that the first flight—I was mentally and physically connected to my air flying machine in order to maintain control. My attention was on commanding the plane.

After takeoff, I flew to the practice area and practiced stalls, slow flight, steep turns, S turns and slips. These maneuvers were practiced often, in the event of loss of aircraft control, the number one pilot error leading to plane crashes. These maneuvers were also practiced to prepare myself for the private pilot practical exam.

In the middle of my flight, I decided to take a time out. I stopped to just soak in all in. I stopped from commanding my air machine to perform, in order to give full attention to my senses to this wonderful moment of life. Here I was all by myself at 3,000 feet ... but I was not really by myself. She—the C-150—was with me. She and I were connected as one. She felt me and I felt her. I sat in her seat; my feet caressed her rudder pedals and I held her with my hands. Sometimes I grasped her tightly and forcefully in order to control her and sometimes, like now, I barely held her in order to feel her sensitive reactions to me. She does not always want to do what I ask of her—she can be rebellious at times—but now she is on her best behavior. She speaks to me through the rumble of her engine and the vibration of her body; although, at times, I feel it is Mother Nature's force of the air and wind that influences her reactions more than me. She and I were enjoying a sensitive, quiet moment together, when inappropriately the other "she," Mother Nature, interfered, unexpectedly dislodging our bonding time with turbulence and a blast of swirly wind, just to let us know she exists. At this solo moment of flight, I felt powerful and fully in control, but she, the mother of all-natural forces, reminds me that she is more powerful than I could ever be and I must respect her. I felt Mother Nature's air pocket jolt me and heard her whisper to me in the wind, which drew my eyeballs outside of the cockpit.

What did Mother want me to see? was my curious thought. The melancholy sky was a friendly pale blue with only a few white, puffy, cotton-ball-like clouds planted in the distance. There was no weather, but that is a bit of a misnomer. Fair weather is weather, too, and this weather was great. Mother just wanted to steal some of my attention from my plane mate.

A brief cross-check scan back into the exciting intellect of my cockpit caught the reading of the Hobbs meter. A Hobbs meter measures the plane's hours of operation. She was not mine; I was just renting her. My hands commanded her to turn 180 degrees and navigate back to Lakenheath airfield, where we entered the traffic pattern. My C-150 airplane, my air transport machine, was commanded to enter downwind, base and onto final approach. On a very short final, I lined up with the centerline and adjusted the air machine's glide path toward my landing aiming point. 50 feet, 40, 30, 20 … then at 10 feet I slowly started to retard the throttle to idle while simultaneously pulling back on the yoke. My eyes started transitioning further down the runway while I used my peripheral vision to judge the rate at which the runway was approaching. My plane started drifting in response to the change in wind vector. I adjusted the left aileron into the wind and applied some opposite right rudder. It worked! The plane landed without incident; I successfully transitioned the plane from flight mode to non-flight mode. The union between planet Earth and I was established, and the runway embraced the airplane's wheels.

On that day, I actually performed four takeoffs and landings, better known as "touch and go's." Simon was probably getting nervous because my first solo flight lasted 1.8 hours. It was similar to the first time I drove my Cheville at age 17. I drove over 50 miles on that first solo drive. He did not anticipate that my first solo flight would last so long. But I was enjoying every minute, commanding an airplane all by myself, that I did not realize how long the flight was taking. How time flies! Ha! Ha!

It was only after that landing that I lost control of my emotions. I'd done it! I conquered flying a plane alone! I had this sense of great achievement, and I was overcome with ecstasy. I aviated, I navigated and I communicated. I didn't screw up (too much); I didn't get lost and did not embarrass myself on the radio. I was smiling hugely just like a four-year-old opening his one and only most requested gift. My head grew, my ego grew and my coolness grew. I felt like some kind of pilot god. This was the best thing that I have ever experienced. This was the best thing I have ever done, and I loved every precious moment of it. Manipulating the controls on an airplane through the air all by myself planted in me the taste of the limitless freedom of flying. Aviation addiction. This experience, *my* experience, afforded to those few elites lucky enough to leave planet Earth and interchange intensely with the regions of space, and the regions of heaven, is so precious. I was re-infected—aviation addiction was solidly implanted in Frank the pilot. It is a fantastic experience to command the controls of an airplane without the instructor there with you. This first solo flight was a turning point in my aviation training experience and an enormous boost to my self-confidence. It even boosted my success in other areas of my life, like acquiring more dates with English women.

After completing that first solo flight, an aviation tradition was executed at the aero club, the back of my shirt was cut off me. My name, the day's date and aircraft tail number were written on my cut-off shirttail. The shirt remnant was hung on the flight planning room wall, celebrating my aviation rite of passage. "Frank J. Donohue soloed in N9611 on June 7, 1981." This first solo flight was a tremendous confidence builder. I was now a cool, big-time pilot with a massive ego; it seemed like I was some superman that could do anything. This was something that I will always remember and never forget.

My definition of the phrase, cool big-time pilot with a massive ego, used throughout this book is a person viewed by others as an awesome, interesting, well-liked and successful person; one who views their self as clever and has high self-esteem, especially when it comes to flying. After a major accomplishment, this person feels like a champion, like a mini-god or like the GOAT (greatest of all time), particularly in regard to their piloting ability. This phrase is used many times throughout this book to indicate the mood swings and self-confidence of a pilot.

The Gouge. My best advice for your first solo flight is to block out the fact that your instructor is not with you. You cannot ask your instructor questions or advice, and your instructor cannot help you now. My best advice is to concentrate on what you have learned about flying and proceed step by step. Be confident in yourself and the training you have received. Try to conduct this first solo flight like other normal routine flights that you've had before, like when your instructor was onboard. Utilize the plane's checklist, as well as your personal, customized mental and physical checklist. The checklist is a pilot's friend and can be a savior. Try to remove your emotions and concentrate on flying the plane, navigating the plane and communicating with air traffic control (ANC). Study the emergency flight procedures beforehand. There may be a few moments of panic; block it out and fly the plane. You will make mistakes; just keep those mistakes minor ones. It is usually a chain of mistakes that contribute to airplane crashes. No one has likely ever crashed because the pilot made a few small mistakes. Those mistakes will teach you that you're capable of making decisions and managing mistakes on your own, further building your pilot-in-command confidence.

First Solo Cross country

Solo student pilots have many weather restrictions dictating when a student pilot is permitted to fly by himself. Good visual meteorology conditions with light winds are two of the most common requirements to fly solo. One of the many requirements for eligibility to take the private pilot's license exam is for the pilot applicant is to have completed at least ten hours of solo flight time. Of those ten solo hours, five must include solo cross-country flying. The student pilot must fly at least one cross-country flight of over 100 nautical miles. There are days, and sometimes even weeks, of inclement English weather that prevent solo pilots from flying. When a pilot is blessed with that block of good weather, which is rare in England, the intelligent, motivated student pilot will drop everything and go fly. Combining time off with good weather in order to log the required cross-country flight time—a requirement for the private pilot license exam—could present a challenge and set the pilot backwards in progress, when the pilot is trying to stay on a forward path. Flying is like doing math—if you do not fly routinely, your pilot skills will deteriorate, especially true for student pilots with low flight time. Go when the weather is good. That is what I did. There was a week of good weather, and I arranged to use my USAF vacation days to fly. My thinking was, *Fly now, get my private pilot license and figure out a way to pay for it later. The aero club may decide to ground me from flying until my pilot flight bill is made current, but they could not take my private pilot license away from me.* Again, I was taking a big chance and investing in myself.

The Gouge. Go when the weather is good. When the weather is suitable for pilots to fly solo, if able, drop everything and go fly solo. Get those required solo and solo-cross country flight hours logged as soon as possible. If the weather is not so good, you can always fly with your flight instructor.

On July 12 of 1981, in a Cessna-150 aircraft (tail number N961L), I commanded my first solo cross-country flight from Lakenheath airfield, (EGULL) to Nottingham airfield, (EGBN) in England.

Gulp—solo cross country. Just me, myself and I.

Was I nervous? Not really. I felt prepared. The instruction had been excellent. As the lone pilot, I do everything. I'm the flight planner, dispatcher, weatherman, mechanic, lawyer and pilot. I compute the flight plan, evaluate the aircraft performance based on weather, check the weight and the atmospheric conditions, plan the route and balance the data. Nottingham Castle is in the woods—supposedly the castle in the Robin Hood movies—and that that will be a good landmark on the way to Nottingham.

I file the flight plan with the estimated time of departure and estimated time of arrival. In case I crash, my filed route will save rescuers time because they will have an idea of where to start looking. From a lawyer's point of view, my flight instructor signs my flight log to verify I am competent to fly solo. I need all paperwork on hand at all times—my signed log book, student pilots' license, airworthiness certificate and lots of other paperwork, including the weight-balance certificate. As a mechanic, I do a preflight on the aircraft to make sure it is safe to fly, looking for anything out of line. Then it's time to start the engine, contact ground control, get taxi clearance and taxi out. Before takeoff, I do an engine run up (to make sure the engine is operating correctly) and then call the tower for takeoff clearance. I'm on my way, with a keen eye out, always looking for a place to land. With one engine, the pilot is always looking for a place to land in case that one engine fails.

In Nottingham, I feel a bit of relief. But it's not over yet. I repeat all the steps—flight plan, aircraft check, everything. I get fresh fuel, check the weather and update the flight plan for the return flight.

Back at Lakenheath, it's difficult to get out of the cockpit. I am feeling so confident and proud, my head swelled with pride and accomplishment. Even though I had flown only a few thousand feet above the ground, I felt like I had the whole world in my hands. Successfully completing this first solo cross-country flight made me feel like a cool, big-time pilot with a massive ego.

I had become completely hooked on flying and became infected with aviation—addicted. The total flight time was 1.2 hours each way. Flight Instructor Simon Dreyfus certified my flight logbook.

The Gouge. Treat the cross-country flight like any other solo flight, except that there is lot more straight-and-level flying, and you will land at a different airport. Study and prepare navigation. Check the weather and recheck the weather, and just before takeoff, check the weather again.

4

PRIVATE PILOT LICENSE

Slice the big pie into small pieces.

How does one become a pilot? First there must be a desire to fly. An introductory demonstration flight is great insight into how badly you want to fly. Most curious individuals will know after that first flight if they want to be a pilot. Afterwards, they will love it and get hooked on flying or they will not.

The private pilot certificate is the most commonly issued certificate throughout the United States. The training needed to obtain the private certificate is comprehensive, covering many areas of pilot knowledge and skill. The Federal Aviation Administration (FAA) has rules and regulations specifying the requirements to take the private pilot's exam. The eligibility requirements are spelled out in federal aviation regulation (FAR) 61.103. The student pilot applicant must have a minimum of 40 flight hours, broken down by instruction time, solo time, night time and instrument time. The applicant must pass the FAA private pilot written test, oral test and flight test. After previously passing the written test, I was scheduled to take the oral test and flight test on the same day.

The practical exam occurred on September 4, 1981, less than five months since I had started flight lessons. Over the past several months I invested a tremendous amount of time and money to achieve my private pilot's license. When the usually noncompliant English weather was good, I took vacation days from work and flew those solo trips. When my soaring aero club flight bill arrived, I paid as much as I was able and continued to fly even as my debt rose significantly. *If my aero club debt rose too high,* I thought, *they could ground me until I paid my debt, but if I pass today, they cannot take my private pilot license away from me.* When my friends wanted to party, most of the time I abstained so that I could study, especially for the private pilot written test, which I took early. The moment of truth had arrived; I had put everything on the line to get that pilot license. Questioning myself, I wondered, *Will my enduring efforts and persistent motivation reap the ultimate reward I am seeking?*

On that day there were many white puffy, cumulus clouds in the partially obscured sky, which did not worry me because clear skies were predicted before my flight was to begin. The previous night I checked the weather several times; this morning I checked the weather several more times, and I would end up checking the weather two more times before we entered the airplane for the flight portion of the exam. As I strolled into the aero club, I eagerly gazed at N961L, the Cessna C-150 airplane that I would fly for the practical exam. FAA Designated Pilot Examiner (DPE) John J. Benton, (known as "Jack") arrived 20 long minutes after me. One of the valuable lessons I learned from my father was, "Do not be late." Dad would say, "If you are not 15 minutes early then you are late," meaning arrive at the jobsite or important event at least 15 minutes before it's to start. I've carried this lesson throughout my lifetime—arrive early or on time, but never late.

Jack was an American but had a trace of an English accent as he'd lived in England for many years. He was big—well over six feet tall—with broad shoulders and a weathered face. He was as big as a brown bear and sometimes roared like one. Jack was full of aeronautical knowledge and experience. One of his impressive pilot traits was his knowledge on all of the runway designators of the surrounding airfields. He drove a 1970 Jaguar E to work, and he owned a 1965 Triumph Bonneville motorcycle, a 1963 Aston Martin DB5 automobile (the classic car seen in the James Bond films) and a 1961 Barron B-55 aircraft. Jack lived in a big old English stone house located off the side of a grass runway, convenient for flying his Barron. In his living room an entire wall was a mural of the famous Red Barron tri-plane in an aerial dogfight. The night following Jeff and Jo's wedding I was invited to Jack's most impressive compound.

Jack and I entered his man cave office to begin the oral portion of the practical exam. The office walls were covered with aviation-related photos, maps and diagrams. Model airplanes were arranged on his desk.

He lowered the radio volume that reported continuous ATSI information or ATC transmissions and receptions, depending on which frequency was selected. This room was oozing with so much treasured aviation and pilot miscellany that I was overwhelmed. Just before the start of the most important test of my life, I realized I was not a big-time cool pilot with a massive ego—I felt small and I started to get nervous, just like when football players' confidence affects their ability to play. To rekindle my self-confidence, I said, "What a great day to fly." Of course, I did not know that if I did not pass the oral test then I would not be taking the flight test.

Jack politely sat me down and we began with the loads of paper work. After checking all my documents, the pilot exam questions began. He began to ask all kinds questions on FARs, weather, airspace, the C-150 normal, abnormal and emergency protocol. What documents are required for flight? What does a private pilot need to do to keep current? What are the operating limits of the Cessna 150? The pilot being evaluated needs to know all the emergency procedures of the airplane that he will execute on the flight test; pilots will always be questioned on emergency procedures.

The Gouge. Sound weak on strong systems and sound strong on weak systems. Let me explain. If you're really strong on the fuel system, when asked a question on the fuel system, then hesitate a little bit before you answer. If the examiner assumes you may be weak on the fuel system, he may start digging, start asking you more fuel-system questions. You don't care how many questions he asks you about the fuel system because your knowledge on the fuel system is strong. If the examiner asks you a question on one of the systems that you are not so strong on, like electrical, answer with confidence. He may assume you know this system well and move on to another. It is better to eat up a lot of oral time on subjects you know very well verses subjects in which you may be lacking. If you get really stuck during the orals, and you cannot answer a particular question, make sure you know where to find the answer. If you miss only a few answers to a few questions but you're able to locate the answer in the airplane manual or FAR manual, then you will pass the oral section of the private pilot practical exam.

I figured the oral exam was over and that I had passed the oral because Jack said he wanted to go somewhere. He requested that I plan and file a cross-country flight. The cross-country flight was planned just as if I were going to make a real solo flight. In fact, I had planned to try to block him out of my mind and make believe that he did not exist while he was in the cockpit. At times that was difficult to do, considering how much space Jack's huge physique took up in the cockpit. After checking the weather again and doing the preflight inspection we entered the airplane to go fly. During the flight test ride, I am acting as pilot-in-command and Jack is acting as a passenger. As I said before, my plan was to ignore that the DPE was there and just try to fly the plane as if I were flying solo. The key to the flight test, and the orals for that matter, is to try to stay calm and be confident in your pilot knowledge and skills. Trust in the training that prepared you for these tests.

The cross-country flight was going well. After I flew past the second waypoint of the flight plan Jack said, "I don't really want to go on this cross-country flight. I heard you were good pilot and I would like you to show me some pilot stuff." After demonstrating my ability to navigate he wanted to see if my air work was up to FAA standards. The cross-country flight was cancelled, allowing me to perform the requested maneuvers. After demonstrating steep turns, stalls, slips and slow flight, I felt really confident because I had had practiced these maneuvers many times before, and I had always executed these maneuvers very well. Everything was great, my large ego and confidence started growing when abruptly Jack pronounced, "I feel real sick, we have to land right away; do you know any airports nearby?"

I cannot believe it, big tough Jack feels sick, I thought, doubting the truth of his statement. *I did not plan for this! What am I going to do?* I contemplated. That self-confident emotional high sank to a new low. That pilot command ingrained in my brain ordered me: *fly the plane.*

According to my aeronautical chart, Thorpe Abbotts Field, a small grass strip airfield, was the closest place to land. After doing all the necessary aviating, navigating and communicating to divert to this grass strip airfield, I entered the traffic pattern and set us up for a medical emergency landing. That self-confidence within me rose from the dead as I said to myself, *This is going to work out perfectly.* However, around 100 feet above the ground, during the approach, Jack shouted, "Oh my God! There's a deer on the runway! We can't land!" Well, I didn't see any deer, but I wasn't going to argue with him, so I executed the go-around procedure to transfer the plane's descent path into a climb path.

Months later, I discovered that Jack's home was adjacent to this airfield. How convenient for him. He was very familiar with this airfield, but I was not. After performing the go-around, I re-entered the traffic pattern to set us up for another landing attempt. During this second attempt, I was spring-loaded to react to any potential deer that may obstruct my landing. Everything seemed to be going as planned, and after performing a nice soft field landing on the grass strip, Jack said, "I feel much better now. Let's go back to Lakenheath."

Once again, after the necessary aviating, navigating and communicating required to return to Lakenheath, I was feeling pretty confident again, saying to myself, *I think the ride is over and I think I passed.* But Jack must have sensed that cool, big-time pilot with the large ego growing within me and decided to put me in my private pilot applicant's place. He moved my hand off the throttle, put his hand on the throttle, retarded the throttle to idle and seriously revealed, "We have an engine failure."

Flying can be "like a walk in the park" when everything is going well. The task of piloting an airplane can be as pleasant as a walk in the park, especially when there are no emergencies, no maintenance issues, no weather problems, no traffic delays, no physical or mental fatigue issues and a whole slew of events that could or may happen. Pilots beware! Just when you think things are going great, always be on the alert for safety threats. The engine had failed, and now I had to make an emergency landing.

We were in England's farm country so it wasn't too hard to pick out a nice, flat, farm field for the emergency landing. After picking a suitable landing point, establishing a glide to that landing point and running the engine failure emergency checklist (always know all your emergency procedures by heart) the examiner seemed confident that I would be able to put the airplane down on my attended landing spot. Jack seemed convince that I would land the plane safely on the field I had chosen. Magically, around 200 feet above the ground during the emergency landing approach, Jack joyfully informed me, "The engine is working now! Let's go back to Lakenheath."

I had been so busy, commanding the operation of airplane during the diversion to another airfield, the go-around, the soft field grass landing and then the execution of the emergency engine failure situation that I didn't know if I was confident, nervous or even happy with my performance. Thoughts entered my head: *I wish I could redo some of the maneuvers with a better performance.* Jack, the DPE, was extremely quiet; he didn't say one word. *Why couldn't he just say nice job, or we're going to have to redo something that I screwed up during the flight?* I reran in my head. During the oral test and flight test I tried not to rush speaking and reacting; I attempted to slow down, think fast, but speak slowly, keep calm and stay confident. I asked myself, *Did I do this while demonstrating and aviating the flight maneuvers and emergencies; navigating the cross-country flight and communicating with air traffic control?* Years later, I discovered that most check pilots are more concerned on how a pilot handles various flight situations, rather than on how a pilot demonstrates their piloting acumen.

We arrived back at the aeroclub, shut down the airplane and walked inside. After an hour-and-a-half oral test and a two-hour flight test, I was mentally and physically exhausted as I continued to ponder, *Did I pass or fail?* Jack called me into his aviation museum, his office, and said, "Well, how do you think you did?" Thinking of an answer I thought, *Do not spill your guts and mention every little mistake I made; the examiner may not have noticed all the mistakes.* My response was, "Well, Mr. Benton, I probably could have done better on certain areas of that flight test, but overall, I am satisfied how things went. We are both back on the ground and safe." Most check pilots look at the overall picture of the entire ride and not nitpick every little "you should have." However, the check pilot will debrief you and at times convince you that you are not worthy of a passing grade.

All private pilot practical exams are different yet similar. All DPEs must test the pilot applicant knowledge on certain subject matters and must test the pilot flight skills on certain flight maneuvers, but the examiner has the discretion on how to conduct the practical exam. This is how my private pilot practical exam went. Most likely, all pilot practical exams will be different, but some things will be the same. The bottom line is the DPE will ask himself, "Do I feel safe as a passenger with this pilot and is this pilot competent to exercise the privileges granted with a private pilot license?"

This was my moment of truth. Did I pass or fail? As mentioned earlier, my thinking was *If my aero club debt rose too high, they could ground me until I paid my debt, but if I pass today, they cannot take my private pilot license away from me.* If I passed, then I would be the happiest man alive. The humongous aero club bill, which I may or may not be able to pay, would be in my mailbox, but in my pocket would be a FAA private pilot license. If I failed, then I may not be back for a retest. If I fail, I may be grounded until I make good on my aero club debt. If I am grounded, then I would not be able to take the required additional flight lessons needed for a retest. After all that hard work, time and money, I was not sure how I would handle failure to meet my goal.

What's on Jack's mind? How did Jack evaluate me? When will he say something? These anxious thoughts repeated within me: *Did I pass or fail?*

Finally, Jack grunted, "I need to see your logbook." I handed it to him and watched in anticipation as he completed the appropriate paperwork. The suspense was killing me! Jack then handed me my logbook, along with a piece of paper I hadn't seen before. Grasping it, my hands shaking, I looked down and a grin spread across my face from ear to ear—it was my private pilot certificate. I passed! The excitement from that realization produced a burst of adrenalin that overcame my heretofore exhaustive state. Triumph and pride swelled within me. What seemed like hours, in reality lasted only a few moments. Jack snapped me out of that glorious euphoria with one word: "Congratulations!" He continued with some words of advice, like continue studying, continue flying, keeping current and a bunch of other stuff that wisped through ear to ear. That newly issued temporary private pilot certificate seemed to have temporarily obstructed my thought process. A temporary certificate is the license; it is paper license until the FAA delivers the permanent card replacing the temporary paper.

I did it! I conquered all those challenges to acquire that private pilot license. My big ego as well as my self-confidence ballooned, giving me this euphoric feeling that I am capable of conquering the whole world— that I was some kind of superman. Everyone congratulated me on passing the FAA private pilot "check ride." Check ride? This was really the first time I heard this term. If you are seeking a pilot career, get used to that phrase, "check ride." During my 36-year pilot flight career, I have probably taken over a hundred check rides. Most of these check rides have not been very fun until after the ride is over, when you have passed and then the ride seemed extremely fun.

The Gouge. Before taking the private pilot practical exam, attempt to locate other pilots that have previously taken the exam with the same examiner who will be testing you. Question those pilots on their orals and check ride experience. Get the gouge from those pilots on their practical exam that may help you on yours. Take the private pilot written test as early as possible in your training process. If a wannabe private pilot fails the written, then there is a 30-day wait time to retake the test. If the student passes the written test, then those test results are valid for 24 months, meaning that the student pilot with a passing written exam grade will have two years to take the private pilot practical exam.

Fly often. Even if you have to postpone the start of the private pilot training program, once you start the program, fly as often as possible—at least once or twice a week. Flight skills are like mathematics; your skills will deteriorate if you do not practice them often. When the weather is good, drop everything and fly those solo flights. Practice, practice and re-practice the flight maneuvers. Practice those maneuvers in the air and as well as on the ground through a "chair flying" technique, in which you're sitting in your favorite chair and practicing flying those maneuvers as if you're in the air in the plane's cockpit. Study, study and restudy all that you have learned. Make your own index cards, checklist and gouge list like ATC, ANC, ARROW, AVIATES, and other acronyms.

ATC
A - Attitude
T - Trim
C – Cross-check

ANC
A - Aviate
N - Navigate
C - Communicate

ARROW
A - Airworthiness Certificate
R - Radio Station License

R - Registration Certificate
O - Operation Limitations
W - Weight and Balance

AVIATES

A - Annual (12 months)
V - VOR Check (30 Days)
I - 100 Hour or Progressive Inspection (if aircraft or flight instruction for hire)
A - Altimeter (24 months) and
A - Airworthiness Directives
T - Transponder (24 months)
E - ELT (12 months)
S - Static Inspection (24 months)

To acquire the total knowledge needed to become a pilot, approach learning in small doses, like that big pie we talked about earlier. Slice the big pie up into many small pieces, learn and master each piece, and then put the pieces together.

5

A Pilot in Development

The pilot license is a license to learn.

I was 20 years old; I had a total flight time of 64 hours, and with this private pilot license, the United States Federal Aviation Administration authorized me to command an aircraft for non-commercial purposes under visual flight rules (VFR)—and I could carry passengers. In other words, the passengers could share the expenses of a flight I was piloting, but they could not hire me in the commercial sense. In order to keep my license current, I had to make at least three takeoffs and three landings within 90 days. I also had to pass an FAA Second Class medical once a year, pass a flight review flight check once every 24 months, operate my aircraft in a safe and legal manner and comply with a litany of Federal Aviation rules and regulations. It should also be noted here that the *private pilot license was just a license to learn.* Even with this license, I was still a beginner in the world of pilots. Beginners make mistakes, and some of the mistakes could cost a pilot his life. The pilot stories in this book will take you into my mind of pilot mistakes that were made and how my flight experiences evolved as a pilot throughout my pilot life. What was Frank the pilot thinking and feeling?

Acquiring that pilot's license was my greatest accomplishment at that point in my life. But all was not well. In the fall of 1981, even though I had my private pilot's license that no one could take away, I was about to get my aero club membership revoked because my aero club flight bill was growing larger than my ability to pay.

I was in debt. To make it worse, I had major car problems too. Things were so bad, that I devised a plan to go AWOL. While hitchhiking during heavy rain of course, to my flat in Bury St. Edmunds, an Englishman gave me a ride.

"Oy, mate, how is it going?" he said.

"Not good," I replied.

"I know what you mean," he said, and he told me his gloomy, sad story. After listening to his story, I had a change of heart and decided to tough it out. "If we all threw our problems in a pile and saw everyone else's, we'd grab ours back," said Reginia Brett.[6] Everyone has problems! My problems did not seem as bad as his. After all, I still had a job with the USAF with income, and I had a private pilot's license. *I am doing better than some, not as good as others.*

The Englishman dropped me off in front of my flat, cracked a half of a smile and said, "Thanks for the chat, mate." Frankly, though, it was not much of a chat, because he did all of the talking—or shall I say, complaining. With sympathy and hope, I responded, "Cheerio, tomorrow will be a better day." As I leaped out of his Morris, I caught that half of a smile grow to a full smile. Trotting up the three flights of stairs to my cold, gloomy flat I contemplated, *Maybe tomorrow will be a better day. I will give it a chance.*

Since then, whenever someone asks me how I'm doing, I reply: "Better than most but not as good as some."

In life there is always someone in worse shape than you, and there is always someone doing better than you. Focus on the good things around you, on what is going well. Don't worry so much; try to be happy with a positive outlook on life.

I was in debt because of my aviation addiction and my car woes. After two years living on non-commission rank pay, I began to understand that I needed a college degree. Graduating from a college or a university does not guarantee financial success, of course. Bill Gates of Microsoft did not finish college. However, statistics show that an undergraduate will earn an average annual salary of almost double that of a high school graduate. Money is what I needed if I wanted to continue to fly; renting planes and hiring flight instructors is very costly.

It is possible to obtain a career as a pilot without a college degree. Even though I haven't figured out what type of pilot I wanted to be yet, I did figure out that I needed a college education. My figuring was that a college education would enable me to secure a lucrative job and make more money, thereby enabling me to pay for the training for a pilot career or something in the aviation field.

Embry-Riddle Aeronautical University (ERAU) had an affiliate in England through the USAF, and this is where I enrolled in college part time. My new dream goal was to finish my USAF commitment and then attend ERAU in Daytona Beach full time to acquire a degree in Aeronautical Science. If I were unable to secure a career as a pilot, then at least with an aviation degree I should be able to secure a position in the aviation field and make more money to pay for my addiction.

After a full day's work for the USAF, I would attend night classes four or five nights a week and sometimes take classes on Saturday. Sunday was often the only day to take care of myself: to wash clothes, buy food and other essentials, go to church and just recuperate. When one is motivated to accomplish a goal, these are some of the sacrifices one must be willing to commit to. Sleep, eat, work, attend school, study, repeat. On Sundays I would take some time off to take care of my body and soul. There were intermediate payoffs through the college classes I attended.

My vivid memory of one aviation class, called "Aviation History" exposed me to fabulous pilots and planes, which solidified my path to a pilot career. This class included a visit to the Shuttleworth collection, located at the old Warden aerodrome near Biggleswade in Bedfordshire, England. The collection included flying machines from before and during the First World War, private and sporting airplanes used between the First and Second World Wars, and aircraft used by the flying services since 1918. A Bleriot XI, the world's oldest airworthy aircraft, built in 1909, is on display there. This plane was built only six years after the Wright brothers successfully flew the first plane. While gazing at this magnificent ancient aircraft I envisioned that in 1909 this plane was state-of-the-art yet still experimental for its time in aviation history. After studying the variety of prestigious ancient and well-preserved aircraft, my feeling was one of amazement. I was astonished by the early rudimentary airplanes that early dare devil pilots flew during the birth of aviation. Flying planes was not very safe in the early 1900s.

On another exciting field trip, we journeyed to visit Royal Air Force Wing Commander Ken Wallis at his residence in Reymerston, where he built and flew a variety of auto gyrocopters. A gyrocopter may look similar to a miniature helicopter, but it uses an engine to power a back propeller that pushes it forward, enabling air to pass naturally through the rotor blades, creating lift.

Commander Wallis was tall, partially bald on top, with white-gray hair on the sides and back of his head that matched his two-inch goatee, and which clashed with his two-tone red rosy pale white smiley face. He presented himself with an upright military posture and spoke with a proper, regal English accent. As he listened to your question, he stared at you, smiled and his right eye twinkled. I do not know if the twinkle was intentional or not, but at times it would distract you during questioning. Commander Wallis piloted a demonstration flight for us in an "Auto gyrocopter" called "Little Nellie." He logged 85 flight hours in the Little Nellie to film the auto gyro sequence in the James Bond film, *You Only Live Twice* (1967).

Commander Wallis used less than a few hundred feet of ground to get the "Little Nellie" airborne. This auto gyrocopter has only three basic controls: the throttle, the rudder pedals and the yoke control stick. It seemed like a very versatile and illusive air machine, kind of like flying a great big bald eagle. "Little Nellie" could "turn on a dime," slow to a near-stop, speed up to 100 mph, perform "High-G" turns, flat-spins, spiral-dives, and it needed very little of planet Earth's surface to take off and land. "Little Nellie" could hide behind big barns, trees and small hills. Although the gyrocopter seemed thrillingly fun to fly, the pilot and air machine has distance and weather limitations. Even if the pilot had an instrument-rating license to fly in bad weather, the gyrocopter did not have the required instruments to do so. This situation would be similar to when I was a solo student pilot; most marginal weather conditions would dictate that I could not fly. The gyrocopter had a limited speed of around 100 mph and a limited distance of around 130 miles. For my travel ambitions, this would not be the tool for me. I preferred to fly planes and to travel farther.

Famous veteran pilot William Fryer visited and spoke to our aviation history class one evening. He fought in WW I and WW II and was awarded the Military Cross. He was a World War I Royal Air Force fighter ace and accredited with 11 enemy aerial victories. He shot down dangerous pilot killer, German Lieutenant Walter von Bulow-Bothkamp who had 28 ally confirmed kills. For some time, Fryer was one of the three pilots claiming to have shot down the famous Red Baron (German Captain Manfred Albrecht Freiherr von Richthofen was the Red Baron) on April 21, 1918. The Red Baron had previously shot down 80 allied (mainly British) pilots through aerial aircraft dogfights. Mr. Fryer admitted there was so much smoke and confusion during that dogfight that he or one of the other two pilots may have shot down the Red Baron.

Mr. Fryer limped with a cane in hand, wearing a battered leather flight jacket into our aviation of history classroom full of curious, eager students. He was aged beyond his years from having flown numerous deadly air battles during the wars. He parked himself on the front chair at a 45-degree angle, facing the rest of us and shifted his half-opened tired eyes towards us. I particularly remember that Mr. Fryer was nearly deaf in his right ear and partially deaf in his left ear from years of flying open cockpit planes. We students had to speak loudly into his left ear. I posed this curious flight question to William the pilot, "Were you afraid of crashing when you landed in those days?"

Mr. Fryer took out his ancient pilot log book, showed us many pictures of various airplanes he had flown and said, "In those days, to land was to crash, because usually the landing gear failed."

I thought, *I give 100% total effort into my landings to avoid landing hard and in an attempt to land smoothly. It never occurred to me that the landing gear could collapse and I may crash. How frightful it must have been to know that your landing gear could collapse on each and every attempted landing.* Yes, landing is the hardest part of flying, especially when the construction of the plane's landing gear had not yet been perfected. It seemed like in Mr. Fryer's aviation days, landing was also the second most dangerous part of flying next to being shot at by the enemy.

He explained that it was not uncommon to fly two or three different types of airplanes in one week because in those days, you may have crashed an airplane on your most recent landing. During Mr. Fryer's time, the history of flying and building planes was in its infancy; it had been only about 15 years since Wilbur and Orville Wright flew the first sustained airborne aircraft flight in Kill Devil Hills, North Carolina, on December 17, 1903. On that date, the Wright brothers were the first ever to "pilot a machine that took off under its own power into the air in full flight, sailed forward with no loss of speed, and landed at a point as high as that from which it started." [7]

William explained that there was no formal training on spins. A spin is an aggravated stall in which the airplane follows a downward corkscrew path. The airplane is basically descending due to gravity, rolling, yawing and pitching in a spiral path. He describes scenarios of return flights to the airfield where he could not see the field because of clouds. He had arrived back to where he thought the airfield was but clouds obscured the landing location. He and other pilots would search for a hole in the clouds and put the plane into a spin maneuver to descend within that hole through the cloud deck. Hopefully, he would see the ground and have enough altitude to recover. These pilots did not receive any spin training from instructors because during these early days of flight by man, this training did not exist. It was only years later that William discovered that the maneuver he used to descend through a hole in a cloud deck was called a spin. Attempting to locate the airfield and land was a dangerous maneuver, but what other choice did he have?

William Fryer had our full attention with every word emanating from his experienced mouth on those early days of pilot history. The words arrived softly upon us with a detection that he was proud of his aviation accomplishments and of his survival. The context of those soft-spoken words created powerful images of "Oh my god" and "I can't believe it!"

He left us with one more shocking pilot story. During those early days of flying, families would have picnics and spend hours at the airports. William and his pilot peers would construct a full-person dummy from old clothes and rags. He would put the dummy in his cockpit with him and fly over the airfield. While flying overhead he would manipulate the flight controls to rock the wings and pivot the plane from left to right, giving the innocent earth viewer the illusion the plane was in trouble and may crash. At the right time, after an enormous crowd gathered, all were standing and pointing towards him, he would then throw the dummy overboard. Imagine the screams and terror among the crowd and the laughter and jubilation among the pilots. Pilots are cool and do cool things! Pilots enjoy having fun and sometimes at others' expense. Later I will regale you with a story of screwing with flight attendants at 30,000 feet.

This was by far my favorite, most enjoyable and aeronautically inspired college course I have ever taken—at least up to this point in my life. This "History of Aviation" class cemented aviation addiction in me and I loved it. There is not a medical specialist on planet Earth who had a cure for my affliction.

While serving in the USAF, I was an accountant using two computer systems to report aviation fuel purchases for all the aircraft at RAF Mildenhall and RAF Lakenheath. It was during this time that, among many of my peers, I was selected "Airman of the Quarter." The selecting board members asked me: "What are the branches of our government and which one is the most important?" Apparently, I was the only candidate who correctly answered, "The legislative, the executive and the judicial branch and they all shared equal power." This "Airman of the Quarter" award earned me an observation air refueling flight on a KC-135 Stratotanker aircraft.

The KC-135 military jet is similar to the Boeing B-707 civilian jet; however, instead of carrying loads of *people*, the KC-135 carried loads of *fuel*. The primary mission of this military plane was to provide aerial refueling to other military bomber jets and fighter jets up in the air. These planes did not have to land to get fuel; they can stay in the air meet up with a KC-135 for refueling.

This observation flight entailed a KC-135 aircraft refueling an F-15 Eagle fighter jet while in flight at an altitude of 30,000 feet. The F-15 is an intercept and fighter jet that can penetrate enemy defense, outperform and outfight enemy aircraft. It is equipped with weapons that detect, acquire, track and attack enemy aircraft. When the F-15 is carrying lots of weapons, it cannot carry large quantities of fuel to fly long missions, hence the inflight fueling, extending the time the jet can fly its mission.

To complete an aerial refueling, the KC-135 and F-15 meet inflight and fly in a front-to-back formation. The F-15 moves to a position behind the KC-135 aided by director lights and directions radioed by the boom operator. A hose that can extend 48 feet from the KC-135, with a funnel-shaped cup attached to the end of the hose, connects to an inserted fitted probe of the F-15 aircraft. An operator stationed in the rear of the plane controls the boom. After a proper connection is made, fuel is transferred from the KC-135 to the F-15. Visualize a baby sucking breast milk from its mother, except that the nipple is receiving the life-saving fluid and the mouth is providing the nutritious fuel.

Witnessing this precision flying and the whole refueling operation was a spellbinding experience for me. I thought to myself, *What type of pilot do I want to be, the KC-135 pilot or the F-15 pilot, a military pilot or a civilian pilot?* There are many types of pilots.

Private pilots are the most common type, which is what I was at the time. There are sport pilots, recreational pilots, flight instructor pilots, banner-tow pilots, aerial photographer pilots, bush pilots, cargo pilots, corporate pilots, commercial pilots, military pilots and airline transport pilots. Jeff wanted to be an airline transport pilot—one who flies commercial airlines for a living.

A bigger plane

Many long weeks had passed since that private pilot practical exam. Somehow, I was able to reduce my extraordinary flight bill down to a point to which the aero club permitted me to rent planes and hire flight instructors again. When I abruptly stop flying, my body was deprived of the joys of operating an air machine above planet Earth, and it required time for me to adjust to functioning without the pleasure. This adjustment period caused me an annoying itch and a yearning to fly. The brutal sentence was over, and I was back in the air again.

This time, I was getting checked out in a bigger airplane and learning about instrument flying. Imagine a new, first-year driver, driving a basic subcompact economy automobile, a vehicle that the driver has become very comfortable and familiar with. Now, imagine how overwhelmed and impressed that driver may feel stepping into a large sophisticated and complicated luxury automobile with new enhanced instrument gauges. It may not seem eventful, but it was a tremendous transition for me, on top of which I was going to learn a new type of flying.

Instrument flying allows a pilot to fly in certain bad weather. In the aviation world, pilots command planes under visual flight rules (VFR) and instrument flight rules (IFR) depending on visual meteorological conditions (VMC) and instrument meteorological conditions (IMC). Basically, a VFR pilot flying in VMC is flying primarily using outside visual references, whereas an IFR pilot flying in IMC conditions is flying primarily by referencing instruments inside the cockpit. A non-instrument-rated pilot, like me, is limited to flying during VMC, when the weather is good. For example, a VFR pilot flying under VMC must maintain a forward visibility of three miles, stay at least 500 feet below clouds, at least 1,000 feet above clouds, and 2,000 feet horizontal from clouds in addition to a number of other restrictions depending on the class of airspace, altitude and airspeed. It seemed like every time I had a day off and planned to go fly, England presented me with clouds and fog, confining me to the ground. I hated that! Obtaining an instrument rating would allow me more opportunities to fly and also make me a safer pilot.

The Gouge. There is a safety factor for all VFR pilots to learn some instrument flying. Instrument know-how can help prevent dangerous disasters, like when a pilot inadvertently flies into deteriorating weather and becomes spatially disoriented. This was probably the cause of John F. Kennedy Jr.'s plane crash of 1999 in a Piper Saratoga P-32R, and many other pilots that have encountered similar situations. Pilots must learn to trust the information provided by the plane's instruments more than the information obtained from visual cues. Visual cues may provide false illusions to the pilot of the plane's situation, whereas a correct interpretation of instrument data provides accurate information to the pilot of the plane's situation. Ideally, the instrument data should match the visual data, but always trust your instruments. All VFR pilots should get some instrument flight training.

To fly in bad weather, the pilot and airplane must be instrument certified. The Cessna C-172 airplane, called the *Skyhawk*, was bigger and faster than the C-150 and could seat four persons. The Skyhawk weighed about 1,500 pounds with a maximum takeoff gross weight of 2,500 pounds. It was 27 feet long with a 35-foot wingspan. The Skyhawk had a 160-horsepower engine that could fly a distance of around 600 nautical miles (690 statute miles), and as fast as 125 KTS (145 mph). It could fly up to an altitude of 17,000 feet. About 42,500 of these aircraft were built.[8] The C-150 had basic instruments in order to fly heading, altitude and airspeed during VMC (or in other words, direction, height and speed during good weather).

The C-172 had more sophisticated aviation electronics, like Navigation Receiver (NAV REC) and a Horizontal Situation Indicator

(HIS) to guide the pilot to fly an Instrument Landing System (ILS) approach and land safely on a runway during instrument meteorology conditions (such as clouds or fog). If a pilot faced limited visibility because of bad weather, he could execute an ILS approach that could guide the pilot safely, via instruments, down to an altitude of 200 feet. High-level, instrument-rated pilots, with certain certified planes and at certain certified airports are permitted, via the ILS approach guidance system, to fly to an altitude point very low above planet Earth in IMC, when the weather is bad. This point is called the decision height (DH), and at this altitude, the pilot has to decide whether or not he can see the runway and land visually. If he cannot see the runway, the pilot must go around and try the approach again or land at another airport.

An electronic signal from a ground-based facility at the airport would be sent to the NAV REC, which would send a signal to the HSI. The HSI instrument would display to the pilot if he were high or low vertically, left or right horizontally from the correct course to the runway. The pilot would make the appropriate adjustments. If the visibility was good, the flight instructor would put a hood over the pilot's head so that the student pilot could only see the interior cockpit instruments, simulating flying in bad weather. At the end of September of 1981, I experienced my first flight in a C-172 (aircraft tail number N14496), my first ILS instrument approach instruction, and my first flight into a big airport (London Stanstead Airport (EGSS).

Stansted is a major international airport located 40 miles northeast of London. The long, wide runways at Stansted provide an illusion to the pilot, like me, who is used to flying into small airfields—that the pilot is higher during the landing approach phase than the pilot actually is. This illusion is one of many other illusions that pilots encounter during certain landings at certain airports. If the pilot is unaware that the plane is actually lower than the pilot interprets using visual clues, then a potential bad landing could occur. This is one extremely important reason that a pilot must interpret and believe the cockpit's instrument data. Stansted is so busy, with big planes coming and going most of the day, that my instructor had to prearrange via a telecom a timeslot for us to practice instrument ILS approaches there.

The ILS approach technology has increased the safety of air travel, reduced air disasters, improved the efficiency and flow at airports throughout the world. Flying an ILS approach is the primary instrument approach that all commercial pilots fly during low visibility approaches to airports. You will not believe it when I discuss, later in this book, how low I was authorized to fly an ILS approach during bad weather in order to land the plane.

Although I may have been initially overwhelmed flying a bigger, newer, sophisticated airplane and flying an instrument ILS approach into a very big airport, I loved the challenge and the sense of accomplishment. Remember the pizza pie? I was mastering the knowledge and another pilot skill—another small piece of the aviation pie, and that gives me pilot satisfaction.

The Gouge. The altitude, trim and cross-check (ATC) technique discussed earlier is more important when flying via instruments, especially flying an ILS approach. The pilot's cross-check (the scan) of the instrument data must increase in speed and rise to a higher level in order to make timely adjustments to the sensitivity of flying instruments; especially for an ILS approach. The key is to scan fast, interpret the data, make minor adjustments and not overcorrect.

6

THE THINGS PILOTS WILL DO TO BUILD FLIGHT TIME

Trust your instruments.

On March 5, 1982, my pilot friend, Jeff Guys, and I piloted a C-172 (the Skyhawk) airplane to Nottingham, England, to spend the night and to return the next day. On the flight to Nottingham, I was the safety pilot and on the return flight I was the pilot-in-command. Our goals were to share operating cost, build flight time, enhance pilot experience and travel to a new interesting English city.

We went out that night to the most recommended local pub in Nottingham. There she was—the most beautiful English woman any human has ever seen. Her stunning, glistening face shined through the pub's partially smoke-filled atmosphere to my mesmerized eyes. My attention was diverted from buying Jeff and me the first round of local lager beer to being completely transfixed to her gorgeous, hazel-blue eyes pulling me in closer. As I arrived within an arm's length to Miss Super Special, her aroma overwhelmed my senses and bodily control. She put a spell on my commands and reduced my body to a museum statue. She smelled luscious! You could see attractive sparkles streaking from her eyes like a fire when it flickers and spews light displays. The hair of Miss Great-Looking was light blonde, like the color of the morning sunbeam, and shaped into the latest, most popular English hair style. Those soft, full, light-pink lips matched the small pearl-like earrings that dazzled in response to her bouncy hair moments. Those mouth-watering lips framed teeth whiter than fresh Alaskan snow and together produced the most alluring, friendly smile. All that was above her waist would have been judged my any human being as the healthiest, well-proportioned perfect female body. I was in love.

Acting confident, like a cool, big-time American pilot with a massive ego, I tried to impress her as I opened our first conversion. This was done during the challenging process of attempting to reduce my racing heart beat and elevated breathing to their normal state. Initially, Miss Gorgeous seemed interested in me, or maybe interested in my foreign New York accent. Miss Beautiful asked several questions: "What's your name? Where are you from? What do you do and how did you get here?" In full brag mode, I answered all of the inquiries of the goddess with heavy emphasis on me being a great, big-time American cool pilot. She melted me with her delicious smile, and then gracefully turned to converse with some stupid-looking English bloke. She was the most beautiful woman in the entire world and wanted nothing to do with a boastful, American pilot. *Was it my accent,* I wondered, *or her other boyfriend? Didn't that insignificant ugly guy know that I was her new boyfriend?* In reality, Jeff and I were poor and barely had enough money for a few pints and a place to stay for the night, but that did not stop a couple of 21-year-olds from bragging like they were highly admired seasoned pilots with over 20,000 hours of pilot time. What do women want and how do you impress them? We left the atmosphere of that fantastic pub empty handed.

The weather deteriorated on the return flight to Lakenheath. We faced torrential rain, reduced flight visibility and increased moderate turbulence due to multiple cumulus cloud decks. Jeff and I were not instrument-rated, although each of us had some instrument training. The ride developed into a rough and bumpy experience, kind of like the experience we had the night before, trying to meet a pair of English goddesses.

Lakenheath was reporting 33-knot crosswinds at the airport that I had to deal with. Jeff was now the safety pilot and I was the pilot-in-command. Landings are the hardest part of flying.

There are two popular crosswind landing techniques: the crab method and the slip method. On that day, the crosswinds were so strong—33 knots—that I combined elements of both landing techniques to get the Skyhawk on the ground. Visualize a plane lined up on the final approach centerline with the wings straight-and-level. If winds are blowing from the left, then the plane will drift to the right of the desired centerline course. To maintain flying on the centerline, the pilot must steer left of course into the wind in a crab fashion. The pilot crabs the plane into the wind to fly the desired runway centerline. When crabbing left, the airplane's nose is aimed into the wind, and to the left, but the airplane's movement is on the desired course.

However, the plane cannot land in a crab position because if the wheels are not aligned with the runway centerline upon landing, then the landing gear will be damaged and possibly cause the plane to crash. Prior to touchdown, the pilot must undo the crab technique and transition to a slip technique. The pilot transitions from flying a wings-level crab into the wind to a low-wing slip into the wind. Depending on the wind and other conditions, this transition usually occurs around 50 to 150 feet above the ground.

The slip technique requires banking the airplane into the wind and applying opposite rudder to align the airplane's nose and the landing gear with the desired runway centerline course. In this scenario, the left hand holding the yoke will be lower than the level flight position and more right-foot input rudder pressure is applied. The upwind main wheel of the landing gear will touch down before the other wheels. It is important that the pilot does not overcorrect banking into the wind to avoid the upwind wing from scraping the runway's surface. During the transition, the pilot needs to adjust the pitch and power of the plane.

The Gouge. During strong, crosswind landings do not bank too much or the wing may scrape the runway surface; use rudder pedal inputs to slip appropriately to avoid sliding left or right of centerline. Land with the upwind wheel touching the surface first. Land with a little engine power and plant the plane firmly on the runway. When landing is strong winds forgo the smooth landing, where floating and drifting are more suspectable, for the firm landing on the targeted runway spot. If at 10 or 20 feet the landing picture does not look good, then go around and get it right the second time or go land at another airport with more favorable wind conditions.

The things pilots will do to build up their flight time

I took Lieutenant Officer Santini and his wife for a scenic flight of the area. Interesting, he was a higher military rank than me, because he was an officer rank and I was an airman rank. He had commanding authority over me through the USAF while on the ground. However, while inflight, I was pilot-in-command and had authority over him. We shared the expenses of this flight.

After my sister graduated high school, she came to England to visit me. As a graduation present, I flew her on a scenic flight of the area. Three friends shared flight expenses with me on a weekend layover trip that I piloted to Brighton Shoreham-at-Sea airport (EGKA) in the C-172. Another friend, Mike Dantz, who showed an interest in flying, shared flight expenses with me on a demonstration flight. By not hiring a CFI pilot and paying the full airplane rental rate, he saved money. Mike's discovery flight sparked a taste of what it would be like to learn how to fly, and of course, I logged the valuable pilot-in-command flight time.

Pilots must take recurrent check rides as required by the FAA, and certified flight instructor (CFI) Jo Rides gave me my first recurrent ride. Jo, a newly hired instructor at the aero club, was a beautiful, blonde, blue-eyed English woman from the Isle of Man. She was my height, smiled with glowing snow-white teeth, smelled deliciously seductive and spoke with the sexiest English dialect. She wore a busty, white button-down shirt with a black tie. There were not many women pilots in 1983, and Jo presented herself as a person who had to prove she was an excellent professional pilot.

She gracefully approached me. Jo engaged her mother-like loving arms around me and embraced her lovely warm hands on my erector spinae. She leaned in, her busty warm breast connected with my smooth, slightly elevated chest and her hot scrumptious moist lips covered my yearning lips. Her fantastic hot body scent combined with a dash of light perfume hypnotized me. Jo, an English lassie, lusciously French-kissed me; just as I dreamed multiple times she would. We were in heaven. This mouth to mouth, tongue to tongue, make out between us lasted hours or maybe all day long. I was unable to calculate time because my internal clock failed. As our clothes disappeared, my uncontrollable body reached maximum arousal, I was just seconds away from making beautiful love to my future wife. "Frank, FRANK watch your airspeed!" Jo disruptively shouted at me! *What? Oh damn! I'm taking a check ride,* were my thoughts that jolted me back into reality. I reengaged and resumed the expected acts of a good pilot: attitude, trim and cross-check.

At the time it was hard for me to separate professionalism with personalism, especially when the other pilot is a gorgeous, sexy Brit. This was my first experience flying with a woman. I really liked her. In fact, I fell in love with her during that first flight, or so I thought. Throughout the check ride I tried to impress her with my pilot knowledge and skills. For some women, fancy flying is not everything.

Months later, Jo married my good pilot friend, Jeff. Not only was Jeff a better pilot than me but he got the best girl. Jo claimed I came in second place. Jeff had me as the best man at their wedding, and I was happy for them.

No worries, all was good. The things pilots have to do to keep flying. The things pilots will do to build up their flight time.

Whore for flying

Several British friends, who had previously labeled me Frank the Yank, started labeling me Frank the Pilot. Even though they and I thought I was a cool, big-time American pilot, the reality was that I was still an inexperienced pilot with low flight hours trying to achieve a career in flying. Are you struggling to get you career off the ground? Are you trying to accelerate the process? Will you do anything to help progress your career? It is import to proceed safely and legally.

When I first started flying, I would do anything to accumulate free flight hours. Because I was addicted to aviation, I was a whore for flying. On January 16, 1983, I hitchhiked to Shoreham-at-Sea airport (EGKA), located about 100 miles south of London on the English Channel. The trip totaled 170 miles of hitchhiking in typical wet, cold, English weather.

From Shoreham airport I piloted a C-150 airplane (N60626), with no navigation aids and no radios during turbulence and strong winds, back to RAF Lakenheath Aero Club. That's like driving for three hours with no smart phone: no voice, no text, no AAPL/GOOG maps, no nothing, and no one with you. During the planned three-hour flight, I would have to circumnavigate London's Heathrow International Airport—one of the busiest airports in the world. I would have to fly with just an aeronautical map and a compass. A compass is susceptible to gyroscopic precession. A gyrocompass uses a fast-spinning disc and the rotation of the earth to find geographical direction; and it is susceptible to precession error, especially while flying in turbulent air.

Everything you see on an aeronautical map, you should be able to see on the ground, but not everything you see on the ground is on the map. Topography and geography change quicker than maps change. After navigating the airplane around London in turbulence and strong winds, I became disoriented (not positive where I was). It is not a good feeling when you are all by yourself, lost, and 3,000 feet above planet Earth. You must know that feeling when you are lost, and do not want to or cannot ask for directions.

I did not have a working radio and you know, "*You just can't pull over to a cloud and ask for directions.*" I was thinking about safety. *Live first! It is better to tell a bad, embarrassing story than to die and not be able to tell a story at all.* I spotted a small airfield below, made a pilot command decision to land, get some more fuel, and get directions.

Not to give myself away, I entered the airport's FBO acting like cool, big-time American pilot with a massive ego. I may have been Frank the Pilot, but to them I was Frank the Yank. Portraying a false confidence, I said to the Englishman working there, "Oi, mate, I need some fuel. Nice airport you have here. How do you pronounce it?" The FBO operator pronounced the airport's name with his English accent, and with my best effort I attempted to repeat the name with similar connotations. Saying the airport's name promoted good international relations, but most importantly, I had the name, and with the name I proceeded to look up the airport's name on an aeronautical map. I plotted a new flight course, paid my fuel bill, and said "Cheerio." Full of actual real confidence, I now knew where I was and therefore where to go. I taxied out, took off and flew the C-150 airplane to Lakenheath.

The Gouge. *It is better to tell a bad, embarrassing story than to die and not be able to tell a story at all.* I lived. I was able to cover up an embarrassing story. I made a command decision to land and used the excuse that I needed fuel when I really needed directions. But most importantly, I was safe and legal. Safety first. Always be safe, and if possible, be legal on and above ground!

During my early flight career, I would do anything to accumulate free flight time. The things pilots will do to build up their flight time. Pilots are whores for flying; they will do anything to fly, and in my case, I would do anything to build up valuable flight time. One time I went absent without leave (AWOL) while serving in the military trying to get a few free flight hours.

AWOL for flying

When advancing or promoting your career, beware of your ego; it could get you in trouble. One Friday afternoon, Jeff and I received Permissive TDY (Temporary Duty Assignment) orders to take a military HOP (a free aircraft ride) to Ramstein Air Base in Frankfurt, Germany, to pick up a plane from the Ramstein, Germany, and fly it back to Lakenheath, England. This was a great opportunity. We could get at least four or five hours of free flight time, spend Friday night in Germany, eat German food, pilot the airplane back to England on Saturday or Sunday and be back to work on Monday.

No problem, what could go wrong? I was thinking.

Generally, Jeff was a good influence on me, but this time, not so much. The HOP to Germany went fine. We met Mike, an aero club member who took us out for our first German meal. This first German food experience was fantastic, but that is another story. At the restaurant, Jeff made the mistake of asking for pepper, salt and ketchup. The cook came out from the kitchen and wanted to know what was wrong with the meal he had just prepared.

The next day, we went to the Ramstein Aero Club to pick up the airplane and fly it to England. One moment, everything about our plan to fly a plane from Germany to England was going great, and the next moment, everything descended into chaos. Bad news. The aero club manager informed us that the aircraft was down for maintenance due to a hard landing made the previous day. The manager explained that he was able to obtain authorization for a special one-time "Ferry Flight" waiver and we could fly the aircraft back to England. We called our aero club manager Jack Benton (That's the John Benton, the DFE, I had passed my check ride with to get that valuable private pilot license) and told him about the situation. Jack did not want the aircraft in a state disrepair.

In that case, no problem. We could stay in Germany another night, eat more great German food and go home Sunday.

Bad news. Guess what? There were no military HOPs to England on Sunday. Plus, because we had permissive TDY orders that would expire on Monday, we would be put on the bottom status of any list of others who wanted to HOP back to England on the limited available seats.

On Monday at 8:00 AM I called my supervisor and said, "Sergeant Rodney Bramilton, I am going to be a little late for work today."

"That's obvious," said Rodney, thinking I was calling from BSE, 17 miles away. "Well, I'm going to be *a lot* late for work today," I said. "I'm in Germany." He shouted, "What!?"

Bad news!

Yes, I was now officially AWOL (a serious crime in the military). My arms and legs began to shake, my voice choked up and I lost a heartbeat or two as I swallowed a whole chunk of useless air. I was in big trouble! *What was I thinking?* For several moments, that seemed like hours, I was very scared and lost for words. I was scared like a young lost boy all alone on a frightful night. Finally, I apologized, "I am sorry, I will do everything I can to get back to England." I let my ego get me into serious trouble. The things pilots will do to build up their flight time.

Through hectic maneuvering to another German base, we did get back to England on Monday night. An AWOL punishment could lead to a conviction with reduction in rank, reduction in pay, expulsion from the military, hard labor or all of the above.

The Gouge. Don't let your big ego get you into trouble. No one is above the law, even military law. When advancing you career, be legal, both when flying and on the ground. Admit when you are wrong and tell the truth. Always tell the truth. There is no cover up in flying.

I was in my third year in the USAF with the rank of only a three-stripe airman, and I went to Germany to fly a plane back to England. Many other higher-rank sergeants and officers were astonished that a three-year USAF airman was leaving the English Isles to go to Europe to fly a plane back. One of those upper ranks said, "Who does he think he is, Charles Lindbergh?" I thought I was a big-time American pilot with a massive ego trying to build up my flight time to advance my chances for a career as a pilot. The reality was that I just a young, inexperienced private pilot—just lowly Airman Donohue serving in the USAF.

Good news. The Generals (the higher ranks) went easy on me and said to themselves, "He is good guy with an interesting AWOL excuse and he had no history of prior trouble." Plus, I told the truth. Lieutenant

Officer Santini contributed a few supportive words on my behalf for my defense. My punishment was two weekends of hard labor, which turned into a blessing in disguise. For the two weekends, I was ordered to paint some of the rooms in our accounting office building. However, to my benefit, I was able to take the leftover paint back to my flat where I put it to good use. I guess I was a good guy with an interesting AWOL excuse and no prior trouble, so they went easy on me. Still, I vowed never to go AWOL again. I am so grateful that I did not get expelled from the USAF or, worse, expelled from the aero club. Always remember, and you will never forget; when advancing you career, Be Legal! The things pilots will do to build up their flight time.

At one of our aero club meetings, I was the keynote speaker. The aero club wanted to present me as a great example of someone who obtained his private pilot's license in less than five months, while flying in English weather. They wanted me to inspire and motivate potential future pilots to join the club and learn to fly. To think I was a cool, big-time American pilot with a massive ego when in reality I was so nervous during my first-time public speaking event that I choked up a few times. My palms were sweating, my cheeks were flushing and I have no idea what I was scared of. Speaking to 50 people is so much different than taking a few people flying. Public speaking is so much different from commanding an airplane.

There are tips to prepare before speaking publicly, tips that I did not follow. Before speaking, you need to know your audience and your purpose for speaking. Eliminate anything that doesn't clearly support your purpose, and don't drown your audience with data. Do everything you can to help them hear and understand you. No one is interested in hearing from an "I" doctor, a person who uses the word "I" in every sentence. It is not about *you*. Talk for the benefit of the *audience*. Like preparing to fly, I should have prepared for that speech. My disastrous example of oration did provide some benefit to our aero club that night. As a result of my sputtering about how I, just a two-striper with no prior flight experience, was able to obtain a private pilot's license, the audience understood that anyone was capable of learning to fly. Five new wannabe pilots joined the aero club that night!

At age 17, I had a near-death experience as a driver, with three friends encountering an auto skid during a snow storm in upstate New

York. At age 21, I had another near-death experience as a passenger with three women in an auto accident enroute from Madrid to Benidorm, Spain. A few months later, I had yet another near-death experience as the driver with three guys in an auto skid on black ice in the Midland Mountains in England. In aviation class, I had learned about Freezing Drizzle (FZDZ), Freezing Rain (FZRA), Hoarfrost (not whores), Rime Ice, and Clear Ice—but what was Black Ice? Black Ice is a thin sheet of clear ice or glaze that is formed when rain falls onto roads of sub-zero temperatures. Black Ice is dark and is very dangerous because the road appears wet rather than icy.[9] You cannot see Black Ice. Under Black Ice conditions, drivers encounter little or no traction, little to no braking and extremely poor directional control.

These experiences influenced me to feel safer with air machines flying than with those on the ground. Flying is safer than driving. According to widely-available statistics, it is estimated that the annual risk of being killed in a plane crash for the average American is about 1 in 11 million. Whereas, the annual risk of being killed in a motor vehicle crash for the average American, is about 1 in 5,000.

Time spent in England

During the three years I spent in England, I had several ways to get around. First, I had a Japanese-made Suzuki 250TS Motorcycle. Next, I had a green English-made Austin Mini car, followed by a red German-made Audi 500 car, then a gray English-made Austin Cambridge car, and finally, a blue American-made Chevy LUV pickup truck with a camper shell. The USAF transported the Chevy LUV truck back to the USA for me. My air transportation consisted of a Cessna C-152 and a Cessna C-172 aircraft. Of course, I did not own those planes. I just rented them on an as-needed basis.

During my free time, I took college courses to pursue a degree in aviation. I also traveled throughout most of the United Kingdom and to Europe, including:

- Amsterdam, Netherlands
- Paris and Fontainebleau, France
- Athens and Mykonos, Greece

- Madrid, Spain
- Venice and Rome, Italy
- Lucerne and Bern, Switzerland
- Salzburg, Austria
- Frankfurt and Munich, Germany

7

CALIFORNIA

Beautiful

This tremendous opportunity, that so few people are granted, had been granted to me. Here I was, flying above the Earth with my hands manipulating the air machine through the atmosphere. My right hand on the throttle, my left on the yoke, and my feet engaged with the rudder pedals. The plane and I are now one, like an engagement. The right hand grants power to the engine, making it roar, and increasing the speed of the plane. Commanding the right hand controls, I can restrict the fuel flow to the engine to slow her down to an idle speed in which the plane and I will barely crawl through the air. With my left hand on the yoke, I can control the direction of the plane. If I push on the yoke, the nose of the plane points down to descend, and the airspeed will increase. If instead I pull the yoke back, the plane will climb, and speed will decrease. With my left hand on the yoke, I can direct the plane's left and right turns while I use my feet to engage the rudder pedals and coordinate these turns. My hands and feet have so much control over the positioning of the plane, and I am only too pleased with this.

On May 31st of 1983, with the C-172 tail number N14496, I piloted my last flight in England. During that two-hour flight I practiced: power-on stalls, power-off stalls, slow flight, 720s, slips, as well as crosswind and soft field take off and landings. I even practiced a few extra things, just for fun; I didn't know yet when I would fly again, and I wanted to savior the experience. Of all that I had accomplished during my three years living in England, this hard-earned privilege to pilot planes above planet Earth pleased me the most.

In June of 1983, I flew as a passenger on a C-141 Starlifter from the Royal Air Force (RAF) Mildenhall station in England, to Dover Air

Force Base (AFB) in Delaware. I used this six-hour flight back to the USA to reflect on my three years in England, and I visualized my future as a pilot; daydreaming, I thought to myself *Maybe someday I will be the one flying a C-141*. Of course, first I would need to finish the last six months of the four-year commitment I had made to the USAF, and my college degree.

After landing in Dover, I utilized public transportation to make my way to Bayonne, New Jersey, to get my Chevy Luv pickup truck. Then I drove it through New York City to my parent's home on Long Island. After staying for a week, my local friend Ralph Saydontyou and I took a long-distance drive to Denver, Colorado, in 48 hours before we moved on to Sacramento, California.

Ralph had been a long-time neighborhood friend of mine, and a fun, good-spirited guy to be around. We're similar in many ways: he is less than a year older than me, of similar height and build, and is full of energy, ambition and imagination. Ralph and I had numerous, extensive and imaginative conversations on what next big idea would make us rich and famous—or at least rich. Ralph also had interest in photography and hang gliding. At the time, he had just lost his mother to suicide, and he needed to get away, so traveling with me across the USA was his perfect out.

So, while we were in the Denver area, Ralph and I indulged in hang gliding with Ralph's glider. A hang glider is a non-motorized kite that a harnessed rider hangs from while gliding down from a high place like a cliff or a hill; it is a different type of air transport that many pilots fly for recreation. Hang gliding is the closest experience we humans can get to flying like birds. The pilot is attached to kite-like wings, similar to the way a bird is. Soaring like an eagle, the pilot manipulates the hang glider to freely swarm, zoom, soar and glide through the air. The updrafts that airplane pilots attempt to evade, glider pilots instead embrace. Hang gliding is one of the most economical ways to fly, but in exchange you must trek the heavy glider up a mountain to start flight, and retrieve it upon landing. My first-time hang-gliding was exhilarating, but I find commanding a plane to fly is both more challenging and rewarding for me.

Then, after our week spent in the Denver area, we continued our drive to California; it was here that, at age 22, I had another near-death experience. On this drive, Ralph and I encountered the ash cloud of one of the worst brush fires to hit Nevada; this caused our terrible life-threatening breakdown on the highway. This rekindled my thoughts on why I would rather operate an air transport machine than a ground transport machine: because planes are more reliable and safer than cars. However, we managed to survive the brush fire accident and made it to Sacramento.

Sacramento: the capitol city of California; and I had arrived in July, the driest month of the year, with temperatures averaging 90º Fahrenheit and plenty of sunshine. Unlike in England though, most days in California are good weather for flying. California is the third largest US state by size, and probably the most diverse state in nature, culture and demographics. There are beaches, mountains, farms, forests, deserts, technology centers, Hollywood and many cities to view. It was here, in Sacramento, that I would be serving the remaining six months of my USAF commitment at the McClellan Air Force Base (AFB).

"Located seven miles northeast of Sacramento, California, McClellan AFB served as a logistics and maintenance facility for a wide variety of military aircraft, equipment, and supplies." [10] McClellan functioned as the main depot for overhauling the Air Force's F-111, FB-111 and EF-111 aircraft, as well as the A-10 Thunderbolt II aircraft. [11] Hercules HC-130 aircraft operated there as well. McClellan had an aero club with Piper Warrior II PA 28-161 airplanes.

Upon my arrival, one of the first things I did was to go to McClellan's aero club and become a member; thus, allowing me to rent a plane and start flying. However, renting a plane is not like the rental car business, where all you need to do is show them your driver's license, credit card and pay a rental fee for them to give you the keys to a vehicle. No one is going to rent out a plane without first checking out the pilot. So, in addition, the pilot will have to pass a ground test, a short oral test, and a mini check ride on the rental plane. This helps assure the renter that the pilot will safely operate their planes and not crash.

The Piper PA-28 is known as the "Cherokee Warrior," or "Warrior" for short. The Cessna C-172 is known as the "Skyhawk." Initially, to me, flying the Warrior was very different compared to the Skyhawk. All my previous flight time was piloting the C-150 and C-172, which were very similar planes; the C-172 being just a bigger version of the C-150. So, switching to the Warrior felt very different to me. In hindsight, the practical differences are minor, but at the time, this was a new type of plane

I had to learn to fly. Each airplane model has its own unique flight characteristics, with a different control panel and the knobs, switches, buttons and circuit breakers all being different. The Warrior could fly up to 15,000 feet going as fast as 126 knots (145 mph) and fly a distance of 525 nautical miles (640 statute miles). Being a low-wing airplane, the Warrior is much sexier looking than high wing airplanes, like the Skyhawk. By comparison, the low wing Warrior has better visibility while performing turns, while the high wing Skyhawk has better visibility to the ground. I observed that the high-wing Skyhawk, which had bigger windows, would be better for sightseeing flights and provides a better view from the pilot-in-command seat. The Skyhawk has two doors, which makes it easier for four people to enter and exit the plane, whereas the Warrior has only one door. The two planes felt different from a pilot's perspective; to me, it seemed like the Warrior was easier to taxi, and easier to land in strong crosswinds—which is beneficial, because landing is the hardest part of flying. In the end, they are different airplanes, but in reality, not as hard to transition between as I initially expected.

Certified Flight Instructor (CFI) Allen Bloor was a cool California guy, who looked just like a young Burt Reynolds. Allen had the same mustache, attractive smile and the general good looks that Burt had. To this day, I still consider that I flew with Burt Reynolds. CFI Bloor's dual mandate was to instruct and evaluate me on the knowledge and skills needed to fly the McClellan aero club's Piper PA-28 safely. He familiarized me with the protocol of the local procedures and area. After passing a ground test and mini oral exam on aero club rules and Piper PA-28 airplane knowledge, we went flying. During the mini check ride, I demonstrated several of the flight maneuvers I needed to perform within FAA flight standards to prove to Allen that I was competent and safe to command one of McClellan aero club's PA-28 airplanes: slow flight, various stalls, engine failure, soft field takeoff and landing, normal, abnormal and emergency procedures. I managed to convince him of my aptitude and, therefore, was granted permission to rent the Warrior: my new best friend—to fly whenever I wished to.

The Gouge. Every time a pilot flies with a flight instructor, the pilot must treat that flight the same as a check ride flight; demonstrate to the instructor/check pilot that you are capable of safely commanding the plane.

After obtaining authorization to rent the aero club's plane, I started doing some things pilots can do to build up their flight time, like taking passengers for a ride and sharing the flight expenses. After meeting some new friends, I would take them for joy rides to view Sacramento and the local area from the sky. Most of these flights were flown for fun. During my six months in California, I was only able to rent the plane seven times and log ten flight hours, because on my meager USAF sergeant's income that was all I could afford.

The weather in England is not known for being a pilot's friend—remember, during my time there I had to take a week of vacation days to accumulate those solo pilot flight hours for when the weather was good. By comparison, California has weather that is much more suited towards private pilots with low flight time. Sometimes in Sacramento, there could be mornings when fog would prevent me from flying but generally, unlike England, most California days were good weather flying days for me.

The view from up above is different between England and California. While flying in England, I observed mostly farms, fields, small rivers, small lakes, old towns and a few castles. My English flight practice area in East Anglia was basically flat terrain. However, the terrain around Sacramento varied greatly; when I flew, I observed majestic mountains, rolling valleys, the sandy beaches of the Pacific Ocean, major highways, small towns and major cities.

On July 20, 1983, I piloted my last flight from California in a PA-28, tail number N43128. The two-factor goal of this last flight were to prepare for flight training at Embry-Riddle Aeronautical University and to maintain my pilot currency. One of the federal legal requirements for pilots to maintain pilot currency is within the preceding 90 days the pilot must execute three takeoffs and landings in the same category and class aircraft. On this flight I practiced many flight maneuvers.

On my return to McClellan airfield, as day turned to night, the sight of a shooting star stole my attention. There was a gap in flight time when I momentarily detached myself mentally from piloting the Warrior; my thoughts drifted towards the shooting star, and I began to dream: as I piloted the airplane, I climbed higher and higher until I reached outer space. As we left Earth's atmosphere, me and the Warrior, we passed our moon, sun, and traveled through our entire solar system to arrive at the boundary of the Milky Way Galaxy—our galaxy. It is only one out of billions. Emotions swelled within me. *Wow the universe is massive! Earth is like a single grain of sand among an entire dune, that represents our tiny place in the universe.*

Humans "wonder about everything: tangible and intangible, tiny and huge, near and far, the past and future as well as the present—the how and why of everything both in this universe and beyond. Human curiosity knows no boundaries." [12] Still hypnotized by the 50 billion trillion stars within the cosmos I wondered, *How did we humans get here?* There I was ecstatically witnessing asteroids, comets, nebulas, planets, dwarf planets, exoplanets, stars, star clusters, neighboring galaxies and dark matter. All of this encompassing me made me feel so insignificant.

Scientists over the years have proved that it took "14 billion years to build up all the resources necessary to make possible the existence of rocky planets, human beings, global civilization, and technology," and that we humans came about 100,000 thousand years ago.[13] Astonishing! Pondering this, I was overwhelmed; I was puzzled by the question: *Why is it that us humans only exist on our special planet, in our special solar system, in our special galaxy within the universe?* A feeling of great significance and self-worth emerged when it hit me, that *we humans are special.* A creator must have planned this; wanted humans to exist, and to give me this opportunity to observe. Stunned by my revelations, my human mind was in a whirlwind trying to comprehend it all, when suddenly human reality broke me out of my intense daydreaming.

"N43128 contact McClellan approach control on 127.8," the Warrior alerted me to the transmission received from air traffic control center. Snapping to it, I responded, "Roger, N43128 contacting McClellan approach control on 127.8." God, the heavens, all the stars, all the planets, and the entire rest of the universe were leaving my thoughts in favor of the reality that was below me. As my dream ended, it was made clear to me that I must descend in the Warrior and return to planet Earth.

The Gouge. Appreciate how special we humans are; savor every delicate moment on planet Earth and savor every precious flight in Earth's atmosphere.

My Own Place

My time in California netted me more than just flight time—it also marked the first time I had my own place. That apartment was mine and only mine. However, I soon learned there are unique responsibilities to living alone. You can come and go as you please, you decide for yourself when to eat and sleep, and who can or can't visit. At the same time, you are solely responsible for paying the bills and maintaining the residence by doing various chores, like cleaning, and I hate cleaning.

The Gouge. To a lot of women, having a clean living space is a high priority. So, it is worth doing the arduous and unpleasant work it takes to keep your place clean.

I took advantage of living in California by traveling around. I went to Lake Tahoe, San Francisco, Los Angeles and San Diego, and, of course, spent time flying around in the Warrior. Soon came December of 1983, and my short career with the Air Force was coming to an end. What had I accomplished in four years? I lived six months in Texas, three years in England, and another six months in California. My travels had taken me all over the United Kingdom and Europe; I'd been to Germany, Italy, Greece, Spain, Switzerland, Austria, France and The Netherlands. I had also been permitted to drive from New York, to California, and then back to Florida. After logging over 110 hours of flight time in England, I logged another ten hours in California; meaning by the end of my four years with USAF, I had logged a total flight time of over 120 hours. In those four years, I had also acquired countless friends and memories.

During my time with the USAF, I was awarded:

- The Commendation Medal
- Good Conduct Medal
- Outstanding Unit Award
- Longevity Service Award
- Small Arm Expert Marksmanship
- Airman of the Quarter (twice)
- An Associate College Degree in Applied Science—Resource Management Technology

More importantly, the Federal Aviation Administration issued me a private pilot license. My time serving was great, but it was time for a divorce. I wanted to pursue a career as a pilot—maybe an airline pilot. In 1983, my options for major airlines were: Pan Am, Eastern, TWA, United, Delta, American, and Republic.

Once again, I was taking a big leap; I was going to invest in myself with time and money for a chance to have a piloting career. At the time, many civilian airlines were laying off pilots and were no longer hiring. Many of my USAF colleagues recommended that I stay in the Air Force and not take that chance. A career as a military pilot would provide me a stable income, medical, dental and eye care, lodging or housing allowance, travel benefits, and 30 days per year of paid vacation, but *Will the airline pilot hiring cycle change?* I wondered. I was driven primarily by four motives: the thirst for travel (especially through flight), the ambition to make career of flying, the desire to learn everything I could about flying, and finally, the fear of failure. Many doubts ran through my mind: *Am I making the correct decision? What if I fail? With all of the time and money I have invested in myself, if I fail at obtaining a career flying, how will I recover? I would I need to move back home and live with my parents; I could end up in New York City selling pretzels on the corner. Are my emotions controlling my thinking? Am I of sound enough mind to make this decision? What could the future have in store for Frank the Pilot?*

During this down time, without any notice, my English ex-girlfriend Linda Sexmiller traveled all the way from London to Sacramento in order to see me. We spent time together and drove across the USA from Sacramento, California, to Daytona Beach, Florida. After some time, I realized that I was not ready to settle down, and so Linda went back to London. I was too focused on my career to have a love life. At age 23, I was likely too immature for a serious relationship anyway; and so, I found myself entering college as a full-time pilot student. In January of 1984, I started undergraduate classes at Embry-Riddle Aeronautical University (ERAU).

8

ERAU

Fifty-four college credits in one year.

In '84 I took 54

In January of 1984 at the age of 23, an age when most college students have already earned a bachelor's degree, I was just beginning my stint in education at the home campus of Embry-Riddle Aeronautical University (ERAU) in Daytona Beach, Florida. That year, I completed a total of 54 college credit hours; I took courses in Aeronautics, Aviation History, Aviation Government, Aviation Law, Navigation, Meteorology, Flight Physiology, Flight Safety, Aerodynamics, Aircraft Engines, Aircraft Systems, Aircraft Components, Aircraft Performance, Federal Rules and Regulations—and more.

The ERAU's original main campus was founded at Lunken Airport in Cincinnati, Ohio; on December 17, 1925, exactly 22 years after the historic flight of the Wright Brothers, stunt-pilot barnstormer John Paul Riddle and entrepreneur T. Higbee Embry cofounded the Embry-Riddle company. The following spring, they opened the Embry-Riddle school of aviation. The school began with a simple plan in mind: to train airplane pilots in a thorough but efficient manner, and to cash in on the booming interest in flying that began at the end of the first World War.

In 1965, with Jack R. Hunt as president, Embry-Riddle consolidated its flight training, ground school, and technical training programs into one location, and moved it to Daytona Beach. In 1968, the ERAU institution was accredited by the commission of colleges of the Southern Association of Colleges and Schools, and two years later Embry-Riddle attained university status.[14] Today, the ERAU is known as the "Harvard of Aviation."

Daytona Beach, famously known as the "World Center of Racing" and home of NASCAR, was also known to college students as the second-best place for spring break on the East Coast. So, every Saturday, busloads of college kids would arrive at Daytona Beach from all over North America to stay for a week. The waves of students came for two months straight; because I lived so close to campus, my spring break consisted of driving five miles to the 23-mile stretch of white sandy beach every day for two months.

The beach in Daytona is one of the few places in the world where you can drive your car just a few feet away from the Atlantic Ocean; the weather is subtropical, with summer temperatures ranging from 70° to 90° Fahrenheit. The winters are dry and mild, with temperatures ranging from the mid-40s to low 70s—a major improvement compared to the cold climate in England.

For us students there were always things to do, such as the Hawaiian Tropic Suntan Lotion Competition, the Daytona Speed Week, the Daytona 500 Auto Race, and the Motorcycle Bike Week; and yes, we still had to make time to fly, take exams and study. So, we had to make tough choices at times—like when to play and when to work. Such as when several teachers selected me as the introductory speaker at the Communications College Night, and the next day there was a veteran's party with free beer and oysters, but instead I decided to stay home and write my term paper for Flight Physiology. The topic I chose was pilot stress.

I was inspired to write about this when John W. Young had given a speech at the university; Young had a long and impressive career as an astronaut, test pilot, naval officer and aeronautical engineer. Young enjoyed the longest career of any US astronaut, and made six space flights, with two as commander on the space shuttle. During his visit I had asked him this question: "Do you think pilots endure more stress due to the increased complexity in the technology installed in the aircrafts commonly flown today?" He answered in the affirmative, and talked in more detail about his experiences commanding different aircrafts, like small airplanes, propeller airplanes, jet airplanes, rockets and space shuttles. I incorporated his response into my paper, which was a good choice and helped me earn an "A."

Mr. Young's speech wowed, impressed and re-motivated me on my pursuit to be a career pilot, and now even considering becoming an astronaut. *What does it take to be an astronaut,* I wondered?

My other term paper was about the spray-on foam insulation used in the thermal protection system of the external tank of a space shuttle. While researching the subject, I learned much about the space shuttle vehicle, and at times found myself reminiscing on when I viewed the first Space Shuttle Discovery launch. That experience influenced my decision to become a pilot. Writing this paper reminded me that the reason I was in here in Daytona Beach was to acquire the knowledge I needed to achieve a career as a pilot, not to party with girls.

The Gouge. Go out late and return early on Monday, Tuesday and Wednesday nights. Most local guys are working or doing schoolwork during the week, so the female-to-male ratio is in your favor. So, the plan that worked for me and a few select friends was to stay home on weekends and go out during the week. We would spend most of our weekends reviewing and studying the previous week's schoolwork, and preparing for the next week.

My goal in writing this book is to share my stories of piloting, and to put you, the reader, in the cockpit seat so that you may experience what Frank the pilot was thinking and feeling. However, my automobile vehicles are a worthy side note in my journey as a pilot, so here is that side note.

Remember the 1972 Chevy Luv pick-up truck that I bought in England, shipped to New Jersey, and drove across the country to California and then back to Florida? Well, after leaving Miami one weekend in 1985, somewhere around West Palm Beach on I-95 en route to Daytona Beach, my engine blew a head gasket. My brother Kevin drove up, towed me back to Miami, and gave me a beat-up 1966 Chrysler Newport in exchange for my newly busted truck. So, I drove the Chrysler back to Daytona Beach. Even though the fuel efficiency was around eight miles per gallon, I would still pull into the gas station and say, "Check the gas and fill her up with oil." At times, it felt like I was regressing with vehicles—going from driving a 1972 Chevy to a 1966 Chrysler—but I needed reliable ground transportation to drive myself to school. Then, after arriving in an old Chrysler ground transport, I would take off in a new Cessna air transport.

The Chrysler had a 440 TNT four-barrel V-8 engine that burned a lot of oil. That boat (another word for a big, American car) was 18 feet long, six feet wide, and weighed 4,300 pounds. However, on a good day the car would go over 120 mph, and you could watch the gas gauge drop. At first, the car ran on only five of its eight cylinders. There were two holes in the rear floorboards, and another large hole on the passenger seat that left the springs exposed. The rear chrome bumpers were bent out like the Batmobile from *Batman*. On the exterior the original blue paint is exposed, along with rust, water spots and bird crap stains. I worked on the engine until it was running proper, performed body repairs, and hand brush painted the exterior.

My pilot peers named the car "The Batmobile," but I called her "Black Beauty." However, one day when I was asked, "Is the Batmobile still running?" I had to reply, "It runs, but it doesn't stop." One day while in a parking lot, my brakes failed—it's a scary feeling to press on the brake pedal and the 4,300-pound vehicle you're driving doesn't stop. Thankfully, there were no injuries or damage. I had survived, but it seemed like I was always having problems with ground transport machines and needing to change. In the previous six years I had owned and operated a 1972 Chevelle Malibu, a 1980 Suzuki 250 TS motorcycle, a 1968 Austin Mini, a 1970 Audi 500 GL, a 1960 Austin Cambridge, a 1972 Chevy Luv pick-up truck, and now a 1966 Chrysler Newport. Once again, I found myself thinking, *I would rather operate an air transport machine than a ground transport machine*. The planes in my life seemed to be more reliable than the cars.

An Embry-Riddle Aeronautical Science degree required 120 scholastic college credit hours plus 12 flight college credits for a total of 132 college credit hours. Those 12 flight credit hours consisted of seven flight courses that every pilot student had to complete. My first flight at ERAU was January 23, 1984. However, I already had a private pilot's license with over 120 flight hours, so this first flight was to demonstrate my pilot aptitude level. The first few flight courses were condensed; I breezed through them and shortly thereafter, I was training towards a commercial pilot's license with an instrument rating.

The personnel at ERAU were very professional and provided the best training that I could have imagined. I would recommend this school as the best option to any civilian looking to train for a career as a pilot. The ERAU is a Part 141 school—which are schools specifically approved by the FAA to teach certain pilot courses in a highly structured and organized way.

The purpose of a Part 141 school is to ensure the highest level of student training possible. There are minimum time requirements for each skill and subject matter; courses are usually taught on a rigid schedule at a fast pace. Each flight lesson is about five hours long, conducted by a flight instructor with two students on board. Flight lessons would consist of: one hour at ground school, 90 minutes of hands-on inflight instruction, another 90 minutes observing a peer receiving the same instructions, and then finish with a one-hour de-brief back at ground school. The philosophy was: hear it, do it and learn it. My daily schedule consisted of about five hours of scholastic classes in the morning and another five hours of flight training in the afternoon—sometimes, flight training was on weekends. As mentioned, I managed to accumulate 54 college credit hours in my one year at ERAU. I had developed an addiction to aviation; I was completely engrossed with everything related to flying. There was no cure for my addiction, but piloting airplanes helped the symptoms.

That December, the last month of my 23rd year, I met a Pan American World Airways (Pan Am) Captain while riding a shuttle service from Daytona Beach to Orlando. We were both traveling to New York: he was commuting to work, and I was traveling home for the holidays. He lived in Daytona Beach, but as a pilot his day job started at JFK airport in New York City.

He sat alone in a row of empty seats; he held up that day's edition of *The Wall Street Journal* to read, and I saw the four silver bars around the wrist end of his dark blue pilot's uniform, which confirmed that he was indeed not just a pilot, but a captain. With curiosity I chose to occupy the seat two positions away from him in the same row. Another confirmation of his rank was the emblem embroidered in his aged pilot's hat, which was resting on the seat between us. He was big and broad, with gray eyebrows and wrinkles from decades of age and experience carved into his forehead. He projected an ambiance of greatness and power, as most well respected people do. *Finally*, I thought to myself, *here is someone who can surely answer all my questions about who pilots those huge commercial jets around.*

I introduced myself: "Hi my name is Frank. How do you do, sir?" In response, he turned his head towards me, lowered his bifocals slightly and said, "Fine thank you." Even though he was, in my mind, a powerful and larger-than-life pilot, he spoke to me with a soft, warm-hearted tone. "I am an Embry-Riddle student pilot," I told him. He lowered the newspaper to rest on his thighs, then turned his attention back towards me and said, "Interesting." I was surprised that this big shot Pan Am captain did not seem to mind having a young inquisitive college kid launching a hundred questions at him.

Throughout our conversation, he explained to me that the hotels where he spent his layovers during his flight trips were paid for by his employer. The company also continued to pay him during these layovers that could range from lasting a half-day to several days. He was also given a per diem amount to cover the cost of food and incidentals while on flight trips. That included free meals in flight while he is piloting. It sounded like to me he was getting paid to go on vacation; except he sat up front in the cockpit instead of in the back with the passengers. He told to me about his schedule—how he gets a lot of time off, typically at least 14 days per month, with senior pilots getting more days, and how he could bid for a different schedule every month to be able to see different cities.

So, after my discussion with this magnificent captain, I was sold! I wanted to emulate him; I wanted to be a big-time airline pilot and fly all over the world. Just days before my 24th birthday, I finally decided what type of pilot I wanted to be. I would become an airline pilot, just like the seasoned and seemingly all-knowing Pan Am international captain that had inspired me. The wheels in my mind started to spin—*a plan, I need a plan.* Just like a pilot needs a flight plan to go cross country, I needed a plan for my career. I thought, *What do I need to do to get one of those fantastic airline pilot jobs?* Starting on that inspiring day, my eyes were locked on the goal of becoming an airline pilot.

After acquiring my first degree (Associate in Applied Science in Resource Management Technology, November 16, 1983) I started accumulating more certifications, and even earned another degree, including:

- May 20, 1985: Commercial and Instrument Pilot License
- July 13, 1985: Aircraft Dispatches License
- Aug. 13, 1985: Certified Flight Instructor License: Airplane Single-Engine Rating. (This single-engine option was a new option under a new program at ERAU; I was the first student to complete this program).
- Aug. 17, 1985: Bachelor in Aeronautical Science from Embry-Riddle Aeronautical University with 298 hours of total pilot flight time.
- Sept. 20, 1985: Multi-Engine Rated License
- Oct. 1, 1985: Ground Instructor License: Advanced and Instrument Rating.

After completing several specific aeronautical college courses at ERAU, I was eligible to take the Aircraft Dispatcher's License practical exam; this license authorizes a person joint responsibility with the pilot-in-command (PIC) for the safety of the flight. Dispatchers assist with planning flight routes, needing to take into account many variables including aircraft performance and loading, enroute winds, thunderstorm and turbulence forecasts, airspace restrictions and airport conditions. They also provide a flight following service and will advise pilots if conditions change. During the practical exam, the applicant is tested on their knowledge regarding all these variables and many other aviation related matters.

My practical test lasted over six hours; I had to plan an entire flight trip for a Boeing B-727 jet. I proved my aptitude with the B-727 aircraft systems, performance, limitations and more. It was a very difficult and comprehensive exam—little did I know that one day I would be commanding a B-727 for a major airline.

Why did I study for so many hours, take the long four-hour drive from Dayton Beach to Miami and pay $200 to take a six-hour practical aircraft dispatcher's test? My thinking was, *If I ever lose my medical license and can't find a career as a pilot, then being a dispatcher for an airline can be my plan B.* My thinking was similar to a flight plan—sure to have an alternate path. This license would also improve my resume and help me compete amongst my peers for that ultimate airline pilot job I was desperately seeking.

As explained in an earlier chapter, a private pilot license authorizes a person to command any aircraft for non-commercial purposes under visual flight rules (VFR), and includes the ability to carry passengers. In other words, passengers could not hire me in the commercial sense, but instead could share the expenses of a flight I was piloting in exchange for coming aboard. A commercial pilot license authorizes a pilot to carry persons or property for compensation or hire. So, holding a commercial pilot license means you can get paid to pilot. On the other hand, an instrument license permits a pilot to file an instrument flight plan, fly in certain airspaces and legally maneuver in turbulent air such as clouds, rain and fog. An instrument-rated pilot must still evaluate weather conditions but is not required to adhere to any specific weather requirements.

A Certified Flight Instructor (CFI) license allows a pilot to train individuals and issue endorsements required for pilot certificates. CFIs are authorized to endorse pilot certificates, aircraft ratings, recency of experience requirements, knowledge tests, operating privileges, flight instructor certificates, flight reviews, practical tests, instrument ratings, ground and instructor certificates. A flight instructor can perform flight reviews, which are required for every pilot to keep exercising the privileges of each certificate they hold. Teaching students how to fly is a great way to receive compensation while building up pilot flight time. Ground Advanced and Instrument Rating licenses authorizes a person without a pilot license or medical license to teach all the required flight ground school that a CFI teaches. *Even if I lose my medical license, I can still teach flight ground school for a career*, I surmised.

A Multi-Engine Rated license authorizes a pilot to operate an aircraft with more than one engine. With one engine, a pilot is always looking for an emergency place to land in case that engine fails, but with two engines, if one fails the pilot has time and options to decide where to make an emergency landing. This license is an add-on to an already existing Private, Commercial, or Airline Transport Pilot (ATP) license or certificate.

A Bachelor's degree in Aeronautical Science from ERAU prepares graduates for careers in areas including aviation design, flight engineering, flight air traffic control, operations, and of course for becoming a pilot. ERAU is considered one of the best aviation and aerospace universities in the world: it is the largest, fully accredited university specializing in aviation. I'd decided that if my flight path as an airline pilot did not work out that I would get that degree to instead obtain a career in aeronautics. Also, with a college degree I could get a higher paying job that would help finance my pilot aviation addiction; I could rent and fly more often. As of August 17, 1985, I had earned a Bachelor in Aeronautical Science from Embry-Riddle Aeronautical University and accumulated 298 hours of total pilot flight time.

9

FIRST PILOT JOB

Forty college student solo flights.

College was a good experience for me, with great professors, incredible classes and wonderful friends. The fun you have in college and the knowledge you acquire can never be replicated. In one sense, I was heartbroken to see college end, but in another sense I was relieved. No more deadlines, no more exams and no more flight check rides!

It was nice to have a vacation after graduation, but the reality of life set in. I did not have a job yet. At times, I was glad to have graduated, but as each day passed, I felt sad that I did not have a job. The cost of college and flight training left me in debt; I needed money! Being broke was getting old and depressing. This situation was getting on my nerves.

When I left the USAF to attend ERAU, not only were the civilian airlines not hiring pilots but the pilots were getting laid off! Two years later, and almost exactly four years after obtaining my private pilot license, I was in pursuit of my first pilot flight position. It was September of 1985; the inside word was that ERAU needed more flight instructors to accommodate the influx of new college students. Others submitted their resume and waited for an interview, but Frank the pilot is not like the others. Dressed up in a professional suit and tie, with resume and completed job application in hand, and without an invitation, I strode into the office of the flight department manager, Paul MacDuffrey. I kindly requested—most likely *pleaded*—for a job as a certified flight instructor.

After introducing myself to Mr. MacDuffrey and expressing my desire to obtain a pilot job with ERAU, we struck up a conversation. He asked me about my background, why I wanted this job, what made me more qualified than other applicants, and how I'd bring value to ERAU.

He shot the questions at me, and I shot back the answers. The questions were all one way, for I did not present any questions other than, "Will you give me a job?" There was no time for me to get nervous, for I was young, naïve, and pumped up, and I was highly motivated to begin my flight career. This exchanged developed into a job interview, the very first job interview I participated in. Beforehand, I did not have a clue about what a job interview entailed nor the protocols associated with it.

It didn't take long. Immediately after the brief interview, Mr. MacDuffrey offered me the position. I flew out of that office elated with enormous self-satisfaction. It was the most precious feeling I've ever had. After that entire struggle, after all that hard work, I finally acquired a pilot position. This was a fantastic first pilot job, teaching ERAU college students how to fly the Cessna C-172 (called the Skyhawk) plane. If I had some money, I would have gone out to celebrate. I did have enough money to call my loving parents to brag; they, too, were enormously proud of me. This was a major shift, boost and accomplishment to my career.

The Gouge. Go for it. If you hear there is a position becoming available that you want, do not wait to be invited. Be proactive and seek to secure that position. By the time some of my college buddies were invited to interview and were hired, I had been flight instructing for several weeks.

My newly acquired Certified Flight Instructor (CFI) license authorized me to train wannabe pilots and issue various endorsements that are required for pilot certificates. One of those endorsements included endorsing student pilot certificates. ERAU hired me as a university professor to teach college students to fly planes, which is a great way to get compensated while building up pilot flight time. Teaching what you have learned, reinforces greater understanding and knowledge retention of those subjects. It leads to deeper and longer-lasting acquisition of that information. Teachers are at the correlation level of learning. Teaching pilots to fly makes the teacher a better pilot.

The pilot courses I taught at ERAU included:

- how to inspect and preflight the airplane
- how to start the engine
- when and how to communicate over the radio

- how to taxi to the runway
- how to take off
- how to depart the traffic pattern
- basic navigation
- basic airplane control of heading, altitude and airspeed about the three basic axes (longitude, latitude, and vertical)
- emergency procedures
- how to reenter the traffic pattern and land

Landing an airplane would be very hard for a total novice. Learning how to make good landings is one difficult skill set to master; to teach another person to land is another skill set altogether.

During takeoff, the plane is accelerating. All a pilot needs to do is pull back on the yoke a little bit, make a few control corrections with aileron and rudder, and the plane becomes airborne. During landing, the plane is decelerating, the pilot needs to manipulate the controls and throttles to transfer the plane from a flying phase to a landing phase at the appropriate time—the time when the plane meets the runway.

Landing is an energy-management challenge and a judgment-skill challenge. The student pilot must learn to put the plane on the right spot at the right speed. The pilot must judge and make the necessary corrections to avoid being too fast or too slow, not to land too long or too short, and to flare the plane at precisely the correct altitude. If a crosswind is present, the student must also learn to manipulate the rudder, aileron, pitch and throttle controls to adjust.

Misjudging distance, over speed, under speed or incorrect crosswind corrections are some of the most common landing issues. Another potentially dangerous problem is landing in conditions above the demonstrated ability of either the pilot or the airplane. The Skyhawk has a crosswind limit of 15 knots and tailwind limit of 10 knots. A pilot or the instructor may install personal limits lower than the airplane's limit. Some student pilots spend at least 20 hours mastering landing and the other required pilot tasks before attempting to fly solo.

First Black Female Student Pilot

In 1986, ERAU had about fifty CFIs and four flight managers. My flight manager was Pat O'Gara. Pat was a jolly, easy-going, likeable boss. The Irish names Mr. O'Gara and Mr. Donohue also encouraged likeability between us. On one particular busy workday, Pat approached me, saying, "Frank, I have a student who is having difficulty with landings. Can you help?"

"Sure, Pat, no problem. We'll get it fixed. What's his name?" He handed me a calendar print out and responded, "*Her* name is Jasmine, and here is her schedule." Scanning the schedule, I noticed that she was available Tuesday at 10:00 a.m., so I set up a flight lesson.

Jasmine and I met in the ground instructor room as scheduled. Jasmine is a black female student pilot—the first black female student pilot at ERAU, and the first for me as well. She has black pasta-like straight, almost shoulder-length, hair, with shiny, smooth perfect black skin. Her dark brown, nearly black, pupils were set in glowing pearl-white sclera, which matched her pearl-white teeth, that appeared with her hello smile to me. Her lips, tongue and nails were pinkish pale.

After briefly introducing myself, I sat down and reviewed her student pilot workbook. This book listed all the pilot lessons and skills taught to her and how she was graded on each skill. All looked good except for landings—she did not grasp the skill to land the Skyhawk.

She was stuck between the application and correlation level of learning of landing the plane. Jasmine had two other flight instructors prior to being handed off to me. Landing was the only skill that prevented Jasmine from taking the course completion final check ride and from flying solo. For some reason, Pat had confidence that I would be able to help Jasmine master the necessary skills.

Jasmine and I departed in the Skyhawk from Daytona Beach (DAB) airport and flew to Flagler Executive Airport (FIN). She entered the traffic pattern and set herself up for the landing. I explained to her that I would follow through on the controls with her, thinking, *If she really screws up the landing, I can make the necessary corrections to prevent a hard landing, or worse, a crash.* Jasmine started the flare too high, reduced too much power too early, and pitched the plane up too high. With my hands and feet, I overpowered her hands and feet by lowering the pitch attitude and increasing some throttle power to avoid a very hard landing. We landed without incurring structural damage to the Skyhawk, taxied to a secluded place on the airport, and shut down the engine. As I recaptured what had just happened during that landing attempt, I thought to myself, *Teaching Jasmine to land is going to be a real challenge, yet otherwise she is a good pilot.*

Jasmine lacked the judgment skill to manage the plane's energy throughout the landing phase. She needed to learn what pitch and performance site picture is incorrect and how to make the necessary adjustments for pitch, flight control and power inputs in order to make a safe landing. While asking her about her judgment of what she observed and the adjustments she made or did not make, a great idea came to my brain. I had a "eureka" moment that pumped me up with hope and excitement.

I leaped out of the airplane and went toward the back of the plane. I slowly pushed down the tail of the plane, which raised the nose of the plane. While doing this, I instructed Jasmine that that was the site picture she should be aiming for to make normal landing. I did this several times while simultaneously verbalizing to her the pitch, power and control adjustments required to accomplish a good safe landing. I varied the rate and height at which I adjusted the cockpit view. At the end of each demonstration, I held the tail for an extended amount of time. This was to reinforce to Jasmine the optimum pitch attitude site picture to aim for as the plane engages the runway. Later on, I started calling this the "holding-the-plane's-tail-down technique."

We went to go fly again, with me demonstrating the first landing while she followed through on the yoke, rudder and power controls. During this first landing, I had her tell me her observations and the adjustments she felt I was making during the landing. Her hands and feet were on the controls with me following my adjustments during the landing. On the second landing she made all the yoke, rudder and power adjustments, and I did the talking of her observations and the control adjustments I felt she should make. I still kept my hands on the controls just in case. For the third landing, I projected my confidence in her landing ability by saying, "You are doing great; show me a great landing without my physical or verbal help." On the third landing, Jasmine made all the yoke, rudder and power adjustments; she did the talking of her observations and the control adjustments. My hands were on my lap, but spring-loaded to take over if needed. On the fourth landing, I directed her to not speak to me but to think the command-and-control thoughts to herself throughout the landing. After about six successful normal landings, we performed more landings on another runway with stronger crosswind components. As Jasmine's self-confidence in executing landings skyrocketed, her self-satisfaction was revealed through her joyful, gleaming smile.

A self-satisfying feeling of accomplishment arose within me as well, from successfully teaching a skill to a student that was having difficulty mastering that skill. Teaching provides an enormous feeling of self-worth, helping and giving back. On a scale of one to ten, the intensity of satisfaction accomplishment as a teacher felt like a ten. The feeling was like the feeling of a woman successfully having a baby for the first time. Of course, as a pilot instructor, this was my job and I was being compensated for it, but this feeling of accomplishment of overcoming a challenge is an additional benefit of teaching. Helping Jasmine overcome her challenge of landing the plane made me feel very good.

Jasmine was able to execute landings to my standards, and more importantly, to the standards of the FAA and ERAU. Jasmine achieved the correlation level of learning, enabling her to pass the course completion final check ride and to fly solo. If I had been smart enough with foresight, I should have followed the promising career path of Jasmine, my first black female student pilot—I did not.

The Gouge. Grasping certain pilot skills can be a challenge to the student. To overcome a student learning block, instructors must adjust, and be flexible, inventive, imaginative, resourceful and creative. Landing can be a huge energy-management challenge and a judgment-skill challenge to a student pilot. The "holding-the-plane's-tail-down technique" to teach landings was an adjustment I made to help a student cope with the challenges in landing an airplane.

Female Versus Male Pilots

My experience with female pilots at this stage of my career was limited. Jo was the first female pilot I had flown with. She was the CFI pilot who gave me my first required recurrent pilot check. Remember how I fell in love with her on that first flight? Jo married my best pilot friend, Jeff. Before Jasmine, I instructed and soloed three other female student pilots. Blue-eyed, fair-skinned, healthy blonde Betty Lou was one of them. During training, I repelled the magnetic attraction between us because I had evolved into a professional instructor pilot. The great wall between business and pleasure was resurrected to maintain my pilot professionalism … and probably my employment as well.

With my limited experience with female pilots, I learned that they differed from their male counterparts. The women studied beforehand and were always well prepared for each flight lesson. Men did not always study beforehand. Most of them figured they would learn all that they needed during the flight lesson.

The female student pilots seemed better at acquiring their aeronautical knowledge with visual skills, through reading and doing, while the males seemed better at acquiring their aeronautical knowledge with spatial skills, through seeing and doing. The women were better at picturing concepts through reading words while the men were better at picturing concepts through seeing objects.

The female student pilots were less willing to take risks than the men. When it was time to take that first solo flight or take a flight test, the women demonstrated emotional low self-confidence. They would admit things they did not understand and claim they were not ready. I would have to give these women a confidence-building pep talk before the solo flight and flight check. The men were full of confidence and pilot self-worth. When we approached the subject of solo, I had to hold them down by the britches until I felt they were ready. At times, the men seemed like they knew it all—perhaps even more than me. They would cover up their weaknesses and omit acknowledging mistakes or lack of understanding of a particular subject. Generally, the men seemed more self-confident. In their own eyes, they were *always* ready to solo.

At times I felt like I had to vary my style of teaching for each sex. Certain techniques of teaching that were successful for the male students were not necessarily successful for the female students and vice versa. The more I attempted to connect with the women's emotions on learning various flight subjects and their reactions to a completed flight lesson, the more effective I became as a pilot flight instructor to women. Women are different from men.

The instructor teaches the student to progress through the four levels of learning: rote, understanding, application and correlation.

Using landing as an example, here is how a student progresses through the levels of learning. During the rote level, the student memorizes and recalls information, like pull the throttles back or pull the yoke back to land. During the understanding level, the student perceives and learns how reducing the engine power throttles reduce the plane's airspeed and how pulling the yoke back increases the plane's pitch attitude. During the application level, the student achieves the skill to apply and perform the use of throttles and yoke inputs to transfer the plane from a descent vector to a landing vector at the appropriate time. During the correlation level, the student associates the learning of current landings to previously learned landings. For instance, the students may have learned on previously landing attempts, that if the throttles are reduced too much, too early while pulling the yoke back too much, too early, then the plane will stall above the runway and a very hard landing or a crash is then imminent. The student's learning experience of previous landings builds the experience to correlate to current landings, enabling the student to perform better.

Recall my first solo flight in chapter 3. I was young, eager and ready to fly that first solo flight. Well, the situation was much different now. As some would say, "The shoe is on the other foot now." I had to decide if the student's performance on multiple maneuvers, including takeoffs and landings, traffic patterns, stall entries and recoveries, emergency procedures, go-arounds, and more met or exceeded the USA's federal aviation standards. The two most important questions I ask myself are: *Is this student safe and competent to fly the plane by him or herself, without my help? Is this student competent to handle a flight emergency and survive?* The first time a student goes out alone can be nerve-wracking for the instructor. My CFI license, that I had worked so hard to achieve, was on the line. Imagine the effect on a pilot instructor's conscience and career if their solo student crashes and dies.

This first flight job came with huge responsibility, which affected my ego and also produced terrifying nightmares. Did you ever have a dream? Dreams have several scales of awareness. At times, you may be unaware that you have dreamed. Occasionally, a dream may be recalled in sharp detail, and other times it is vague. You may experience a dream that is so lucid that you think the events are real—it's so vivid that you cannot initially distinguish between the reality of the dream and the reality of the awake life. In your dream, you see, hear, feel, and touch. The effects or feelings that we experience in our dreams can persist after we are awake and can seem as real as anything in the awake life.

In those days, my nightmares always involved my solo students crashing into the Atlantic Ocean of Daytona Beach. These dreams were triggered by my concern that I had signed off too early, that they weren't ready to operate the C-172 aircraft solo. These nightmares produced strong feelings of fear and anxiety. Just as it seemed that my respiratory system stopped and I started to panic for air, my eyes started to blink open. Slowly and unbelievingly, I started to realize that I was transitioning from a nightmare to the reality of awake life—*somewhere, sometime, somehow.* This was one of the stresses that came with the responsibility of teaching college students to fly airplanes all by themselves.

With an aircraft that has only one engine, the pilot is always looking for a field in which to land, in case that engine fails; or in my dreams, my student pilots were looking into the Atlantic Ocean for an emergency landing. Once the student has mastered these skills, maneuvers and procedures, the certified flight instructor (*moi*) would certify and endorse the student's logbook, permitting the student to fly solo—all by him or herself. The endorsement read:

> *I have given Mr. John Ace Pilot Doe the flight training required by CFR 61.87 (n). He has met the requirements of CFR 61.87 (n) and is competent to operate a Cessna C-172 aircraft in solo flight during daytime at Daytona Beach Airport (DAB). This endorsement is valid for ninety days effective (date).*

In the nine months I was employed with ERAU, I instructed and signed off 40 students for solo flying. I loved my job so much that I was instructing eight flight hours a day and ground instructing four classroom hours a day, six days a week—a total of 72 work hours per week.

The Gouge. Instructors should keep track of their hours of work on a knee clipboard, to keep legal with the Feds. CFIs are limited to maximum of eight hours of flight instruction per day and 12 hours of total instruction, including ground instruction per day within a maximum of 6 days per week. CFIs are required by law to have at least a 24-hour rest within a seven-day period.

What a deal. I was a college professor at the "Harvard of Aviation," teaching college students how to fly airplanes. As well as earning a paycheck, I was logging precious pilot-in-command flight time. This first pilot flight job helped me to meet girls as well. I was a cool, big-time pilot with a massive ego.

First Aviation Catastrophe

The first *aviation catastrophe* I observed was when I was instructing two students, and our flight position was 4,000 feet above the Ormond VOR (OMN). Ormond VOR is located on the Ormond Beach Municipal Airport, and it's less than 80 miles from the Kennedy Space Center at Cape Canaveral.

While in flight, we observed the Space Shuttle Challenger (STS-51 L) blow up—a devastating sight. At the time, I knew something did not look normal, but we were not cognizant of having just been witnesses to the death of seven people.

The catastrophe occurred on January 28, 1986—a scant 73 seconds into flight and above the Atlantic. The accident remains NASA's most visible failure. It was the world's first high-tech catastrophe to unfold on live TV.

Adding to the anguish was the young audience; school children everywhere tuned in that morning to watch the launch of the first schoolteacher and ordinary citizen bound for space, Christa McAuliffe. McAuliffe and six others on board perished because of the failure of an O-ring seal and feeble bureaucratic decisions. It was, as one grief and trauma expert recalls, the beginning of the age when the whole world knew what happened as it happened.[15]

The crew compartment shot out of the fireball, intact, and continued upward another three miles before starting to plummet. The free fall lasted more than two minutes. There was no parachute to slow the descent. There was no escape system whatsoever. NASA had skipped all that in shuttle development. In the public view, space travel was becoming ordinary and routine.

In a horrific flash, the most diverse space crew ever—including one black, one Japanese American, and two women, one of them Jewish—was gone. NASA had safely launched shuttles 24 times previously. The launches were being taken for granted, despite the enormous risk involved. The name of NASA's second oldest shuttle was forever locked in a where-were-you moment."[16] My students and I were 4,000 feet above the ground and less than 80 miles from the disaster. It was easy to see from our vantage point that something had gone wrong with the launch. It wasn't until I had landed and was changing students and aircraft that I learned I had watched seven people die. Yes, I was changing students and aircraft, and I was going back up in the air to flight instruct another two students. Pilots, at times, have to block out non-flight events and concentrate on flying the plane. Pilots must compartmentalize flying the plane from all other non-flight thoughts.

Hearing the news was very difficult to absorb, but you never know when your number is up. Afterwards, the thoughts and emotions of viewing the space shuttle explode with seven people onboard, while I was flight instructing two students, affected me. Later that night, I spent valuable precious time studying the emergency procedures for the Cessna C-172 airplane.

Although the young male urge to go out and have fun was very strong within me, the self-survival human need motivated me to stay home and study. It is possible that I may be faced with a live-or die-flight emergency, and I wanted to be prepared to survive such an encounter. When something goes wrong up there you just cannot just pull over to a cloud and check the oil. Astronauts, like pilots, make their money above planet Earth, and it is serious business. Safety first.

This is when I began to realize pilots are always studying and not just studying to pass a flight check ride or other pilot tests. Pilots are always studying multiple complicated emergency pilot tasks that you rarely and hopefully never encounter, but if you should encounter such an emergency, you would be prepared and, hopefully, be able to survive. One example of such an emergency was Sully Sullenberger's miracle on the Hudson.

The Gouge. Continue to study, and study not just to pass a pilot check ride. Set up a weekly or at least a monthly schedule to study. Pick one aircraft system or emergency procedure a week to study. Like that big pie we talked about earlier; break it into small pieces, conquer each piece, and put it back together again. Strive to be that pilot, like pilot Sully, that if you should be faced with a flight emergency, you will be prepared and survive.

10

BANNER-TOWING

First pilot emergency

The things pilots will do to build up their flight time. If you love piloting planes, then you are willing to accept some risk. I had chosen to be a pilot, which says something about my level of risk tolerance. Moonlighting as a banner-tow pilot increased my level of risk. In pursuit of additional flight time, I started moonlighting with a company that towed advertisement banners over Daytona Beach. The planes flew out of New Smyrna Airport (EVB). As well as being a flight instructor pilot, I was going to be a banner-tow pilot too. Others said, "You already had a good pilot job at ERAU. Why go fly banners?" I would respond, "Flying banners pays me a whopping $10 per hour, helps me build up my flight time, and besides … flying banners is really cool."

While taking a break between instructing lessons at EVB, I met Chuck Heygether. Chuck may have been admiring me, an ERAU CFI, but I was definitely admiring him, a banner-tow pilot. As we started a conversation in pilot dialect, all I heard was, "Flying banners is really cool!" Chuck projected an addictive, upbeat, easy-going, happiest-guy-on-planet-Earth attitude. He explained how the plane is flown at both very fast and very slow speeds, how the flight controls are manipulated to fly acrobatic maneuvers, the unique takeoff and landing procedures, and the visuals of all the gorgeous visiting spring break women on Dayton Beach from 200 feet above.

He finished with, "Frank, we are looking for pilots like you, and we pay $10.00 an hour." Days later I parsed his statement, "We are looking for pilots like you." Chuck had no idea what type of pilot I was. What he meant to say is, "We are looking for *any* pilots." However, my only short-term memory was, "Flying banners is really cool!" Because of Chuck, Frank the young pilot started to earn extra money moonlighting as a banner-tow pilot over Daytona Beach, Florida.

Have you ever looked up and wondered how those pilots tow those banners? Here's how the tow operation worked.

The pilot would first take off with the banner hook in the airplane's cockpit—no banner yet. The hook was tied to a rope and the rope was tied to the aircraft. Once in the air, the pilot would throw the hook out the window and make a dive-bomb attack (like a kamikaze pilot) toward the banner poles. The banner was built onto a long strap that had a huge loop at one end and the banner attached at the other. The banner could be as large as 35 feet high by 100 feet in length. The huge loop would be set atop two 10-foot poles, and the poles would be set upright, about 20 feet apart, and the rest of the banner would lay flat on the ground. The operation entailed flying directly over the huge loop that was set on top of the two 10-foot poles. Flying at top speed, as the aircraft passed over the loop, and just as the hook was about to snag the loop, the pilot would pull the airplane's yoke back so that the aircraft would pitch high toward the sky above the airplane's stall attitude. While transferring all your kinetic energy to potential energy, the airplane's airspeed would slowly decrease as the banner was lifted off the ground.

To prevent the aircraft from stalling (when the aircraft loses all its lift and will no longer fly) and to tow the banner at a slow speed, the aviator would slowly reduce just a little attitude as the banner was being lifted off the ground. Lifting the banner into the air would greatly increase the aircraft's drag force and weight force, thereby reducing the aircraft's thrust force and lift force. Then, the pilot would depart from the aerodrome's traffic pattern and navigate to the Daytona Beach shoreline, flying at only 200 feet above the Atlantic Ocean, and about 200 feet from the shoreline at the slowest possible speed (usually only five to ten knots above the stall speed—even though it's really the aircraft's angle of attack or attitude that determines the actual stall). Flying at a low altitude at a slow speed was the optimum way to present the banner to all those sun-bathing customers on Daytona Beach. The key was to keep a safe distance from the other aircraft and the beach, while maintaining a safe airspeed.

Flying low and slow increases the banner-tow pilot's level of risk. Height above planet Earth is potential energy, and speed through the atmosphere is kinetic energy. Flying high and fast is usually the safest flying. Flying high and slow is fairly safe. If the plane stalls, there is plenty of altitude in which to recover. Flying low and fast is fairly safe; one must just avoid flying into mountains, buildings and towers. Flying low and slow is the most dangerous scenario of the four. The pilot is flying very slow and close to stall attitude, and the pilot only has a few hundred feet in which to recover; therefore, the pilot must be alert of all times for a potential stall. Flying too close to another banner-tow pilot could cause a stall from that plane's wake turbulence. To be perfectly honest, I do not recall the dangers; I only recall the benefits. There are fantastic views of planet Earth and its people from 200 feet above.

Pilots must pass routine eye exams, and flying banners helps exercise scanning, fixation and distance adaption skills. Scan the beach, fixate on a particular view and adjust eyesight for distance. A vision of 20/200 means if an object is 200 feet away, you have to stand 20 feet from it in order to see the object perfectly clear. So, 200/20 is the vision I was trying to master. From a distance of 200 feet, I was hoping to see what a normal person could see at 20 feet. I especially hoped to clearly see the pretty college girls on spring break. Towing banners across the 25-mile beach resort strip helped me pinpoint where the most beautiful female sunbathers were stationed. After my final landing for the day, I knew just what part of the beachfront I wanted to explore to increase my odds of meeting the next gorgeous woman of my life.

On a side note, you would be surprised the number of times I sighted sharks mere feet from people in the water. This is not to scare you, because it is my understanding there are over 500 species of sharks, and only 15, or fewer than 3%, have been known to attack humans.

After making six or seven passes over the strip, it was time to return to the New Smyrna Beach airfield to get another advertisement banner and fuel. Approaching the field, the goal was to fly as low as possible to safely drop the banner by releasing the hook, using the hook release latch located in the airplane's cockpit. After releasing the hook, to detach the banner, the aircraft's thrust force and lift force would drastically increase due to the loss of the drag force and weight force. The pilot could then climb and enter the downward leg of the traffic pattern, then the base leg and then the final leg in order to land on the runway.

Most banner-towing is flown with planes called taildraggers. The viewing public may notice that the landing gear and wheels are positioned differently from most conventional airplanes, most of which have a tricycle gear landing system with one or more landing wheels up front and two or more pairs of wheels in the back. Taildraggers have two wheels up front and one wheel in the back near the end of the plane's tail. The airplane's tail appears to rest on the ground.

The center of gravity (COG) of conventional tricycle gear airplanes is in front of the main gear, and the COG of taildraggers is behind. Landing a taildragger requires a completely different landing technique. With tricycle gear planes, the pilot touches down on the back paired main landing wheels and then lowers the front nosewheel onto the runway. With taildraggers, the pilot stalls the plane with both front main wheels and the back tailwheel touching down on the runway at the same time.

One Day I Became the Hero

Pilot beware! Too much self-confidence and a massive ego may get you in trouble. Here's a kicker story to towing banners. One day I became the hero—a cool, big-time pilot with a massive ego among my banner-pilot peers.

That day, after dropping the banner, instead of continuing on an easterly heading to follow the normal route to land on the 5,000-foot runway 24 (RWY 24), I made a snap aerobatic decision. At around 50 feet above ground level (AGL), I viewed the remaining 2,000 feet of the 4,000-foot runway 20 (RWY 20) out of the corner of my eye and decided—*I could land on that!*

I banked the C-150 airplane 45 degrees, turned 90 degrees right, pulled the power to idle, extended all my flaps and attempted to land on the remaining portion of RWY 20. A few of the other banner pilots observed most of this aerobatic flight display and were immensely impressed. They bragged about me for weeks, and a few attempted to replicate my maneuver.

My id psychic function probably made the decision to land on RWY 20, my ego psychic function probably executed the landing maneuver, but my super ego psychic function certainly influenced me to tell the whole story of what happened that day. You see, I actually unintentionally taxied off the end of RWY 20, and almost ran into the grove of trees ahead. However, as I approached the hard, grassy ground at the end of the runway, I released the brakes, grabbed the yoke full aft so that the nose wheel would stay off the ground, and made an immediate left turn onto the taxiway. This was a technique I had learned from flight training in England on actual soft-field, grassy runways. Yes—confess! *Tell the truth!* Always tell the truth! Not only did I want to be safe, I wanted my peer pilots to be safe too. If one of those other pilots tried to copy me but messed up and got hurt, that would bother me. When I told the whole story, some of the banner pilots were even more impressed with the soft-field landing and taxiing technique.

The next time you look up and see a plane towing a banner, think of Frank the pilot and why he told the truth.

The Gouge. Unless your air machine is on fire, most of the time, pilots do not need to be impulsive, so think before you act. Always tell the truth. Do not let your stupid flying stunts influence other pilots who may get hurt or crash and die emulating your flight maneuvers.

First Emergency

One beautiful sunny day, while happily working on my scanning, fixation and distance adaption eye skills at 200 feet above planet Earth, I smelled something strange—an acrid smell of burnt metal wire and plastic rubber. This unpleasant stench grew in intensity. This smell is far worse than the smell of food burned from overcooking. Within seconds, before my pilot brain had a chance to deduce the cause of the odor, electrical smoke emitted from the cockpit dashboard. Smoke from burning wire insulation is toxic. An airborne fire can kill you.

Smoke and fire are the worst phenomenon that could occur on any airplane, especially with aviation fuel on board and no fire trucks to rescue you. No problem. I would just turn off the avionics master switch, I thought, and that would turn off all the avionics. Something was probably overheating.

Big problem!

The burning smell and puffy white smoke, only inches from my shocked face, was not extinguished.

During a flight emergency, the human body readies itself for survival. The breathing rhythm increases, the heart rate increases, the blood pressure increases, the pupils dilate and adrenalin kicks in. The body becomes primed with greater strength, heighten awareness, and quicker reaction time to survive the emergency. The human instinct is to live. During an emergency, the pilot is usually unaware of these bodily changes and unaware of his/her feelings because the pilot is totally engaged with handling the emergency and landing the plane safely. Most likely, I was probably really scared and was unaware of those feelings at the time.

I thought, *I do not want to drop my banner on the sunbathers and I do not want to land in the water, what shall I do?* I was positioned at the northern part of the banner-tow pattern, the furthest point from New Smyrna Beach airfield. The closest airport to me was Ormond Beach Airport (OMN). Although there was a residential neighborhood between me and OMN, OMN was the nearest place to land. I made a pilot-in-command decision to divert to OMN.

To conserve battery power and to contain a potential fire, I turned off every switch in the aircraft and only turned on the radio on an as-needed basis. Therefore, I would aviate the plane, navigate to OMN, but I would not communicate unless it was absolutely necessary.

As I entered the OMN pattern to land, I encountered yet another problem! There were ERAU flight instructors with student pilots flying in the same traffic pattern.

Why was this a problem?

Simply put, I was not supposed to be moonlighting while being employed by ERAU as a flight instructor. So, I did my best to disguise my distinctive New York accent, declared an emergency, dropped the banner on the OMN airfield and landed safely. Afterward, I called my boss for a car ride and requested that they fix the airplane and arrange for someone else to fly that airplane back to New Smyrna Beach airport.

Apparently, some of the avionics were hot-wired to the battery and not through the avionics master switch, which is the correct way to wire the avionics. So, with the Cessna C-172 avionics dropout relay, if you start the aircraft's engine when the battery voltage is low, then the relay will fail to energize, which will let voltage spikes reach your avionics and cause them to overheat.

Afterwards, during the self-pilot debrief, my reflections ignited my feelings of dropping the banner on people, getting fired from ERAU, crash landing in the ocean or short of the ORM airfield and possibly catching fire in flight. My feelings on this incident were like a child having a great day playing with all his/her favorite toys and someone not only takes away all the toys, but implies possible future punishment. After reassessing what happened, I resigned from my banner-towing position and stayed with the one job—flight instructing at ERAU. Otherwise, flying banners is really cool.

The Gouge. My first *aviation emergency* was an emergency landing at Ormond Beach Municipal Airport (ORM) due to avionics smoke in a Cessna C-172 aircraft while towing banners. There is always risk in aviation. Ignore your massive ego and make good, safe pilot decisions. Do not make impulsive decisions up there. If I had to, I would have dropped the banner on the beach or ocean, but I was able to tow it to an airfield. I was prepared to drop that banner at any moment on my way to OMN airfield. ERAU was not privy to this banner-tow pilot incident. If they were, then I would have probably been fired for moonlighting. Block out what others may think about you or any possible consequences and land the plane safely. Safety first! *It is better to tell a bad, embarrassing story than to die and not be able to tell a story at all.*

On that day I lived and landed the plane safely, but others weren't so fortunate. Hedrick Nickelson lost his C-150 G aircraft on April 14, 1985. His aircraft lost power while he was towing a banner off Daytona Beach. The pilot applied carburetor heat and checked the fuel controls. But the engine quit completely. Since the beach was crowded, the pilot elected to ditch the airplane into the rough sea water. The aircraft sank. The pilot survived, but the wreckage was never recovered.[17]

In 1986, the major airlines were American, Delta, Eastern, Northwest, Pan Am, TWA, United and USAir. There were many regional airlines as well as the turbo jet airline companies. My first choice for a job was Pan Am, for one reason—they flew all over the world. My second choice was Eastern because they flew the most varied routes and most varied types of aircraft. Then there was TWA, which was a first-class operation and also flew to Europe. USAir had the highest-paid pilots for the equipment type they flew. American Airlines, based in

Dallas, was still a small airline, but growing. Northwest was in the process of merging with Republic Airlines and was not hiring. United was not hiring white males at the time, and Delta had an anti-nepotism policy. Because my sister was employed with Delta, I would not be eligible to work for Delta unless my sister resigned her position. I had many good choices for possible employment, and there were other national and regional airline companies such as:

- Air Atlanta
- Air Kentucky
- Air Midwest
- Air Tran Airways
- Atlantic Southeast Airlines
- ATA Airlines
- Braniff Airlines
- Colgan Airways
- Frontier
- Jet American Airlines
- New York Air
- Ozark Airlines
- People's Express
- Piedmont Airlines
- Presidential Airways
- Southwest Airlines
- Sun World International Airways
- Texas International
- West Air Commuter Airlines
- Western Airlines

There were many options, but one big problem. Nearly all of these airlines required that pilots have minimum jet flight time and/or multi-engine flight time experience and preferably pilot-in-command time. This was the hole in my resume that I needed to fill. Part of my flight plan to acquire an airline pilot job was to dress up my resume to be competitive among my pilot peers.

In pursuit of acquiring multi-engine or jet flight time and after receiving a substantial pay raise of four dollars an hour, I resigned from my first flight job at ERAU.

On April 21, 1986, I wrote:

> *Dear Mr. MacDuffrey:*
>
> *After serious consideration, I have reached a definite decision to resign from the Embry-Riddle Aeronautical University employment, effective May 5, 1986. You will readily understand my decision in view of my personal goals.*
>
> *My time with Embry-Riddle Aeronautical University has provided stimulation and challenge. I enjoyed working with you, and I regret very much the necessity of leaving because of the economic trend. I must seek a higher salary and a position with the opportunity for advancement in the line of work that best suits me.*
>
> *I am sure you will find that my work was satisfactory with the Embry-Riddle Aeronautical University, and I hope that I have proved worthy of the confidence you placed in me.*
>
> *If at any future time a problem should arise, I shall be happy to assist in any way I can.*
>
> *Sincerely,*
>
> *Frank J. Donohue, Jr.*

With almost 1,000 hours total pilot flight time and 25 hours of simulator time, I resigned from my first pilot job without having another pilot job lined up. This was risky. I was taking a big chance to dress up my resume with more quality flight experience. At ERAU, the only flight time I logged was single-engine pilot-in-command time. If I stayed at ERAU, it would be several years before I would be eligible to flight instruct in multi-engine aircraft.

I was taking a big chance on myself; I was going to give up a lucrative, stable pilot job with benefits at one of the best aeronautical universities in the world to invest in myself with a chance to acquire multi-engine flight time, time that would make me more competitive for a chance get that ultimate airline pilot career. At the time, airlines were starting to hire pilots again. Hoping and wishfully thinking to myself, *Will this airline-pilot-hiring cycle change be an opportunity for me to get one of those fantastic sought-after pilot careers?"*

11

TRANSAMERICAN AIRWAYS

Building flight time.

I drove to airports in Orlando (ORL), Ft Lauderdale (FLL), Miami (MIA), and Jacksonville (JAX) looking for a multi-engine or a jet-engine pilot job.

College pilot friend Bill went to People's Express Airlines in New York, accepting a position as a Second Officer on a B-727 aircraft. College pilot friend John went to American Eagle Airlines in San Juan, accepting a position as a First Officer on a multi-engine turbo prop aircraft.

It didn't look good for me.

I thought I was failing and would end up on some corner in New York City, selling pretzels. With my resume and letters of recommendations in hand, I drove Black Beauty to Atlanta, Georgia.

Going from airport to airport like a door-to-door salesman, a door finally opened.

On May 9, 1986, I accepted a position with Transamerican Airways as a Certified Flight Instructor to instruct all phases of single-engine and multi-engine flight students under Federal Aviation Regulations, Part 61.

As mentioned before, Part 141 flight schools like at ERAU teach certain courses in a highly structured and organized way. The pilot student must conform to their full-time flight program schedule. Part 61 flight schools are more flexible and are typically smaller than Part 141 schools. Students have more control over their training timeline because flight instructors are typically more willing to work around the student's usually part-time schedule. Generally, Part 141 schools require fewer minimum flight hours and cost less to acquire pilot licenses. Generally, Part 141 schools are big operations and require full-time attendance versus Part 61 schools, which are small operations and accept part-time attendance. There are other pros and cons to Part 141 versus Part 61 flight schools, and each is suitable depending on the particular needs of the student pilot.

ERAU had a huge flight department that included about 50 flight instructors, four pilot flight managers, a secretary, a chief pilot and over 50 Cessna C-172 and Seminole PA-44 planes. At ERAU, I was well compensated with the great benefits, and I always had the opportunity to flight instruct up to 72 hours per week.

Transamerican Airways had four airplanes, a Cessna C-152 and C-172, a Piper PA-28 and a Piper Seminole PA-44, a company owner, a secretary and two flight instructors. One of the flight instructors was due to leave shortly after I started. There were many college grads in a similar situation who had to decide whether to take employment with a big, stable company with great benefits, but poor opportunities for promotion (like my situation at ERAU), or take a chance with the small startup company (like Transamerican) that may go out of business, and offers few benefits, but with great opportunity for personal growth.

At ERAU, I was making great money, plus extra money towing banners on the side. At Transamerican, there were many days when I only had one flight lesson to teach. During my six months at Transamerican, I made the least amount of money and had the lowest standard of living of my entire life. I had to share a small apartment with four girls and a guy. One time, I ate at McDonald's for a whole week because it was all I could afford. The calculations of these risk/reward scenarios can rarely produce the correct answer for the correct decision. Sometimes, you just have to take a chance and go with your gut feeling. The final outcome was that this pilot position was a big break and a big plus for my resume, mainly because of that Piper Seminole PA-44 multi-engine plane. Multi-engine flight time experience is a valuable requirement that most airlines require of their pilot job applicants.

The Multi-Engine Rating License I had obtained in 1985 authorized me to fly multi-engine aircraft, but it did not authorize me to teach students in multi-engine aircraft.

One of the best ways to accumulate pilot-in-command, multi-engine flight time is to enroll flight students to pay you to teach them how to fly those planes. Therefore, I worked out a deal with owner, Benjamin Butler the owner of Transamerican, to rent the Piper Seminal aircraft (PA 44-180) at cost so that I could get the required flight hours to take my Multi-Engine Flight Instructor Rating exam.

On July 2, 1986, I passed the Multi-Engine Instrument Instructor (MEI) flight check ride in a Seminole PA 44-180 airplane, tail number N810K. This was a very challenging practical exam. The oral exam was two hours, and the flight exam was more than two hours, including five landings. The oral exam followed the typical pilot exam procedure; the designated pilot examiner attacked with the questions, and the pilot applicant defended with the answers. However, the flight exam is unique from most others because the pilot examinee must both *do* and *teach* during the flight, such as if the test examiner retards one of the engine throttles to idle to simulate an engine failure. The test taker (*moi*) must teach the test administrator how to identify which engine has failed; how to verify which engine has failed; how to feather the failed engine; and how to secure the failed engine while performing these tasks, and all to FAA pilot standards. The test taker, for the multi-engine instrument instructor's license, sits in the right seat and teaches the rote, understanding, application and correlation levels of learning for each pilot maneuver conducted to the test examiner as if the examiner were the student pilot.

After more than two hours of flying and having taught numerous pilot maneuvers, I was exhausted and my voice became hoarse. The exhaustion I experienced felt like what a Boston marathoner encounters after crossing the finish line. To date, his was the most challenging flight check ride I had accomplished.

This new MEI license authorized me to instruct basic and instrument students in multi-engine airplanes. Instructing enables you to build up flight time while getting paid, and multi-engine pilot flight time was extremely valuable in strengthening my resume in order to get hired by a major airline company. Passing this MEI ride was the second biggest break I obtained in my pursuit of a major airline pilot job. That first pilot job at ERAU was my first big break.

The Gouge. Do and teach at the same time. For the MEI practical exam, the pilot applicant must teach while demonstrating instrument, commercial and multi-engine flight skills and knowledge. During the exam, constantly speak like a teacher, explaining your thoughts and what you are doing during each phase of each flight maneuver. The MEI ride is like the CFI ride except instrument, commercial and multi-engine task are additionally tested.

After obtaining the Multi-Engine Certified Flight Instructor (CFI-MEI) Rating License, I started teaching all types of multi-engine student pilots. Experienced military pilots who flew sophisticated fighters, bombers and transport planes needed training in order to acquire the civilian Airline Transport License (ATP). All commercial airline pilots have an ATP license. I instructed many military pilots in their pursuit of earning their ATP license.

At Transamerican, we offered an accelerated ATP program mainly utilized by military pilots. For one price, we offered unlimited ground flight instruction, knowledge preparation and test training, and three or four flights of ATP multi-engine flight training. Afterwards, most of these military pilots were able to take and pass their ATP practical exam. The Airline Transport Pilot (ATP) license is the highest level of aviation pilot license one can obtain. All airline captains have an ATP license. The ATP multi-engine flight instruction enabled me to log very valuable multi-engine pilot-in-command flight time.

At this small flight school operation, I instructed all phases of single-engine and multi-engine flight students. When working at a small startup company, be prepared to wear many hats. One time, Benjamin, the owner, and I flew a Cessna C-T210 aircraft from Atlanta, Georgia (ATL) to Kerrville, Texas (ERV) to pick up new student pilot Eric Manson. The seven-flight-hour trip covered 750 miles and was the longest flight I have ever piloted.

Eric's mother was quite wealthy and was the second largest landowner in the state of Montana at one time. At the time, Mrs. Manson lived in Kerrville, and while we were there, she arranged for us to get a private tour of the Mooney aircraft factory. When Eric's mother asked Eric what he wanted to do for the summer, he expressed his desire to learn to fly planes. Some kids are lucky if they get to attend summer camp for a week or two. Eric was very fortunate to attend our flight school for the summer.

With that C-T210 plane, I flew 16-year-old Eric back to Atlanta and spent the summer teaching him, along with my other students how to fly planes. The minimum age requirement is 16 to solo and to earn a private pilot's license is seventeen. Eric was the youngest flight student I had instructed.

At the time, Eric was an owner of a pickup truck and an all-terrain vehicle, which contributed to his natural ability to learn how to operate an airplane. He looked upon me as an older brother; he told me so. He admired me and he presumed I knew everything about flying. To him, I was the pilot god.

At 16, Eric was lanky and energetic, with brown eyes, short brown hair, pale skin and a few distinct freckles scattered on the outskirts of his juvenile smile. He was intelligent, a fast learner and very inquisitive. He constantly presented me with questions. Of the hundreds of questions Eric asked me, I will never forget the last question he had for me: "Frank, what would be a good first plane to buy?"

12

MIDNITE EXPRESS

Career-ending emergency.

The day I heard Midnite Express Airline was conducting pilot job interviews, I arrived professionally dressed without an invitation. This was becoming a little habit of me, showing up and seeking a pilot job without a prior invite to interview.

Mentioning college pilot friend Robert Valaro as a personal reference, I politely requested an interview. Robert and I attended ERAU together, and he was currently employed at Midnite Express. Robert's position there had helped him land a better job at United Airlines later on. Rob is from Long Island like me, and we bonded well together.

That day, Midnite Express interviewed and gave airplane simulator check rides to eight candidates. I was one of two pilots hired on October 9, 1986, by Midnite Express to fly Cessna C-402 aircraft under Federal Aviation Regulations Part 135. My job as the pilot-in-command (the captain) was to command the C-402 multi-engine aircraft as a solo pilot, during all weather conditions, five nights a week from Mobile, Alabama (MOB) to Atlanta carrying cargo freight.

So, I resigned from Transamerican Airways with 1,300 hours of total pilot flight time, over 100 hours of multi-engine flight time and 1,160 hours of pilot-in-command time (PIC).

The Cessna C-402 airplane was the largest airplane I had ever flown. Its wingspan was 44 feet, and the plane was 36 feet long. It had a max takeoff gross weight of 6,850 pounds. The Cessna C-402 had two 325-horsepower, turbo-charged and fuel-injected engines. It could fly at 230 knots (265 mph) as far as 1,200 nautical miles (1,380 statute miles) and as high as 26,900 feet.[18]

The C-402 nicknames are the "Business liner" and "Utiliner." The C-402 had a seating capacity of ten passengers, but the plane I would fly was configured with only two seats so it could carry as much freight as possible. The nickname I gave to my C-402 was "U-Till" short for "Utiliner." "U-Till" as in a "tool," and this was my new tool I used to produce income.

My main route left Atlanta Hartsfield International Airport (ATL) around 6:00 a.m. and headed to Pensacola, Florida (PNB) and then to Mobile (MOB). At around 9:00 p.m. I would fly the return route from Mobile to Atlanta. This was a Monday-through-Friday operation, so Mobile became my new residence.

During my employment with Midnite Express, I logged some of the most valuable flight time and encountered some of the most valuable flight experiences ... and almost died. I logged multi-engine time, night time, instrument time, instrument approaches and all of it was pilot-in-command time. Accepting this cargo pilot position, that entails flying at night through all kinds of weather, had increased my level of risk. During my employment with Midnite, I experienced my first missed approach (MAP), my second almost-career-ending pilot emergency, my attack from a flock of seagulls and I obtained the Airline Transport Pilot (ATP) license. These nine months catapulted my flight career. In fact, I believe something that happened to me at this job helped me acquire an airline pilot job later on.

First Missed Approach

Fog can prevent you from getting to your destination. Fog is like a low cloud close to the ground. Fog forms when the air becomes saturated with moisture, when the air contains more moisture than it can hold for that temperature, and there are light winds present. When temperature and dew point move close together, either the dew point rises until it equals the temperature, or the temperature decreases to match the dew point, but in either case, fog forms. There is radiation fog, advection fog, steam fog, upslope fog, precipitation fog and freezing fog. Fog can be extremely important to a pilot ... and to you. Bad weather like fog can prevent the pilot from seeing the runway, causing the pilot to wait for better weather or go to another airport to land, which can disrupt your plans for the day.

My first missed approach occurred while flying an Instrument ILS Approach into Atlanta on the Cessna C-402 as a single-pilot captain for Midnite Express.

Aviation Route Weather Report (METAR) is an observation of current surface weather designed to give accurate depictions of current weather conditions. It is reported in a standard international format. There are two types of METAR reports. The first is the routine METAR report that is transmitted in regular, usually hourly time intervals. The second is the aviation selected SPECI. This is a special report that can be given at any time to update the METAR for rapidly changing weather conditions, aircraft mishaps or other critical information. A typical METAR report contains information in sequential order. Below, you will find the METAR for Hartsfield–Jackson Atlanta International Airport (ATL). Notice that the temperature dew point is close and there are light winds. The pilot raw data is what pilots read and interpolate. Below the raw data, I have decoded the data for the non-pilot to comprehend.

The METAR read: Pilot Raw data: KATL 111454Z 07003 1/2SM -RA BR OVC 002 20/19 A 2990. Decoded for the non-pilot, this means: on the eleventh day of the month, 10:54 a.m. local time, wind 070' (east/northeast) at 3 knots, visibility 1/2 statue mile, light rain and mist, with clouds overcast at 200 feet, temperature 20° Celsius, dew point 19° Celsius, the barometric is 29.90 inches of mercury.

The air traffic controller instructed me to fly 170 knots (almost 200 miles per hour) to the outer marker final approach fix. The 170 knots airspeed is about 40 to 50 knots faster than the normal approach airspeed in this aircraft. We would generally fly this faster speed to the final approach fix (FAF) in order to maintain constant flow control with other jets, which normally fly at faster speeds then twin-prop planes into this very busy major international airport.

Most final approach fixes are about five miles from the end of the runway. Usually, the pilot has sufficient time to slow the aircraft to the normal final approach speed before landing. My final approach speed was about 125 knots, and I had slowed down to that speed before reaching the Decision Height (DH) on the ILS Instrument Approach to runway 26R. Remember, the DH is that point where the pilot decides whether he can see the runway or the runway's environment. The DH is the point when the pilot decides whether he is in a position to make a safe landing or he must execute a go-around procedure. The DH is usually around 200 feet above the ground and around a half a slant mile from the runway.

On this particular landing, the weather was bad with very poor visibility. It was so foggy that night that at the DH, I could not see the runway. All I could see was the red halo glow of the "Fly Delta" light sign on top of Delta's maintenance building, which was located in the middle of the airport. There was this landing expectation I had within me and now I could not see the runway. One of the things pilots always do after getting up in the air is land; at least the surviving pilots do. This is a solo pilot operation; there is not a co-pilot on board for me to confer with. I thought, *What am I going to do? I was expecting to see the runway and land, as usual.* My cool big-time pilot attitude with the massive ego waned; I felt small. I did not like this new feeling. I was expecting to land.

My prior flight training included practicing go-arounds in *simulated* bad weather. This weather was *actual* bad weather. I made the pilot-in-command decision to execute a missed approach and go around. This was my first actual go-around in real-life bad weather. It is not a good feeling when you are all by yourself, at night, in bad weather, and you cannot see the runway to land. During this event there was no time to reflect on my feelings—I had to fly the plane. My thinking was consumed with commanding the C-402 to execute my first actual missed approach and go around. I had to aviate the plane, navigate the airspace and communicate my intentions to the air traffic controller.

The go-around procedure is a transition from a descending landing phase (the plane is configured to land in a descent vector with slowing airspeed) to a takeoff climbing phase (the plane is configured to climb in an ascent vector with increasing airspeed). There are many things a pilot must do as well as think.

My thoughts were, *Will I attempt another ILS Instrument Approach again, see the runway and land? Or will I have to fly to another airport with good weather and land there? How much fuel do I have?*

The missed approach procedure (MAP) tells the pilot in detail how to navigate the airspace with directions on headings, altitudes and turns to fly. As I was executing the MAP, the communication from air traffic controller inquired, "Midnite N2713K would like to attempt to fly a second ILS Instrument Approach to runway 26R?" The weather was still above minimum landing visibility requirement, and the fuel gauges indicated that I had enough fuel for another attempt. "Yes, Atlanta Midnite N273K would like to attempt another ILS approach for runway 26R," I transmitted.

On the second ILS approach attempt, the controller authorized me to fly at any speed, at my discretion. I slowed to my normal final approach airspeed a few miles before the FAF. I configured the aircraft for landing early and glued my eyes forward to detect the approach lights and runway. This time, I saw the approach lights and eventually I saw the runway. I was relieved! My eyes popped wide opened, a grateful smile spread across my face and my sweaty hands re-clutched the plane's yoke and throttles. My current expectation, to miss approach and go-around instantly, transformed to the glorious expectation to land. The realization that I was going to land on planet Earth made me feel bigger. My self-worth was growing within me. Once again, I started feeling like a cool big-time pilot as my massive ego grew and grew. With absolute confidence, I decided to continue and land.

It may have taken two attempts, but on that terribly foggy night in Atlanta, I landed on planet Earth and re-engaged with my pilot comrades. All of my pilot peers had loads of more instrument flight experience than me, and that night, landing in bad fog seemed routine to them; therefore, I did not brag. They also knew that it took two attempts for me to see the runway and land. Those pilot friends cuddled me as if I were a puppy dog afraid of the bad weather and congratulated me on a job well done. They did not give me a treat like a dog might have gotten, but they boosted my self-esteem. It was as if I were a rookie football player who fumbled the ball during the first game, and they were the seasoned experienced ball players supporting me as I was growing into an experienced pilot right before their eyes.

It's always a good feeling to touch down on planet Earth, especially when it is very challenging to see the runway due to bad weather. One of my favorite trademark sayings, came back to me then: *When you get up there, don't forget to land.* Landing is good!

The Gouge. Pilots, pay close attention to the temperature dew point spread and winds of aviation weather reports for the runway on which you intend to land. Expect fog when the temperature and dew point spread are about 5° Fahrenheit (3° Celsius) apart and there are light surface winds. Review the missed-approach procedures and go-around procedures for your destination airport runway beforehand. Be prepared not to see the runway and go missed. Stay calm. Aviate, navigate and at your discretion, when you are ready, communicate. ATC is usually very helpful at assisting the pilot to fly back around a second time and attempt another approach to landing. During my commercial airline career, one of the first pilot actions I performed before I flew to an airport was to check the visibility forecast and then check the lowest instrument approach minimums for the airport to which I intended to fly. This technique was one of the pilot habits I developed that helped me determine the risk factor of landing there.

Crash Landing Emergency

Life is great … sometimes. One glorious morning, on December 13, 1986, I was thinking, *I have the greatest job in the world. Flying is as easy as walking in the park. I get to see all this.* Feelings of joy and total job satisfaction swelled within me as I consumed all the glories of the beauty of Mother Nature from a height of 5,000 feet. It was the last flight of the week—a short flight from Pensacola International Airport (PNS), Florida to Mobile Regional Airport (MOB), Alabama. My weekend of additional fun would begin soon after finishing that last, short, wonderful flight. The strong desire to get to a destination can override a pilot's logic, sound decision-making and basic instinct. Good pilots fight the dangers of the negative effects that "get-home-itis" can have on safe flying. On that particular day, "get-home-itis" was winning the battle.

Just 5,000 feet below me, I took in the amazing view of a Spanish Fort, a place where battles were fought during the American Revolution and the American Civil War. Maybe I will visit there this weekend. The final descent of the final flight of the week had begun. Under me was Highway 10, but my attention swayed left to the shrimp boats on Mobile Bay. *Maybe I will go fishing this weekend.* With U-Till's nose pointed downward, during the descent in the far distance, New Orleans comes into full view. Ah, there is where I will indulge myself this weekend. These and other options on how I will enjoy my days off excited me. I was looking forward to having a fun weekend.

Upon approaching MOB, the Air Traffic Controller (ATC) cleared me for a visual approach to runway 36. After executing the pre-landing checklist, I extended the landing gear. There are three square light indicators that turn green indicating that each landing gear is down and locked. This time, however, the landing nose-gear light did not illuminate. Drawing the file from my brain on my landing gear system knowledge, I pressed the landing light indicator button. The bulb lit up, verifying that it was working properly. I turned the plane onto the final approach and recycled the landing gear, and ... again, the same result—only the two main green lights were illuminated. Technically speaking, the lack of a green illumination of the nose gear indicating button means "the nose gear had not extended properly." The nose gear of U-Till, my plane, failed to extend! All symptoms of "get-home-itis" faded as I was forced to deal with a potential catastrophic emergency. A nose-gear-up landing could destroy U-Till, and wouldn't be doing *me* any favors, either!

"Mobile Tower, Midnite 32 (the call sign for Midnite Express aircraft tail number N320AR) needs to abandon the landing and depart the traffic pattern for few minutes," I stated. Mobile tower responded, "Midnite 32 fly runway heading, cleared to 2,000 feet, what is the problem?"

"Cleared runway heading climb to 2,000 feet," I acknowledged and continued in a timid voice, "I have an indication that the front nose gear is not down." With sympathetic understanding he inquired, "Do you want to fly a low approach for me to visually check if your gear is down?" Thinking, *This is a good idea*, I agreed, "Affirmative." The tower instructed me, "Descend to 1,200 feet, turn right and enter the traffic pattern for runway 32."

"Wilco," I complied. Wilco is a pilot term meaning I heard you, I understand you and I will comply with your instruction.

While flying the downwind leg in the traffic pattern, I attempted to manually extend the landing gear. Still no light! Damn! I checked the circuit breaker, which was in its proper position. An additional attempt to verify the malfunction was made by retarding the throttles below 13 inches manifold pressure and extending the flaps past the 30-degree position. With the throttles retarded and the flaps extended, if all three landing gears are not down and locked, then a warning horn will sound. To my dismay, the "Gear-Not-Down-Warning" horn blasted. Damn! What a terrible sound. After exhausting all my ideas based on my aircraft system's knowledge, I opened the emergency checklist manual to the "Nose-Gear-Not-Down-and-Locked" section. I executed all the checklist items.

I turned base, then final and descended to about 50 feet above the runway. The air traffic controller is perched about 50 feet high in the control tower. During the low approach just abeam the control tower, I banked U-Till to expose her precious underbelly for the ATC to visually ascertain whether the nose gear was down. Waiting for a response, I had a few seconds to accept the fact *this might not end well.*

Finally, he reported, "The nose gear does not appear to be fully extended. It looks like landing gear is cocked to one side." My heart dropped, my eyes closed, my brain went blank, but my speech function, probably out of habit, responded, "Roger." Like an emergency doctor approaching a patient in severe pain. ATC inquired, "How can I help?"

Of course, my brain re-engaged, for I was determined to win this battle and survive. Looking at my fuel gauges, I calculated I had about twenty minutes of flight time remaining before I was going to return to planet Earth, one way or another.

"Midnite 32 needs more time to troubleshoot the problem," were my words, my decision and best course of action. Helpfully, ATC granted my request, "Midnite 32 fly right-hand turns west of runway 32, altitude at your discretion. Keep us updated on your status."

"Wilco Midnite 32, I will get back to you," I transmitted. I went off into my own little world to try, once again, to solve the flight emergency at hand and to prevent a catastrophic event and potential death. Poring through the Cessna Emergency Checklist, I spent approximately 15 minutes troubleshooting the situation. I went through every detail three times. My logical brain and creative imagination produced one more final idea. This was not in the checklist; this was my idea. With my feet, I implanted aggressive left then right rudder movements to yaw U-Till left and right. With my hands grasping the plane's yoke, I initiated erratic nose-up and nose-down to pitch U-Till up then down. My idea was to use aerodynamic forces and the weight of U-Till and me to force the nose gear to lock down in place. Damn! This did not work either.

I requested, received permission and executed another low approach. The reported status of the nose gear did not change. As I finally accepted the fact that my landing nose gear was not down and would not come down, a fog of misery and disappointment filled the cockpit. The affliction bestowed upon me and my possible disastrous fate was disturbed by the voice from ATC; "What are your intentions?"

What are my intentions? What could I do? I felt inadequate. With my heart sinking and my worry level rising, I declared, "Midnite 32 is declaring an emergency; I will need emergency ground crew and equipment!"

This was mentioned before, and I am reluctant to repeat it again, but the reader needs to be aware of the gravity of a pilot flight emergency. During a flight emergency, the human body readies itself for survival with an increase in breathing rhythm, an increase in heart rate, and an increase in blood pressure; also, the eye pupils dilate and adrenalin kicks in. The body becomes primed with greater strength, heightened awareness, and quicker reaction time to survive the emergency. The human body and the person within does not want to experience pain and death. All bodily functions and symptoms contribute to the survival mode.

During the emergency, the pilots are usually unaware of these bodily changes and unaware of their feelings because the pilot is totally engaged with handling the emergency and landing the plane safely. Occasionally, during an emergency, pilots may briefly connect with their feelings and emotions, but within seconds, the pilot must reengage with the motor skills and thought process to land safely. While troubleshooting and handling most inflight emergencies, I rarely connected to my feelings that I may crash, burn and die; I was too busy thinking and utilizing my pilot skills to land the plane safely. Most likely, I was probably really scared and was unaware of those feelings at the time. However, this time, the stimuli of crashing, burning and dying briefly overwhelmed my pilot-in-command duties of flying the plane and landing safely. During this emergency there was a moment or two when I did connect with the state of my body and mind. I felt the fear of death, and I did not like the feeling. That moment or two passed briefly as I re-engaged with Frank the pilot to fly the plane, land safely and live.

The tower spoke again, "Understand Midnite 32 is declaring an emergency. The men and equipment will be standing by. What runway would you like?" With wind direction of 40 degrees and 12-knot strength, I requested, "Runway 36."

"Fly heading 120 for a vector to final approach to runway 36, and descend to 1,200 feet," he instructed me.

After I relayed back the clearance to ATC, I stated, "Be advised all electrical switches would be turned off after my final radio transmission."

After deciphering my statement, ATC said, "Roger, we will talk to you on the ground."

The tower forecasted a hint, an innuendo, a slither of trust that I would survive. Did he have more hope in me than I had in myself?

I completed all the necessary checklists, aviated and navigated U-Till, communicated with ATC, and now I was lined up on the final approach to runway 36. After crossing the runway threshold at 75 feet above the runway, I completed the last remaining checklist; the "Final Shutdown" checklist. This entailed shutting down both engines. At 75 feet above the runway, I shut down both engines, utilizing my depleting kinetic energy (my engines were no longer producing power) and decreasing potential energy (75 feet above the runway and descending) to land the plane. Winds, aerodynamic glide and ground effect were the forces I had to battle with the flight controls. The goal was to dissipate as much forward energy as possible, touchdown softly, and hold U-Till's nose up as long as possible.

I am committed. My engines are shut off, and there is no option for a go-around. Planet Earth and I will meet one way or another, pleasantly or otherwise.

At 50 feet above the runway, I am lined up with the centerline: 50 feet, 40, 30, 20 ... then at 10 feet, I slowly started pulling back on the yoke and adjusting the unpowered plane's glide path toward my landing aiming point. My eyes started transitioning further down the runway, as I used my peripheral vision to judge the rate at which the runway was approaching. My plane started drifting in response to the change in wind vector. I adjusted the right aileron into the wind and applied some opposite left rudder. I have no engine power to assist me—only rapidly depleting potential and kinetic energy power.

Although I may have been clutching tightly to the plane's yoke, I was utilizing the feel of my fingertips to make small changes to the aircraft's attitude in response to the changing outside forces affecting my flight path. These sensitive finger receptions and small-brain command responses were crucial to me successfully transitioning the plane from flight mode to non-flight mode, especially without engine power.

Times up! Zero feet!

The rear wheels did touch down at the softest slowest speed possible, and I did hold the plane's nose off the runway for as long as possible. So far so good. All my goals, on how to conduct this emergency landing, were accomplished. Finally, I had to let the nose down. The aerodynamic forces of lift and the control I had to hold the nose off the concrete were being depleted. To prevent the aircraft's nose from slamming onto the runway, I eased the nose down not knowing what to expect next.

U-Till lightly kissed and then forcefully embraced the runway. The momentum of the plane's forward motion caused U-Till and me to skid about 100 yards. Through my peripheral vision, I could see blazing sparks igniting from the metal propellers scraping against the gray concrete runway surface. Wishing, *I hope those sparks do not ignite a fire with the fuel I have on board.* My brain cells were computing, *How long will this skid last before I can get out? I want to get out now!*

The skid time of the plane's metal scraping the runway's concrete surface seemed to take forever. Finally, after what seemed like an eternity of my mind playing flashbacks of my life, the plane came to rest. The time between airplane nose contact and the aircraft arresting to a full stop seemed as if my whole lifetime were wrapped up in those precious seconds. So many vivid emotional memories packed into a short period of time were happening all at once. It was as if I were having a near-death experience. My human mind did separate these memories into different events. Always in the background of these events was a blazing fire. Fire, fire trucks and fire truck water hoses flashed in the background of these images during this near-death experience. Somehow, the central theme during the entire time of these flashback memories was that I knew I wanted to get out of the plane because the plane was going to catch on fire. I did not want to catch on fire and burn.

Upon full stop, I evacuated immediately. I jumped out and fled the crash site like a jackrabbit fleeing for its life. The emergency men and the equipment were there on full alert. Just a few feet away, there were fire trucks with firemen ready for action. But there was no subsequent fire. I did not catch fire! I did not burn! The feel of my feet connected to planet Earth felt good. The flash of a sunshine ray onto my face felt satisfying. The light northeast wind brushed across my lips as I breathed with the surface atmosphere. My breathing rhythm settled to a normal rate. The deep, rapid pounding of my heart slowed to a normal rate. The accompanied extraordinarily high blood pressure entered the normal range of an adult human being. All of my human body systems and functions were returning to normal. The adrenalin, created from the flight emergency to land and survive, was wearing off quickly. Relief, gratefulness and thankfulness were the three greatest emotional feelings I was experiencing. I did not experience burning fire, pain or death. I was alive!

The nose-gear-up landing was a controllable crash landing, and I joyfully survived. It is better to tell a bad, embarrassing story than to die and not be able to tell a story at all. I thought, *I did not die, and I would be able to tell this story, but would it be an embarrassing one? Did I do something wrong, something embarrassingly wrong? Was it my fault that the landing nose gear did not extend to the normal position?* These conflicting, double-doubting, self-imposed questions were interrupted.

A huge, husky fire chief anxiously bolted toward me saying, "Are you all right?" After reassessing my mind and body I responded, "Yes, I am fine." The considerate fire chief reassured me, "There are no imminent signs of a fire."

"Great! I'll be right back," I replied.

Thinking of my brain bag (my pilot's flight bag), I re-entered the aircraft, removed it and my other belongings. A pilot's flight bag is filled with numerous, valuable pilot stuff that is needed to fly planes; it is so valuable that pilots call it their brain bag. Before I exited U-Till, I took a mental picture of the unusual nose down cockpit view of the runway. A plane's nose usually sits parallel to the runway surface. However, with the landing-nose gear collapsed, the plane's nose was pointing approximately 45 degrees to the runway's concrete pavement.

Poor U-Till! Her nose is smashed and her propellors are bent. My means of producing income and my best friend has been disabled. She incurred major damage while I came through the catastrophic event unharmed—at least physically. She protected me and **she did not catch** on fire and explode. I am thankful for that, but couldn't help wondering, *Will she ever fly again?*

A logical deduction spilled through my thoughts: *I guess I am not going fishing this weekend.*

Officers from the Mobile Police Department approached me and requested my name, address, phone number, aircraft tail number, the name of the aircraft owner and my company's name. After I provided all the information the police requested, I requested a ride from them to the Aero One flight station. At Aero One, I called Midnite Express part-owner Mario Spaghetti and reported the incident. Mario directed me to call maintenance Chief Skip Wallace, which, of course, I did. Then I phoned the airport manager to obtain permission to move the aircraft and remove its cargo. After receiving permission, I removed the cargo from the aircraft and transferred the cargo to the customer. Landing the plane and surviving was great, but I still had a job to do. The customer packages must get delivered. Aero One moved the aircraft to their premises. Mario released me and I went home.

During the emergency and shortly afterwards I was too busy doing stuff to debrief myself and reflect on what happened.

A few days later, Midnite Express asked me for copies of my flight logbook. This was a tense time. For over a week, no one said "good job" or "bad job." For over a week, I kept thinking, *Did I do everything right during the emergency? Was I safe? Was I legal? What should I have done differently? Was it my fault that the nose gear did not extend and lock down?* Although I could not find fault in myself for the landing-nose-gear malfunction, a sense of guilt haunted me.

During that post-crash week, sadness with feelings of helplessness and hopelessness grew intensely within me. There was a loss of interest in activities that I once enjoyed, like I had time to fish but I did not want to fish. There were times I felt worthless. The effects of these concerns gave me a loss of appetite and a loss of sound sleep. During several nights, I awoke recalling a variety of flashback dreams of the landing and skidding. Blazing fire, fire trucks and fire truck water hoses were in all my various dreams. I had no one to talk to for help in dealing with my situation. I had just recently moved to Mobile, Alabama, and did not know anyone. I did not want to bother my parents.

I had an emergency crash landing that may have been my fault, and I was convinced my aviation career was over. All that hard work and money building a pilot career seemed like it was going down the drain because of one crash landing. What was I going to do? Again, the image loomed of a New York City Street corner and yours truly as a vendor of pretzels.

About 10 days after the crash, I was summoned to Midnite Express headquarters in Atlanta, Georgia. My deductive reasoning was that I was being called in to get fired. At headquarters, before my hearing with the bosses, I was approached by the head mechanic, Skip Wallace. Although I had spoken to Skip via the telephone, I had never met him in person.

Skip asked me, "Are you Frank Donohue?"

"Yes," I replied. Skip congratulated me, "You did a great job saving the C-402 from total loss." With a sigh of much needed relief, I said, "Thank you."

This was the first time anyone, and not just anyone but the chief airplane mechanic of the company, said "good job." The enormous, almost uncontrollable, semi-state of depression within me subsided. The extremely high physical stress and psychological stress that had consumed me since the emergency crash landing, came flooding out. My shoulders rolled upright; my gaze was once again directed skyward. I smiled. That smile developed into glowing, wonderful self-confident gigantic smile. At that very moment, I once again became that big-time, cool pilot with a massive ego.

These are some examples of the ups and downs of a pilot's life. This was my second major, almost-career-ending pilot flight emergency. Moments before, I was convinced my pilot career was about to end, and now, I had renewed hope that one day, I would obtain a pilot's position at a major airline.

Upon entering chief executive officer Robert A. Milton's office, I received handshakes, job well done statements and the following:

> *Dear Frank:*
>
> *I wish to personally express to you the gratitude of all of us at Midnite for the excellent and truly professional manner in which you handled a very challenging situation this past Saturday, December 13, 1986. Although the professional pilot is*

clearly expected to handle difficult occurrences, I have received feedback from several individuals, both from within and outside our company, indicating that the skill demonstrated in your landing of our Cessna 32, N320AR, after a nose-gear-extension failure, was nothing short of remarkable.

It has also come to my attention that the reason for the gear failure was probably caused when a torque tube in the gear extension mechanism was bent during a towing. Clearly, this is most regrettable and we must strive to ensure that an unnecessary incident such as this never again occurs at our company.

We can ask no more of any employee, than the thorough attention to detail which you took prior, during and after your emergency landing. Please keep up the good work and please accept the small gift enclosed as a token of our genuine appreciation.

Sincerely,

Robert A. Milton

Chief Executive Officer

That small gift of $100 was quite valuable to me, but not as valuable as keeping my aviation career. Besides, who wants to sell pretzels on a corner in New York in December? Remember this very important story because later in this book I will reveal how this crash-landing emergency had a major influence on the outcome of my pilot career.

The Gouge. Be safe and legal. Treat every flight like an FAA flight check ride, and be prepared for an FAA ramp check after each flight. After a flight emergency, all the paperwork and logbooks will be scrutinized so always keep those in order. Strive to fly every flight to FAA check ride standards; fly airspeed within 10 knots, heading within 10 degrees and altitude within 100 feet of target. Strive to fly legally and be prepared to show the documents to the FAA after each flight. Always look for flight threats. Just when you think flying is as easy as walking in the park, an emergency can occur. All that hard work of learning, studying, flying and testing can go down the drain with one bad flight emergency. Pilots have died making incorrect decisions during pilot emergencies. Flying is precious, delicate, valuable and unpredictable—savor each flight because one day it may be your last.

Attacked by birds

My second missed approach occurred at Craig Field in Jacksonville, Florida. I was flying a VOR Non-Precision Instrument approach in a Cessna C-402 aircraft to runway 32.

With a precision approach, the ILS system guides the pilot laterally and vertically to a point usually around 200 feet above ground level and around a half a slant mile to the end of the runway. At that point, the idea is that the pilot will be able to see the runway and land.

With a VOR Non-Precision approach, the VOR only guides the pilot laterally to a position at which the pilot *may* be able to see the runway. A VOR is the acronym for "VHF omnidirectional radio range." A VOR is a type of a short-range radio navigation system, transmitting and receiving radio signals in the very high-frequency band (UHF) from ground radio beacons to the aircraft's receiver unit to help a pilot navigate his aircraft position and stay on course. The system was developed by the United States in 1937 and is used worldwide.

An ILS approach provides more precision guidance; therefore, it is called a precision approach. A VOR approach is called a non-precision approach.

While executing a VOR approach, the pilot directs the airplane's vertical flight path based on reading of a pre-approved Federal Aviation Administration (FAA) authorized procedure. The procedure dictates when to descend and to what altitude. The instructions will vary based on the aircraft's airspeed, time and distance flown during the VOR approach.

The pilot uses a diagram that depicts the plan view and profile view of the procedure. The VOR receiver instrument in the cockpit displays the lateral guidance to fly, but the pilot must aviate the airplane vertically, based on interpreting the paper approach on the diagram.

The pilot flies this procedure to a Missed Approach Point, which is different from Decision Height Point. The Missed Approach Point could be anywhere within a mile from the end of the runway, and can also be much higher than the Decision Height—at a higher altitude of up to 700 feet above ground level. [19]

On this day I was executing a runway 32 VOR approach to Craig Field Airport on a bad weather day. Fog again.

I descended to 400 feet and flew to the missed approach point at which I had to make a decision: *Can I see the runway, and am I in a position to make a safe landing?*

I could see the runway, but I was 400 feet above, on top of the approach end of the runway. I was not convinced I was *in a position to make a safe landing* on the 4,000-foot runway.

My thoughts flashed back to that snap aerobatic decision I made at New Smyrna Beach, at 50 feet above ground level with 2,000 feet remaining of a 4,000-foot runway, I was convinced— *"I could land on that!!"* Revisiting that shocking image of me running off the end of the runway towards a forest of trees help shape my current split-second decision. Remember that runway overrun incident in New Smyrna Beach as a banner-towing pilot? Learning from that experience, I decided I was not going to make the same mistake twice. Great pilots learn from other pilots' mistakes and their own. There is no law preventing two pilots from learning from one mistake. Sometimes, small pilot incidents early in a pilot's flight career pays great dividends later on.

I executed the missed approach procedure, did a go-around, and attempted a second approach. On the second attempt, I saw the runway and I was in a good position and continued to land. But there was one problem. Around 20 feet above the ground, out of the right corner of my eye, I spotted a flock of seagulls standing in a V formation on the ground. All of a sudden, the flock took flight, and headed in my direction. Those menacing birds flew right smack in front of my flight path. This startled me and evoked an instant alarm.

Not only was I committed to land, but I had started my landing flair. U-Till's (my C-402 plane) throttles were being reduced to idle as her yoke was being pulled back. About 10 feet above the runway, while initiating the landing flair, about twelve seagulls were about to make contact! Those long-winged, white and gray feathered seabirds slammed into us like torpedoes slamming an aircraft carrier. Have you ever been shot at? It felt like a slew of torpedoes slamming into the thin membrane that were protecting my engines … and me. U-Till banked and rolled slightly, as I sat shell-shocked for a few milliseconds of precious time. My thoughts were, *What just happened?* Without any conscious direct pilot command, some of me naturally reacted. My hands closed tighter onto the controls, and my feet pushed the rudder pedals to counteract the uninvited bank and roll. As my hazel blue eyes enlarged, my vision shifted from looking down the runway to land, to my peripheral vision, sooner than planned, to view my attackers. All of this happened so fast that I was too busy to acknowledge that I may have been fearful of the plane crashing. I reoriented myself to continue to land, and with steely concentration, U-Till and I landed successfully.

Why were these gulls here and not out at sea? Pilot stuff can happen at any time, anywhere, even at 10 feet above the runway. If those birds had decided to ram me at 20 feet or higher before my transitioning to landing the plane, it's possible that the airplane would have stalled, and I would have crashed. Birds have caused havoc to numerous planes. Bird strikes on US Airways flight 1549 ("Miracle on the Hudson") caused both engines to fail and the captain had to perform an emergency water landing.

After I had taxied in to a full stop, I informed the mechanic of the bird strikes and possible airplane damage. The aircraft mechanic spent hours cleaning seagull remnants off the airplane. The control tower closed the runway for several hours to remove bird parts from the asphalt too. Soon after, the FAA issued and published this warning for Craig Municipal Airport (CRG):

> "Birds periodically on or near airport, increasing activity during inclement weather."
>
> and
>
> "Wildlife on and in vicinity of airport."

These pilot advisories, called NOTAMs, still exist today for Craig Municipal Airport. A NOTAM is a notice to airman or a notice to air mission. The notice is filed with an aviation authority to alert aircraft pilots of potential hazards along a flight route or at a location that could affect the safety of flight.

Earning a Pilot Call Sign

Later that night, in Atlanta at our small Midnite Express hub, I told this story to my pilot comrades. Our pilot group consisted of about ten pilots, who were like brothers to me—sometimes I liked them and sometimes I did not. We met there nightly, spoke pilot language for a few hours and then each of us departed with freight onboard our aircraft to fly to the cities where we lived. Picture a bicycle wheel, a hub and spoke operation with Atlanta as the hub and various cities attached to the spokes. My spoke, or route, at the time was Atlanta to Craig Airport, Jacksonville, Florida.

These are just some of the pilots in this group. Rob, a fellow ERAU colleague from Long Island like me, was funny, smart and a good pilot. Rob later landed a career with United Airlines. Eddie was a smart-aleck, full of wisecracks and usually complaining. He was eventually fired or politely forced out. Von, from Sweden, was here to build flight time with a plan to return home to secure an airline flight career. It was probably my imagination, but the way he described Swedish women, I believed they were all gorgeous angels and sought-after goddesses. Barron, from Germany, had a similar game plan to Von. Barron told loads of great pilot jokes, but with his German accent and his choice of English words he would often have to explain the joke afterwards, which was at times very funny. And lastly, there was Chris, a true southerner from Georgia—a long, slinky and timid guy. His father flew for Northwest Airlines, and often Chris corrected us on the real happenings of airline pilots.

As I told this second missed-approach story to my pilot peers they started chanting, "Seagull, Seagull, Seagull." They were not interested in the missed approach or the dangers of the bird strikes. *Why are they singing seagull in harmony?* I asked myself. The madder my temper seemed to grow, the louder they seemed to sing, "Seagull, Seagull, Seagull." My pilot comrades planted a call sign on me: Seagull. In my lifetime I've held many titles—sergeant, instructor, sir, coach, boss, captain, brother, son, husband and dad. The title that gives me the most pride is "Dad." Being a father to my sons has been my greatest challenge and my greatest reward in life. Although I was born with the name Francis, I am also known as Francois, Franco, Francisco, Fran, Frankie, Frankolino, Frankenstein, and most commonly, Frank. During my life in Britain, initially the English called me Frank the Yank and after I earned my private pilot's license, I was tagged with Frank the Pilot. This motley pilot group labeled me with the call sign "Seagull." Years later, I would earn two more names: Fast Frank and FedEx Frank.

Call signs are a unique fixture of the aviation community and are normally assigned to military aviators. The call sign is a specialized form of nickname that is used as a substitute for the pilot's real name. USAF and USN pilots use their call signs to communicate on the radios. It's for both operational security and identifying the pilot. Call signs are awarded to pilots for a variety of reasons and are usually earned based on how badly a pilot screwed something up, a play on their name, some personality quirk, or some unusual fight episode, like killing over a dozen seagulls.

In the original *Top Gun* movie, most of the characters aren't recognized by their actual names, but by their call signs. Among the most memorable call signs were "Goose," "Viper," "Iceman," and "Maverick." Nick "Goose" Bradshaw is laid-back, self-deprecating and lovable; Mike "Viper" Metcalf is a no-nonsense instructor, spiteful to his enemies; Tom "Iceman" Kazansky is cool, calm and collected; and Pete "Maverick" Mitchell is independent and unorthodox, who lives dangerously, and doesn't play by the rules. On account of the bird incident at Craig Airport, the Midnite Express pilots issued me the aviator call sign "Seagull." There are worse ways to get yourself an aviator call sign.

The Gouge. Learn from pilot mistakes—both your own and others.' Reading and watching aircraft pilot accidents reports will help educate pilots: learn from and avoid their mistakes. Be safe first! Even though the runway was in my sight, I was not convinced that I was in a position to land safely; I did not want to make the same mistake I made in New Smyrna Beach and run off the end of the runway. NOTAMs are notices to pilots warning them of various types of potential hazards to an airport, service or procedure. Read the NOTAMs and pilot advisories for the departure and arrival airports beforehand. Craig Airport has a new pilot advisory: *"Birds periodically on or near airport, increasing activity during inclement weather,"* and *"Wildlife on and in vicinity of airport."* If a call sign is going to get planted on you, try to manipulate the name. Do not complain and moan about your new call sign or you'll probably get a new nickname you'll hate even more! Being called Seagull is not so bad.

ATP License

At age 25, with just over 1,500 hours of total pilot flight time, I passed the rigorous written exam for the Federal Aviation Administration (FAR)

Air Line Transport Pilot (ATP) license. Then, I arranged a deal with the Midnite Express owners to rent the Cessna C-402 company aircraft at cost, so that I could take the Airline Transport Pilot flight exam.

The Airline Transport Pilot (ATP) license is the highest level of aviation a pilot can obtain. Just as in school, one may progress from a high school diploma to an associate to a bachelor to a master and to a doctorate, a similar progression occurs in the world of pilots: from a student pilot certificate to a private pilot to a commercial to a flight instructor to an airline transport pilot license. The ATP is like a PhD level of education in aeronautics, aviation law, physiology, aeromedical factors, meteorology, aerodynamics and a slew of other aviation subject matters. It is possible for a pilot to obtain an airline pilot position without a college degree if he has an ATP license, but without an ATP license, no university degree in the world will get you in the door. Most major airlines require a college degree *and* an ATP. The ATP authorizes you to act as pilot-in-command of a scheduled air carrier's aircraft, having a max gross weight over 12,500 pounds or having over nine passenger seats. All airline captains have an ATP license.

The ATP license applicant is tested on Air Law, Aircraft General Knowledge, Flight Planning and Monitoring, Human Performance and Limitations, Meteorology, Operational Procedures, Principles of Flight, Communications (IFR and VFR), Performance, General Navigation, Radio Communications, Radio Navigation, Instrumentation and Weight and Balance.

On February 2, 1987 in Jacksonville, with a total pilot flight time of 1,650 hours, I passed the Airline Transport Pilot flight check ride exam, which requires the highest level of pilot ability. The exam took place at Jacksonville International Airport (JAX) with a two-hour oral and over an hour of flight time plus one hour of simulator flight time. In the previous months, I had logged several hundred hours of multi-engine, actual instrument pilot-in-command time in the C-402 plane, so my flight skills were sharp and I felt very comfortable in the C-402 plane. I would not say that this was the easiest practical flight exam I experienced, but I did feel really comfortable and confident throughout. The check pilot examiner detected my pilot swagger throughout the exam and that seemed to work to my benefit.

Obtaining the ATP license is a great achievement. With the ATP license and a college degree, two of the three major pieces of my flight plan to secure an airline pilot position were accomplished. Building more quality pilot flight time is the third piece of the plan I was determined to implement.

The Gouge. Obtain the ATP license as soon as possible, for one never knows when a big pilot hiring cycle begins, and pilots with ATP licenses are in short supply and in high demand.

13

ATLANTIC SOUTHEAST AIRLINES

Five pilot jobs in two years.

In January of 1987, I purchased a pilot-hiring service from Future Aviation Professionals of America (FAPA). Again, I was investing in myself. Without any guidance, you can waste valuable years trying to gain knowledge and practice on how to obtain an airline pilot career. This service was like a mentor-protégé relationship, one of the most productive forms of learning because it helps streamline the learning process by doing so in a concentrated manner.

This service educated me on the current pilot airline industry and helped me become more competitive to acquire one of those pilot positions. Louis Smith was the president, and the phone number was 1-800-JET-JOBS. FAPA published pay listings for major, national, jet and regional airlines, including starting, second-year, tenth-year, and captain's pay. They published pass-and-jump-seat privileges, and also included information on flight hours, duty rigs, pay guarantees, days off, per diem rates, recall rights and profit-sharing.

FAPA had a computer database for storing all your flight time, the type of aircraft flown, airplane ratings, education and so forth. They would match this data with potential airlines that were hiring pilots. The airline pilot hiring cycle was on an uptick. The airline industry was entering a phase of great demand for airline pilots at a time when few pilots were available. Was I lucky to be in the right place at the right time? No, I was in all places all the time trying everything to get my dream airline pilot job. FAPA started conducting pilot hiring seminars in conjunction with airline companies across the USA. These pilot seminars are commonly known as job fairs to other professions, except there is no hiring at these seminars. Each airline has its own special hiring process, and the hiring is conducted at the company's headquarters. The second such seminar in March of 1987 was held in Atlanta, and I attended. Unlike the majority of other pilot job seekers who attended, I did my homework and was well prepared. Virtually all of the job seekers showed up, picked up a job application and dropped off their resumes with the representative at the various airline companies.

I did some work upfront. I needed an edge among my pilot peers who were competing against me for these great airline pilot jobs. I obtained the various job applications and learned the names of the individuals who would represent the airlines that interested me. Virtually all the major airlines were of interest to me. My philosophy was to apply to all the airlines, pass all the interviews and then decide which job offer to accept. So, at the seminar, I had a completed job application, a personalized cover letter for each company, a resume, photocopies of my pilot licenses, a medical certificate and copies of three letters of reference. All were arranged neatly in a large brown envelope.

Professionally dressed in a dark gray suit, I approached each airline representative, introduced myself and personally hand-delivered a completed pilot application package. The majority of the other pilots at the seminar were collecting job applications and handing out their resumes. As the representatives flew back to their headquarters, they had my complete application package—the only one they had received at the seminar with photocopies of all necessary documents. The airline transport license (ATP)—I had that; the college degree—I had that; the extensive quality pilot experience—I was constantly working on that. Maybe, I didn't have all the tens of thousands of pilot-in-command multi-engine jet time that some of these airlines were looking for, but I had everything else documented in a completed application package sitting in their lap.

At this Sunday seminar, I met the chief pilot, Donald Doolittle of Atlantic Southeast Airlines, Inc. (ASA). ASA is a regional airline. Don is a congenial person with a sympathetic ear toward young pilots seeking a pilot career at an airline. He displayed signs of being stressed out. ASA was rapidly expanding its route system with the new planes arriving every month. Not only was Don responsible for hiring new pilots to fly those new planes, but he had to hire pilots to replace the pilots ASA was losing to the major airlines. He was very busy, yet he spent time talking to me. During our conversation, I mentioned Bob Ycraz as a personal reference. Captain Ycraz flew regional jets for ASA was my flight instructor at ERAU, and my friend. As Don shook my hand, he said he would call me on Monday about arranging a pilot job interview.

At the seminar, I felt so empowered and full of pride strolling among hundreds of other pilots. Even though we were all competing in some way for a better pilot career, it made me feel special to belong to this prestigious professional group. All the chatter of new planes, new routes, higher pay, great career benefits, and the increasingly high demand for airline pilots, instilled this feeling of hope, or almost as if this rite of passage was the future guarantee for me.

Eventually, I exited that building full of enthusiasm for what may lie ahead, with the belief that my airline job would soon be in hand. Like when you exit a concert hall, it takes a while for the music to fade away and one starts to think clearly of the reality of life. My brain was thinking, *How long will it take before those airlines invite me in for an interview? What if I never get an invite? It could be years before I get the invite. Don from ASA said he would call me for an interview.* Would you expect a highly motivated person, like Frank the pilot, to sit by the phone waiting on that call?

The next day, dressed in that same gray suit, with another completed pilot job application package in hand, I showed up at the office of the chief pilot of ASA (located in Atlanta). Anxiously I had arrived a half hour before Don had arrived to start his workday.

Upon Don's arrival, he observed me waiting for him, which convinced Don that I was highly motivated to secure a pilot job with ASA. He called me into his office. Don had a few questions for me, mainly about my flying experience. Don knew the chief pilot at my company, Midnite, and he knew that I had to pass a check ride with him before Midnite would let me fly their planes. Don waved the ASA's simulator check ride hiring requirement. He probably deduced that if I could pass a check ride with Midnite's chief pilot, then I could pass the potential new hire simulator test. Don shook my hand as he offered me a job as a First Officer, flying Embrea EMB 110 aircraft. At ASA I would be responsible for flying passengers to and from Dallas International Airport under FAR Part 135 operations.

Midnite Express had provided me the opportunity to increase my multi-engine pilot flight time to 600 hours, my total pilot flight time to nearly 1,800 hours, and my pilot-in-command time to over 1,600 hours, but it was time to move on to a bigger airplane and a bigger company and better pay. My thinking was, *If I am not able to acquire the ultimate goal of a major airline pilot job, then ASA would be a good place for a pilot career.* ASA checked many of the boxes I had in my quest for an airline pilot career.

The Embrea EMB-110 Bandeirante was the largest airplane I had ever flown. We pilots that flew her called her "The Flying Bandit," or sometimes just "The Bandit." In fact, the FAA requires two pilots to operate the aircraft: a captain (the PIC, the pilot-in-command) and a co-pilot, professionally called the first officer (the SIC, the second in command)—me. Aircraft are categorized by their maximum gross takeoff weight (MGTW), which is the most weight a plane is certified to lift off the ground with, including the crew, passengers, cargo, and fuel onboard. By federal law, aircraft with a MTGW of 12,500 pounds or more require a two-pilot operation. The captain must have an airline transport license (ATP).

Two 750 HP Pratt and Whitney turboprop engines enable the EMB-110 to fly as fast as 248 knots (285 mph), as high as 22,500 feet, and as far as 1,000 nautical miles (1,150 statute miles). The aircraft's max takeoff gross weight was 13,000 pounds, with a wingspan of 50 feet and a length of 50 feet. There were 500 EMB-110 aircraft built.[20] The EMB-110 was configured to carry 19 passengers and two flight crewmembers. Guess who was the flight attendant? Yes, moi.

The first flight attendants, hired in the 1930s, were all registered nurses and were called "stewardesses" or "air hostesses." A flight attendant is mandated by federal law to ensure that safety instructions are provided for the flight. On large aircraft, at least one flight attendant per 50 passengers is required. For planes with 19 or fewer seats, including the Flying Bandit, which had 19 passenger seats, there is no requirement for a flight attendant. Theoretically, I was not a flight attendant. Obviously, I am a first-officer pilot, but I did greet passengers as they boarded the plane, directed them to their seats, ensured that all carry-on items were stowed appropriately and informed them of the safety procedures. I made safety briefings to passengers. The most important thing I learned about passengers is that they want to feel reassured that their lives are safe in the hands of competent pilots. This is especially true with passengers flying for the first time. For your safety concern and information, the federal pilot requirement standards in the USA are one of if not the highest in the world.

The captain and I are responsible for the passenger's safety. Occasionally, I had to move a few passengers around to comply with the weight and balance operating limitations of the airplane. Weight and balance calculations are a federal law requirement to demonstrate the airplane is capable of safe operation on the takeoff runway and the landing runway.

From the pilot's perspective in the cockpit, flying a plane with passengers is no different from flying a plane with cargo. Passengers complain more than packages, and a pilot may try to avoid some predictable turbulence for the passengers' sakes, but otherwise, there is no difference in the way pilots fly passengers versus cargo.

After training in Atlanta, I drove my 1966 Chrysler Newport Miss Black Beauty to Dallas. My ERAU pilot friends called my car Miss Black Beauty because I hand painted the car with black gloss, Rust-Oleum paint. My Miss Black Beauty was a boat, weighing over 4,000 pounds, was over 18 feet long and did not always fire on all eight cylinders. Once again, I was driving a beat-up old car for ground transportation and flying new airplanes for air transportation. I would rather fly than drive. How did that car make the trip? I'll never know. She was tough.

Summers in Dallas can be brutally hot, with temperatures of up to 117°F. The terrain is flat with warm, dry air blowing from the north and the west, while warm and humid air can blow in from the south, causing temperatures to rise. An approaching cold front can be seen from miles away and looks like a tidal wave (like those on the old *Hawaii Five-O* TV show), kicking up a dust storm or forming a tornado. Dallas also had more beautiful women than Atlanta. There was nothing to do outside of Dallas, so when the women turned of age, like 18 to 20 years old, they all moved to Dallas. Maybe that's why the Dallas Cowboy Cheerleaders are able to obtain one of the best selections of girls for their cheerleader squads. Texans speak much slower and differently from New Yorkers. In New York, the girls say, "You can." In Texas, the gals say, "You all can." Pilot friend Bob Ycraz and I shared an apartment. We had so much fun barbecuing, playing water volleyball and making margaritas that we rarely left our thriving apartment complex. Interestingly, there are *dry* counties in Texas. No one but no one can buy or sell alcohol of any kind in a *dry* county. This could be a challenge to a pilot on days off from work. Yes, pilots like to have fun on their days off, maybe even more than the average worker because flying planes is demanding and can be really stressful at times. At the time, my life was going great; what could go wrong?

Turbulent Landing in San Angelo

Flying into thunderstorms can kill you.

On May 13, 1987, Captain Phil Flipping and I operated the Bandit, tail number N404AS, with 19 passengers from Lawton Regional Airport, Oklahoma (LAW) to San Angelo Regional Airport, Texas (SJT). Before takeoff, I had briefed the passengers on bad weather in SJT and instructed them to remain seated with their seat belts fastened securely.

Phil and I are a two-pilot operation; he is the pilot, the captain, and I am the co-pilot, the first officer. There are pros and cons with a one-pilot operation versus a two-pilot operation.

As a CFI at ERAU and a solo pilot captain at Midnite Express, I was able to make all the pilot decisions during the flight. However, that meant I had to be on my game.

Flying single-pilot forces the pilot to really know their air machine, know the emergency procedures by heart, be extra cautious on decision-making, and not rush in order to enhance safe flight operations. There is no oversight or checks and balance on a possible mistake in a single-pilot operation. For a single pilot, flying by use of instruments only during bad weather, especially when entering a busy airport (like Atlanta International Airport), the radio calls and clearances combined with aviating and navigating the plane can become overwhelming. The workload increases tremendously, especially during an emergency. To have another pilot with me during that nose gear up emergency crash landing would have been extremely helpful. Flying single-pilot operations requires a lot of mental discipline; those pilots must be on their game.

Flying planes with more than one pilot decreases workload, increases oversight and increases safety.

Large, complex, sophisticated aircraft require more than one pilot to help reduce stress, fatigue, and mental saturation by dividing the workload. Each pilot completes their part of the flight operations with more concentration to detail. With big, older planes like B-747, three flight crewmembers were required for operations. Today, two flight crewmembers are required on most big planes because the workload has been reduced with the modern advancement in technology in avionics, cockpit ergonomics, flight automation and navigation.

With two pilots, the workload is reduced; one pilot flies the aircraft and the second pilot monitors the aircraft, communicates with air traffic control and ensures the aircraft and navigation are configured correctly. By splitting the duties, it allows each crewmember to focus on the task at hand. This becomes especially important during an emergency. One pilot aviates, one pilot communicates and they both navigate the plane.

With a two-pilot operation, there is oversight on each other. One pilot reads and ensures the checklist are completed, while the other pilot completes the checklist items. Working together ensures the smooth, accurate and efficient management of the aircraft and its systems. The use of crew resource management (CRM) improves flight safety. I will discuss CRM in more detail later.

Two-pilot operations are required by federal law because they are safer.

Also with a two-pilot operation, there are two distinct personalities onboard. Phil is easy-going, friendly and approachable. He talked really slowly, and I often found myself waiting quite some time for him to finish. He used phrases like "howdy" and "y'all" often. If the plane was not performing the way he expected, Phil would say, "This dog won't hunt." He wore black cowboy boots though I was not sure if the company uniform policy allowed this.

Frank the pilot, on the other hand, is ambitious, goal-oriented, and energetic. He is a fast-paced guy. He walked fast, talked fast and lived a fast-paced life. He is always upbeat, projecting a positive attitude.

Phil was forecasting negative outcomes about the flight to SJT before the plane was airborne.

He showed signs of stress and worry, telling me, "The weather doesn't look good in San Angelo."

"Yeah," I replied, "but I heard there are beautiful women and good food there."

San Angelo's weather forecast was for gusty winds, cumulonimbus clouds and thunderstorms in the area for our estimated time of arrival. The weather report read:

Pilot Raw data: KSJT 132135Z 26018G25KT 1SM -TSRA BR SCT020 CB BKN035 OVC040 30/21 A2992 RMK FQT LTGICCCCG OHD-W MOVG E RAB25 TSB32 CB ALQDS SLP132 P0035 T03020210. Which means the 13th day of the month, at 3:35 p.m., local time, winds 260° (west) at 18 knots, gusting to 25 knots, visibility 1 statute mile, thunderstorms, light rain, clouds scattered at 2,000 feet, cumulonimbus clouds broken at 3,500 feet, overcast skies at 4,000 feet, temperature 30° Celsius, dewpoint 21° Celsius, the barometric pressure 29.92 in inches of mercury. The report indicates that there is frequent lightning in clouds, cloud-to-cloud, and cloud-to-ground overhead the field from the west moving east, rain began at 25 minutes after the hour, a thunderstorm began at 32 minutes after the hour, there are cumulonimbus clouds visible in all quadrants of the sky, the precise temperature is 30.2° Celsius, and the precise dewpoint is 21.0° Celsius.

As defined by the National Oceanic and Atmospheric Administration, which provides the National Weather Service, a thunderstorm is a local storm produced by a cumulonimbus cloud and always accompanied by lightning and thunder, usually with strong gusts of wind, heavy rain and sometimes hail. Severe thunderstorms can produce funnel clouds, tornadoes and wind shear. Wind shear is a rapid change of wind direction and wind strength with clouds of different levels moving in different directions. The updrafts and downdrafts can produce microbursts. A pilot considers wind shear severe when an airspeed change is greater than 15 knots, or a vertical speed change is greater than 500 feet per minute, or the aircraft's pitch attitude changes greater than five degrees. Some microbursts can exceed the performance capability of all aircraft, and even the best pilot would not be able to escape.

Enroute to San Angelo, I was thinking about Delta Flight 191, an L-1011 aircraft that crashed in Dallas/Fort Worth with 134 fatalities on

August 2, 1985, because of thunderstorms, wind shear and microbursts. According to International Civil Aviation Organization (ICAO) statistics from 1970 to 1985, at least 28 aviation accidents with 700 fatalities occurred because of low-level (near the ground) wind shear.

In the cockpit, we have a weather radar instrument that helps us see and avoid severe weather. The radar transmits beams out in front of the aircraft to detect precipitation and reflect that information back to the cockpit for the pilots to interpolate. The pilot uses the Antennae Tilt, Range, Gain and Radar Mode features to operate the radar. While flying as a captain on the C-402 for Midnite Express, I had accumulated valuable flying experience using radar. However, I had been flying the Bandit for less than a month, and I was not the captain; I was the first officer. My job was to support and help the captain in any and all ways, but the captain would be making all the decisions. Also, I did not have any radar experience with thunderstorms in this part of the country. The radar displays colors that reflect humidity, but not necessarily turbulence. The radar is good at detecting moisture, rainfall and wet hail, but it is not good at detecting ice crystals, dry snow, clear air turbulence, dry hail or wind shear.

Thunderstorms are categorized by levels one through five, with five being the most severe. So, if a pilot was familiar with flying in the Northeast United States (like New York) and familiar with viewing a Level Three or Level Four thunderstorm on the radar scope, that pilot would adjust his flight path and avoid the thunderstorm cells. If this same pilot was flying in the southwest United States (like San Angelo) and viewed a Level One or Level Two thunderstorm on the radar scope, that pilot might not adjust his flight path, thinking the thunderstorm cells were small and did not contain much dangerous energy.

However, that pilot would be wrong, because thunderstorms in the southwest usually contain dry moisture, and the radar is not good at detecting this. Therefore, viewing a category Level One or Level Two thunderstorm in the southwest could be as dangerous as a Level Three or Level Four in the Northeast.

San Angelo was about 20 minutes away, and our radar scope did not show much severe thunderstorm activity—or so we thought. Each individual cell in a thunderstorm can last approximately 30 to 60 minutes and has three stages: the cumulus stage, mature stage and dissipating stage. It is the microburst produced in these stages that can bring down an aircraft because the numerous updrafts and downdrafts can cause the aircraft to lose airspeed. The most severe, deadly microburst might last only 6 to 8 minutes, but it can be severe enough to where the best pilot in the world cannot recover.

As we approached San Angelo from the east, thunderstorms loomed southwest of the airport. The radar display and tower-reported winds were not that bad. We had just received a PIREP (pilot report), which provides notice of actual weather conditions encountered by another pilot while in flight. This one was from a Learjet pilot who said that landing on runway 36 was not that bad.

We turned onto final approach and set up for the ILS runway 18 approach. During the approach, we encountered non-threatening heavy rain, sporadic wind gusts and we saw some miniature lightning strikes. Then we encountered some occasional light to moderate turbulence.

With the runway in clear view, Phil seemed less worried. Within a New York minute, our flight conditions changed drastically. We were approaching SJT from the east while the bad weather was approaching SJT from the southwest. Even with the runway still in sight, that humongous thunderstorm from five miles away started spewing hailstones in our direction. As our distance to the airport decreased, long, sizzling lighting strikes struck more often and lasted longer. Bandit started to disobey the captain; she started rolling, banking and pitching in reaction to the explosive turbulence.

That mysterious thunderstorm didn't look that bad on our radar scope. That unpredictable, evil thunderstorm contained tremendous unstable energy and dry moisture, which the radar is not good at detecting. Phil presumed this thunderstorm to be a tamable, Level-Two thunderstorm, when, in fact, it was probably a dangerous Level-Four thunderstorm. That ferocious storm showed us her true colors. Behind her veil, she was dark, unstable, mean and fiercely offensive. She shot nickel-sized rock-hard hailstones at us, like Rambo's bazooka shooting deadly hail at our innocent and defenseless Bandit. And her aim was good!

As I heard and felt the hammering—BOOM, BOOM, BOOM—the Bandit started weeping and limping. Bandit did not like it; I know

Phil did not like it and I certainly did not like it. In the back of my mind, I was thinking, *Go-around, let's get out of here,* but I did not suggest it and I was not the captain.

Rock-'n'-roll.

The Bandit rocked-'n'-rolled like a dancer at a concert only in a horizontal position. Unlike a dancer that has a floor under their feet to help maintain balance, we had Mother Nature's unstable air all around us. We were getting bounced around like a wine cork in rough ocean waves. All the time, I kept saying to myself, *This doesn't feel good, I don't like it!*

Mother Nature, probably at God's command, gave us a one-minute time out, like in football. The hail stopped, the turbulence stopped, the wind became calm and the lightning may have stopped, though I did not know because all of my five bodily sensors were fixated within the confines of the cockpit where I was assisting Phil to save our lives. My left eye caught a glimpse of a brief smile of relief that Phil displayed. Bandit resumed obeying all of Phil's commands. Bandit was happier under the influence of Phil versus under the influence of the bad turbulence. During that brief time of soundlessness and solace, I remembered, *We have passengers, I wonder how they are doing?* There were no conversations going on in the back of the plane—all of the passengers were soiling their pants, and/or praying for their lives. It's amazing, that in times of sensing that life may end soon, everyone attempts to connect to God.

That very angry thunderstorm resumed her offense, with the same momentum of self-confidence as before time out, to destroy us. Hail, rain, wind, turbulence and reduced visibility were her weapons of attack. Again, Phil looked extremely worried. You learn something new about a person every day. Phil is a fighter and he had great pilot skills to fight with, and by the skin of his teeth, managed to command control of the aircraft.

I can't believe we're doing this, we may be in over our heads, I said to myself.

Yank and bank—the captain fought Mother Nature with the Bandit's aircraft's pitch and power. I did everything possible as a first officer to support the captain—I wanted to live too. With purpose and care, Captain Phil deliberately landed firmly on the soaking wet runway. Phil won! His pilot skills enabled Bandit, him, me and all our passengers to land safely.

Just as we thought the unwanted nightmare was over, Bandit, without notice, started to skid. Pouring rain reduced the friction coefficient between Bandit and San Angelo's runway to nil. We encountered hydroplaning, but Captain Phil was able to maintain steering control. At long last, with some runway remaining, Phil slowed the plane down and exited the runway. While taxing to the arrival gate, night turned to day before it should have because the apocalyptic thunderstorm blocked the sun's light. That incalculable evil thunderstorm positioned itself directly above us.

God must have been pissed off.

Strong, gusty winds, heavy rain and hailstones pounded the San Angelo airport. Shortly thereafter, the ATC tower closed the runways, preventing all planes from departing and landing at SJT. We came to a full stop at the gate. Turning towards Phil, his eyes full of relief, I proudly proclaimed with congratulatory voice, "You did a great job getting the plane on the ground!" He withdrew his hands and feet from Bandit, turned towards me and released a long breath of air, "Thank you."

All the passengers thanked us, especially the captain, for getting everyone safely on the ground. One of the passengers hugged and kissed me, and she was stunningly pretty. That cute, lovely-smelling Texan probably mistook me for the captain. A captain's uniform displays four-stripe bar epaulets, whereas a first officer's uniform displays three. All the passengers thanked us with authentic emotions as if we had saved their lives.

In the aviation industry, you will often hear the phrase: "That's why he gets paid the big bucks," meaning he, the captain, earns a high salary to compensate for his expertise and critical decision-making skills that make it possible to transport passengers and the plane safely to their destination.

We make our money above planet Earth, and it is serious business!

We also have a vested interest too. We want to live.

The Gouge. Thunderstorms can kill you inflight. They can kill even the best pilots. Pilots—never forget, "*Recognize and avoid thunderstorms.*"

Thunderstorms in the southwest usually contain dry moisture, and the radar is not good at detecting this. Utilize the range and tilt functions of the radar instrument to see and avoid severe thunderstorms. I like to adjust the range and tilt of the radar so that there is some ground return depicted on the top edge of the radar display. Very strong thunderstorm cells will attenuate (or block) returns of any objects, including the ground. If the view looks clear on the backside of the cell and a ground return is depicted on both sides of the cell, then most likely the cell is so strong that it attenuates all that is on the other side of that cell or group of cells. Avoid this route and deviate around these strong cells. Passengers: if your Captain encounters thunderstorms or any bad weather and lands the plane safely, then thank the captain. Thank the captain for his expertise and critical decision-making skills. Thank the captain for getting you to your destination safely.

I am so grateful that I learned about thunderstorms early in my flight career. On those occasions when I was not able to avoid them, I was able to recover and land safely. Later, I will tell you a frightening story about a deadly, hair-raising, wind-shear microburst.

The Airline Interview

In June 1989, Flying Tiger Line, Inc. (FTL), a major airline, invited me to a pilot job interview in Los Angeles, California. Note, this was the first official written invite I had received for a pilot job interview. At ERAU, I requested to see the chief pilot for a CFI job. The banner-tow job evolved from a friendly, inquisitive conversation I had with the owner of the company. The Transamerican Airways job I obtained as I was searching door to door like a salesman looking for a multi-engine flight time pilot position. The Southeast Airlines job I weaseled out of the chief pilot, by showing up at his office after meeting him the day before at a pilot hiring seminar, instead of waiting for a phone call invite. People say you were lucky, you were at the right place at the right time, but I say I was at *every* place *all* the time.

Prior to this interview, I purchased, read and studied the book *Sweaty Palms: The Neglected Art of Being Interviewed* by H. Anthony Medley. At the time there were not many books available on interviews, and my knowledge on the subject was very limited. By investing in myself with this book knowledge, I wanted to make me shine among my competition during any possible future airline interviews. After working so hard to acquire college degrees, pilot licensees, quality flight hours and this interview, I did not want to blow my chance for that ultimate airline pilot job simply because I had failed the interview.

The interview process consisted of five parts: a personal interview, a pilot board interview, a simulator test, a personality test and a medical exam. First, Beth Mentor, an employment specialist with a master's degree in psychology, interviewed me on a one-on-one basis for about an hour. Beth asked me why I took 54 college credit hours in one year. This question surprised me. *Why did she ask me this question?* I was dumbfounded and was knocked off my self-confident stool. New knowledge that I just recently absorbed from the *Sweaty Palms* book formed my response. Like a politician, I turned the question around and answered the question to my advantage. "I observed that the airline industry was rebounding and that there would be a need to hire more pilots so I wanted to get a competitive advantage over my peers by increasing my qualifications at a faster rate."

Then, I was interviewed by a three-pilot board for around an hour and a half. Captain John asked me if I ever had an emergency. The C-402 nose gear failure landing was the best emergency story I could think of, and I told that story. At the end of the story, I kept silent, looked at the pilot board members, and held my ground. One of the other pilot board members wanted to know what happened afterward.

I paused. I wanted the job. I didn't want to come across as an "I" doctor, one of those guys with a PhD in "I" who brag, "I did this, I did that, I was it, I am the best, I am the greatest," et cetera.

It's always best if you have someone else brag for you.

So, I pulled out a copy of the letter written by Robert Milton, the CEO of Midnite Express, and handed it to the pilot board members. That gear-up airplane emergency that I feared would end my pilot career, was now positively affecting the outcome of my airline pilot career. Even though I was being interviewed for a second officer position, these pilot interviewers were looking for future captains. They are looking to hire career pilots who can safely operate jumbo jets and who can make good command decisions during emergency situations. Months later, I learned that the Flying Tiger pilot board were also looking for likable personalities. They were looking for pilots who could get along with each other during twelve-day flight trips.

"Impressive," said one of the pilot board members. In order to proceed to the next phase of the pilot interview process, the pilot board must provide a favorable recommendation on the job applicant. Many pilot job applicants do not progress beyond this pilot board interrogation. After the pilot board interview, I was put in a Boeing B-747 simulator for a 45-minute test on my pilot skills.

The Cessna C-402 has two engines; the cockpit is about four feet by four feet and required one pilot. The Embraer EMB 110 has two engines; the cockpit is about five feet by five feet and required two pilots. The Boeing B-747 has four engines; the cockpit is about ten by ten feet and required three pilots. A captain, a first officer and a second officer are required to operate this mammoth ship. The bigger the ship, the more flight crewmembers are required. There are a least five crewmembers on Star Trek's Starship Enterprise bridge or cockpit. There are five seats, three pilot seats and two jump seats, in the huge B-747 cockpit. The B-747 cockpit is gigantic.

As I eased into the captain's seat, I felt like a small first-time conductor, all by himself, in the biggest concert hall. Propeller airplane engines produce power and the throttles control the plane's power. Jet airplane engines produce thrust and thrust levers control the jet's thrust. The B-747 has four thrust levers, one for each turbojet engine. The front instrument panel has four: N1, EPR, N2, and FF gauges, two radar altimeters, a whole bunch of lights on the light warning panel, and a sophisticated upper-mode control panel. The airspeed, altimeter, heading and vertical speed instruments did look somewhat familiar to me. *How will I conduct and command this enormous air flight machine?* I asked myself. *This could be do or die,* I thought. I must conquer this task if I want a chance towards achieving my ultimate airline pilot career goal. Like Kirk commanding the Starship Enterprise, I had to command this jumbo ship.

I had never been in a B-747 cockpit before. I had never flown a jet before. Thinking outside the box, I petitioned the simulator pilot evaluator for attitude, pitch and engine thrust settings. The examiner obliged. Flying a jet airplane is so much different from flying a propeller airplane in so many ways, but mainly jet airplanes are more responsive to pitch and thrust commands. A flashback to that first experience of transitioning from a single-engine plane to a two-engine plane reminded me of the initial challenge of monitoring two engines. Now, I had four jet engines under the control of my right hand and four engines for my eyes to scan. A scary thought struck me—*Maybe I am in over my head.* Another thought followed, *Is this jumbo jet maybe too big for me to handle?* The opportunity for an airline pilot career was here in my hands, so the least that I could do was to give my best effort.

With the limited flight experience I had with smaller planes, I flew this larger plane just like any other airplane. Utilizing the Attitude, Trim, Cross-Check, and adjust the Pitch and Thrust accordingly method, I commanded the Boeing B-747 jumbo jet as if I were flying a Cessna C-150 plane. The key to flying a B-747 jumbo jet is to scan the instruments quickly and often, and make small pitch and thrust adjustments. The B-747 jet is sensitive to yoke and thrust inputs. When velocity is added to this large jumbo jet mass, it creates huge momentum. Because of this huge momentum, when a pilot input is made to direct the B-747 for a turn, there is a delay for the remaining part of the jet to follow the cockpit. It's like watching an aircraft carrier or cruise ship turn; it takes a while for the whole ship to move. This, and the reaction time of pitch and thrust, presented me with an immediate learning process. Constant adjustments were made to try to anticipate the reaction of the jet to my pitch and thrust inputs.

The simulator test included a takeoff, some vertical S turns, a non-standard holding entry and holding followed by an ILS approach to a landing. After the simulator test, I do remember the instructor pilot saying, "Nice job." Wondering if that was the generic comment presented to all the applicants, I said, "Thank you, that is one fine plane."

How did I feel about my simulator test performance? Part of me was overwhelmed, like maybe I was in over my head trying to fly a B-747, but part of me felt that I did a pretty good job. At the time, my pilot skills were sharp from all the recent EMB 110 and C-402 flying. Surely the simulator check pilot could ascertain that I did not have any B-747 flight experience but that I did display good pilot skills.

With doubts swirling in my mind on how they viewed me, I was guided into a room to take a paper, pencil and thinking test. This next part of the interview process involved completing the Minnesota

Multiphasic Personality test. The purpose of this test is to determine a person's personality psychological profile. The test took 90 minutes to complete and was comprised of almost 600 true or false questions. Three times, a variation of a question on stealing appeared throughout the test: "Have you stolen anything before? Have you stolen something small once? Have you thought about stealing?" Without any prior experience with this type of test, all I could do was not to lie about my answers and to be consistent.

It had been a long, exhausting eight-hour day, and I was looking forward to retiring to the nice hotel funded by Flying Tigers. Before leaving the premises, I was given instructions to report, with other pilot candidates, to a medical facility on the following day. The final part of the hiring process was a medical exam.

The medical exam was extremely thorough: we had to fast, give blood and a stool sample; our sight, hearing, cardio endurance, heart, and a bunch of other stuff were tested. The lengthy comprehensive medical exam seemed extremely evasive, but they did not bother me, for I was distracted by the two nurses conducting the exams. The two nurses were number ten models in disguise. Thoughts of wishing to secure a date with one of those beautiful models pretending to be nurses were squashed by the thought that this may disqualify me from being hired. This may be the final interview test, testing pilot morality with fraternization. To date my possible future wife or to secure a possible future airline pilot job was the conundrum I faced. I chickened out; I did not pursue her.

The two-day event ended, and I was on my way back home to Dallas, wondering, *How did I do? Did I wear the right color tie?* The right color tie is an inside pilot joke. Afterward, other pilots would pose numerous questions about the interview and finish with, "What color tie did you wear?" Pilots were well aware that airlines interviewed many more pilots than they hired and no one could figure out what the secret formula was to passing the interview and being offered a pilot position. Why did Wilbur get hired and Orville did not? It must have been the tie. What color tie did you wear?

The Gouge. If able, get the gouge from other pilots on that particular airline interview process, beforehand. Gather as much information on the airline you are applying for, like aircraft types, fleet size, etc. Practice and rehearse your answers to the most common interview questions. Turn the interview questions around and answer the questions to your advantage. Keep up to date with the latest airline industry news.

Wear your best professional suit. Be well-groomed and put a $100 dollar bill (probably a $500 bill today) in your pocket to feel like a king. Walk in like a confident captain and conduct yourself in a professional and courteous manner at all times.

Bring your pilot licenses, medical, logbook, letters of recommendation, and any other supporting documentation. During the simulator test, strive to fly all the flight maneuvers with the least number of deviations from ATP standards. Use ATC (Attitude, Trim, Cross-Check) and ANC (Aviate, Navigate, Communicate).

Do some investigative research on the Minnesota Multiphasic Personality test. I will admit I did not know a thing about this test beforehand. I did not lie and I was consistent with my answers, which worked in my favor. If you have any health issues beforehand, rectify those issues. Those pilot medical exams are very comprehensive, and all health issues will be revealed.

14

FLYING TIGERS

Pilot goal in six years.

Moving Up and On

Flying for Atlantic Southeast Airlines was my shortest aviation pilot job, lasting only 100 days. One Friday evening, I received a call from Flying Tiger pilot Gary Stearns, and he offered me a position as a Boeing 747 Second Officer with the Flying Tigers Airline, Inc. (FTL). At first, I thought it was one of my friends playing a practical joke, but this was the real deal.

This was fantastic news, but I kept the news a secret for a few days until I received the official offer letter via US mail. With the letter in hand, I exuberantly gathered a few friends and we went out to celebrate. This news, to my parents, made them extra proud to have me as their son.

The edge I created at the FAPA seminar paid off. The chances I took to invest in myself paid off, as did the chance I took to leave the USAF to go to ERAU to earn a college degree and pilot licenses and ratings; the chance to leave my first pilot job at ERAU, without another job lined up, to search for quality multi-engine flight time; the taking 54 college credit hours in one year; the chance to take vacation days when the weather was good, in England, to go fly solo flights; and the chance to put myself in financial debt, to acquire that private pilot license. So, at age 20, I was inflicted with aviation addiction and decided to be a pilot. I flight instructed for ERAU and Transamerican Airways, I towed banners, I flew cargo for Midnite Express, I flew passengers for Southeast Airlines and flew for just about any reason to build up flight time.

Here I was just over six years later, at age 26, with my ultimate airline career goal accomplished. This is written not to sound braggadocious, but to motivate career seekers to achieve their career goals, even if those goals are not to be a pilot. At age 18, I left New York with a high school diploma and a driver's license and returned at age 26 with two college degrees, several pilot licenses, pilot ratings and an airline pilot job. If I can do it, you can do it. Knowledge, education, and skills are important, but motivation is the most important trait when attempting to achieve your goals.

The Gouge. Make a flight plan for life. Even if you do not want to be a pilot, make a plan. Devise short-term, medium-term and long-term goals for yourself, and then execute the plan. I belong to a pilot group, and each month I interview a pilot and write their story. It is amazing the multiple different paths each one pursued to become a pilot.

There was widespread envy, jealousy and curiosity among my peers at Atlantic Southeast Airlines. After all, I had only been employed with Atlantic Southeast Airlines, a regional airline, for about three months. That, and I was leaving to go operate a Boeing B-747 jet with a major airline.

My name became popular with several Dallas-based pilots, as you might imagine. Here is the chatter of a conversation between pilot James and pilot John.

James began, "Did you hear Donohue just got here a few months ago and he is leaving for Tigers?"

"Flying Tigers? You're kidding me," John replied with surprise. He inquired, "Is that the Italian-looking guy with an Irish name?"

James answered, "Yea, he looks like Robert De Niro, except Frank has shiny, hazel-blue eyes. He talks with that same New York slang."

John said, "I know the guy. He is energetic, always has an upbeat attitude and speaks fast. He is funny with the jokes and good with the ladies. I saw him with a beautiful red-headed Texan in her convertible sports car. I think they call her Beth, Crazy Beth."

James continued, "Well go figure, he just got here and now he's leaving for the majors. There's hope for us. I am going to update my resume and send out applications."

John finished, "Me too; I wonder how he did it. I wonder what color tie he wore to the interview."

Many other pilots approached me to ask how I pulled it off. I jokingly told those pilots that "the airline just dropped their hiring standards and I wore the right color tie that day." But the real reason was taking chances with investing time and money in myself and my persistent pursuit and motivation toward advancing my career. I had a goal—and I stuck to it.

Major airlines generate billions of dollars in revenue every year. National airlines are smaller than the major airlines, and regional airlines are smaller than the nationals. Flying Tigers is a major airline, and Atlantic Southeast is a regional airline.

I had moved up to the big boys—the boys who flew the big metal all over the world. My body had to support my new big head because, in my mind, I had become a cool big-time pilot with a massive ego. Within my ignorant massive ego, I had evolved into the GOAT—the greatest pilot of all time. Lessons learned throughout my flight career, as you will read, set the record straight; I am just an average pilot. A flight emergency, a medical issue or a violation could end it all. My motivation to become a big-time airline pilot may have been extremely strong, but in the end, I am just an average pilot.

In 1987, the average age of a new-hire pilot at a major airline was 32, and the average total pilot flight time was 3,800 hours. Ironically, the average age for a new-hire pilot at a national airline was 35 with an average total pilot flight time of 6,300 hours. The airline industry and pilot hiring cycle were in the early innings of a big upswing. The airline pilot cycle had turned from laying off to hiring pilots. The industry was growing and pilots were needed.

At age 26, I had a total pilot flight time of just over 2,000 hours including 600 hours of multi-engine time including 250 hours of turboprop time and 250 hours of second-in-command time. These flight hours may seem like low numbers, but those hours contained high-quality flight hours. Those 600 multi-engine solo pilot-in-command flight hours during all kinds of bad weather is extremely valuable—almost as valuable as military jet time.

Flying Tigers

The Flying Tigers airline was started in 1945 by Robert W. Prescott and a group of pilots who were formerly members of the First American Volunteer Group (AVG) of the Chinese Air Force in 1941 and 1942. The 1st AVG were comprised mainly of volunteer US pilots who went to help the Chinese fight against the Japanese in 1942. This AVG pilot group was famously called the Flying Tigers because of their uniquely painted P-40 aircraft and their extraordinary kill-to-loss ratio.

Over seven months, the AVG fighter squadron shot down more than 300 Japanese fighter planes over Burma, China, Thailand, and French Indo-China while losing only 12 of their P-40 aircraft in combat.[21] Watch the *Flying Tigers* (1942) movie starring John Wayne, for a historical perspective.

After the war, Bob Prescott and a handful of these pilots raised $89,000, and with the financial backing of Samuel B. Mosher, they purchased 14 World War II, Budd Conestoga aircraft from the US military. They started a daily, scheduled all-cargo service under the name of the Flying Tigers Line, Inc. (New York stock symbol FTL).

In 1949, the Flying Tigers purchased 18 Curtiss C-46 aircraft, and in 1950, the airline purchased a large fleet of Douglass DC 6 freighter aircraft. In 1957, in another wave of expansion, the Flying Tigers bought 15 Lockheed Super Constellation aircraft, allowing them to fly non-stop transcontinental schedules.

In 1965, the Flying Tigers acquired Boeing B-707s, and in 1968, Douglass DC-8s. Flying Tigers eventually purchased Boeing B-747 aircraft and Seaboard World Airlines, allowing Flying Tigers to provide worldwide air freight service.[22] Flying Tigers has a proud, impressive history and a unique pilot culture. Continue reading for more interesting information in the next chapter on the pilot culture.

On my new hire date of July 7, 1987, Tigers (short for Flying Tigers) had six DC-8s, twelve B-727s, and thirteen B-747s. Shortly after being hired, the B-727 fleet expanded to sixteen aircraft, and the B-747 fleet expanded to twenty-one aircraft. Two B-747s were configured to carry passengers used for Military Airlift Command (MAC) charters. Tigers operated the B-747 passenger MAC flights with 498 passengers and 17 crewmembers on board. Rarely did any airline carry more than 500 people on board in 1988 (or even today, for that matter). At Tigers, pilots could bid on trips to fly cargo or passengers. Tigers operated big jets all over the world and they were expanding.

Pilot Code of Ethics

When hired by a major airline, the airline pilot must comply with the Federal Aviation Rules (FAA regulation Part 121). Most airline pilots join the Air Line Pilots Association (ALPA) Union, which negotiates a contract with the airline company, and the pilot must also comply with that contract. The Air Line Pilots Association was started in the 1930s in the interest of safety for pilots. These George E Hopkins quotes appears in several publications.

> *The 1930s was a decade of great significance for airline pilots across the United States, Canada, and beyond. It was the decade when a professional union of pilots was born to protect the interests of airmen during a decade marked by "pilot pushing," horribly unsafe flying conditions, and a company mentality that pilots were an expendable commodity. Fly at all costs, under all conditions; just make sure that the mail is delivered on time."[23]*

In 1931, Captain David L. Behncke, a pilot for Boeing Air Transport, met with 24 other pilots considered "key men" in Chicago, to officially launch a new pilot organization to protect pilot rights.

Among other items, the pilots approved the name Air Line Pilots Association and adopted a motto (Schedule with Safety). More than half of the 24 "key men" would later perish in aircraft accidents.[24] Since the 1930s, ALPA has been the leading aviation safety advocate protecting the safety interest of airline pilots and passengers in the United States and around the world. ALPA had created its own engineering and air safety department and was instrumental in creating the following:

- Air Traffic Control Center
- Standard T Instrument layout in the cockpit
- NTSB National Transportation Safety Board
- GPWS Terrain Awareness Warning System
- Fasten Seat Belt signs in the aircraft
- HAZMAT standards
- Master Minimum Equipment list for aircraft

- Improved Standard Taxiway signage
- Standards and procedures for ground de-icing
- Color Aeronautical Charts for depicting high terrain
- ALPA and ERAU International Aviation Security Academies

… and many more aviation safety-related enhancements to air travel.

The Federal Aviation Regulations (FARs) stipulate the following: the pilot must pass a first-class medical exam every six months, pass a simulated check ride every six months (today, every nine months), and pass a flight check ride every year. In addition, if you fly too fast, if you turn to the wrong heading, if you level off at the wrong altitude or if you do anything that is considered careless and reckless by the Federal Aviation Administration, you can be heavily fined or even lose your license—and your job.

Pilots are the most regulated professionals—more so than in any other career. There may be over a million doctors and over 1.3 million lawyers in the USA, but there are only about 160,000 airline transport pilots in the United States of America. We are an elite group of professionals. We work above planet Earth, in the air. Our jobs involve serious business. You can't pull over into a cloud and check the oil.

The pilot's contract is negotiated between the pilot group and the airline company. The pilot's contract contains written legal language that spells out pilot pay provisions, travel expenses, relocation expenses, vacation, training, hours of service, seniority, scheduling, crew rest, retirement and so forth.

The primary goal of my job is to fly safely and legally—and then attempt to be reliable and efficient.

This is the ALPA code of ethics that pilots live by:

Code of Ethics

An Air Line Pilot will keep uppermost in their mind that the safety, comfort, and well-being of the passengers who entrust their lives to them are the pilot's first and greatest responsibility.

An Air Line Pilot will faithfully discharge the duty they owe the airline which employs them and whose salary makes possible their way of life.

An Air Line Pilot will accept the responsibilities as well as the rewards of command, and will at all times so conduct themselves both on duty and off as to instill and merit the confidence and respect of their crew, their fellow employees, and their associates within the profession.

An Air Line Pilot will conduct their affairs with other members of the profession and with ALPA in such a manner as to bring credit to the profession and ALPA as well as to themselves.

To an Air Line Pilot, the honor of their profession is dear, and they will remember that their own character and conduct reflect honor or dishonor upon the profession.

Having endeavored to their utmost to faithfully fulfill the obligations of the ALPA Code of Ethics and Canons for the Guidance of Air Line Pilots, a pilot may consider themselves worthy to be called an Air Line pilot.[25,26]

Yeah, I know in reference to the first code, I fly mainly cargo. The passengers I carry on my jet are usually other pilots riding on the jump seat, and not paying passengers. The question I pose to you, "When you drive an automobile with passengers versus with groceries, do you drive differently?" With small children or a precious, fragile lamp you may drive more cautiously. With a full passenger load of adults—or full load of heavy lumber—you may be restricted to driving the vehicle at slower speeds. However, a license to operate is a license, no matter what you're carrying in the back. Fly safely, drive safely and don't break the law.

Flying cargo can be more difficult than flying people because the aircraft is routinely flown at the aircraft's maximum gross weight. There were many times we departed with the maximum takeoff weight of 820,000 pounds and landed (after fuel was burned off) with the maximum landing weight of 630,000 pounds, carrying tigers, racehorses, racecars, cows, chickens, whales, oil rigs, computers and other stuff.

On July 7, 1987, along with 23 other new-hire pilots, I started my basic indoctrination class for Flying Tigers. Basic indoctrination is the initial introduction of the newly-hired flight crewmembers to the company, covering rules and regulations, what is expected of the pilot, pilot benefits, who's who at the company, training schedules, bidding and many other things. It is a fun week.

As the first week ended, reality set in. *This is really serious*, hummed in my mind, like a catchy tune you can't seem to shake. It is time for me to grow up and become the professional pilot demanded of me by Flying Tigers. There is a pilot contract and a pilot code of ethics I would have to comply with, plus I had to absorb the knowledge to operate a B-747. The B-747 ground school is an accelerated school, like four months of college material packed into several weeks. The course material for the B-747 included bulletins, description, emergency equipment, limitations, anti-ice and rain protection, auto flight, axillary power unit, communications, electrical, fire protection, flight controls, flight instruments, flight management, hydraulics, landing gear, miscellaneous systems, navigation, oxygen, power plant, radar, weight and balance, performance, passenger aircraft, supplemental procedures and differences. This was just the ground school system knowledge for the B-747 plane. There was plenty of air school knowledge that I had to learn as well. Thinking, *Getting here was hard, staying here may be harder*. The fear of failure is a very strong human motivator, and I did not want to fail training. The fear of failure with the thought of ending up on a New York City Street corner selling pretzels was the greatest incentive for me to succeed. This vigorous training was very challenging.

My 23 classmates were great; we were not competing with each other, and we were helping each other learn. Actually, they helped me more than I helped them. All of my classmates had more pilot experience and knowledge than me, and they gave me **"the Gouge."** Kris L is the San Diego surfer dude; I body surfed with him several times at Huntington Beach. Steve B is the Long Island guy who had an aircraft maintenance license and a plane business. Gary D from Florida provided all the Boeing B-747 jokes. Kip M, also from Florida, is goal-orientated, competitive and likes his toys, which consisted of cars, boats, motorcycles and all-terrain vehicles. Brad C from Washington kept us straight with all rules of the pilot's contract. Joe C from Cleveland owned a Stearman airplane and had an airstrip on his property. Easy-going Henry A from Chicago owned a six-passenger-seat airplane; he flew his family to Orlando, Florida for vacations. Norman G is younger than me, had more flight time than me, is smarter than me, and helped me the most to get through school. Donald D is the smartest pilot of all of us; we called him "the brain," because he had the correct answer on every inquiry of every B-747 subject. Larry F from Mississippi is very conscientious, practical and an analytical thinker; he could predict possible emergency scenario outcomes from the result of system failures of the B-747 jet. John S's parents were doctors, and his parents were disappointed that he pursued a career as a pilot, not as a doctor. John loved flying planes and talked about flying all the time. John J is the most laid-back California guy in the class; nothing seemed to bother him. Joel F left Eastern Airlines for Tigers; he pointed out all the pros and cons of the two airlines. Kip M is an ex-military fighter pilot, who spoke in military acronyms; it was like he was speaking in tongues. Michael J to me is the star performer Michael Jackson; he looked, spoke, acted and danced like the famous singer. Don J is the son of a Tiger pilot, who provided us with all the inside rumors of the company; he also told us some fantastic, unbelievable Tiger pilot stories. Tom H from Atlanta had flown for a regional airline; he spoke with a distinctive Southern drawl and spoke of the potential real-estate deals he would purchase with the increased pay he would receive at Tigers. Austin W from Houston also spoke with a Southern accent; he wore a permanent smile, and I could not determine if he was smiling *at* me or *with* me. Jeff L is the youngest classmate, and he had loads of pilot flight time because he started flying at such a young age; I think he started flying before he was born. Dave L from Nevada, according to all women, is the perfect looking Earthman created by God. When we went out together, I would follow behind him to try to scoop up the leftovers. His leftovers, the women who were not up to his standards, were well above *my* standards, and perfect for me. The two women pilots were Renetta L who knitted in class and Ellen G, the sweetest person I'd ever met.

All of these pilots came from different backgrounds with different pilot experiences and I savored that. An author could write an entire book of 24 chapters, one chapter per pilot, and the book would be extremely interesting. Unfortunately, today most of ground school training is conducted one-on-one with a computer. It is not the same as training face-to-face with other pilots, mainly because the student misses out on the personal interaction and shared pilot knowledge that helps each pilot student succeed. There is not a personal connection with a computer, and the computer does not have cool pilot stories.

Oddly enough, all 24 of us graduated ground school, simulator school and initial operating experience school. At the start of 1988, I officially received my permanent Flight Engineer license with a Boeing B-747 turbojet rating. The Boeing B-747 jumbo jet airplane, also known as "the whale," was for many decades the largest commercial airplane in the world. *I will always remember and never forget*; I left New York at age 18 with a high school diploma and a driver's license. At age 26, I returned to New York with a couple of college degrees, a handful of pilot licenses and a major international airline pilot job as a second officer pilot on the B-747 jumbo jet airplane. Part of me wondered, *Who did I fool to get this job?* The other part knew that I had studied hard, worked hard and had performed well. There was that persistence of not giving up and the consistent motivation to get that airline job. There were times I took chances to invest in myself that paid off. There were four motives I was driven by: the thirst for traveling, especially with the aid of a plane; the ambition to succeed in making a career of flying; the desire to learn everything about flying; and the fear of failure. The fear of failure was the strongest motivator in my struggle not to fail in flight school. That motivator of fear was vanquished upon my graduation from B-747 flight school. Now, I was ready to satisfy that thirst for travel.

Would you like to travel with me?
Would you like to fly with me on my first trip around the world?
Come join Frank the Pilot on the B-747.
Come fly with the crew and me.

15

AROUND THE WORLD IN TEN DAYS

The sun rose and set during the flight.

Over 98% of the population has no concept of what it is like to fly a jet around the world. So here is an attempt to describe—or provide a taste—of my around-the-world trip in 10 days at age 26.

The itinerary was New York to Brussels (Belgium) to Dubai (United Arab Emirates) to Hong Kong to Tokyo to Anchorage to Chicago and back to New York.

Kirk is the captain, the one who makes the decisions. Kirk always took his duty as captain very seriously, with his main concern in any crisis being the safety of his crew and plane. Despite his strong sense of justice, Kirk will disobey aviation laws to do what he thinks is best for everyone's safety. He is level-headed and multi-talented.

Captain Kirk was called "Junior" by the other senior captains because when Kirk was 23 years old, he was the youngest B-747 international captain at the time. In his forties on this flight, I remember him as being a smart, ambitious investor. He had purchased a Navy ship and was converting it into a commercial yacht. He had also purchased a large tract of land and was subdividing the land into trailer home lots. Finally, he had also purchased 10,000 shares of Flying Tiger's company stock.

Spock is the first officer. He is a calm, logical, and caring person. During this trip, numerous times Spock asked me, "Frank, how are you doing, do you need help with anything?" He had served in my position before and handled me, a new guy, with care and understanding. I liked that caring trait in him. Spock has a deep capacity for compassion for all people.

First officer Spock lived in Alaska, part-time. He was an airline pilot and a bush pilot. He owned and operated a plane that could be configured with floats to land on Alaskan lakes, and it could be fitted with skis to land on snow-covered mountain strips.

Spock loved to share his thoughts and memories with others, especially about hunting. Spock had a license to hunt brown bears, and his passion was to shoot a trophy Kodiak bear, the largest land-based predator. Spock's great pilot analytical skills extended to his detective work with hunting bears. Spock vividly described many close bear encounters and potential rifle shots that he did not take, because the bear was less than ten feet tall. He had superior physical strength and endurance—traits needed to hunt ten-foot bears. As I absorbed these stories, I became overwhelmed by the presence of these larger-than-life jumbo jet pilots. Contemplating my situation, I concluded, *Maybe I am in over my head, flying with these pilot gods on the largest jumbo jet in the world.*

I kept my mouth shut.

I owned a small plot of land in Florida, and I fished for 20-inch fish.

The three of us, with our distinctive personalities and backgrounds, started to bond with each other as we crewed the B-747 jet airliner to Brussels. Upon landing, and before exiting the cockpit, a pilot spirit whispered, "This may be our last day, so we better have the most fun of our lives in Brussels."

Brussels is a truly European city with its own currency—the Belgian Franc (the Euro is the currency now). Brussels has beautiful medieval and gothic buildings such as the Guildhalls on the Grand Place. Also, every street seemed to have a butcher, a hairdresser, a pharmacy and a restaurant. Kirk and Spock had been flying to worldwide international cities for years and knew the best places to eat and drink. We had the best mussels in Brussels and washed them down with the best Belgian beer. Afterward, Kirk treated his crew to the most exclusive piano jazz lounge in all of Brussels. From that experience, I was able to describe Kirk as charismatic and charming with the upper-class young ladies. He also maintained a light-hearted attitude and formed a cohesive bond with his flight crew.

The next morning, we ate Belgian waffles for breakfast and departed for Dubai.

The seeds of pilot camaraderie were being planted in me. What I did not know then, I found out later; I would be acquiring more brothers—

lots more brothers—throughout my flight career. My family was growing and I was not even married.

The flight crew had a two-day layover in Dubai, and before I exited the jet, I heard, "This may be our last day, so we better have the most fun of our lives in Dubai." Dubai is a Middle Eastern city in the United Arab Emirates, located on the Persian Gulf adjacent to the Arabian Desert. It is about 1,100 miles from Mecca, the birthplace of the Muslim religion and Muslims' most sacred place.

During my layover in Dubai, we toured the fish market and the Gold Souk. Using their currency, called the Dirham, we purchased and tasted fantastically cooked kabobs with pita bread. My eyes were fixed on the women in Dubai, who wore long black robes with headscarves that covered their necks and part of their heads. Most of the women covered their faces, revealing only their eyes. In this part of the world, religious laws outline the way women live their lives on a day-to-day basis. We heard the "call to prayer" horn, alerting people to one of the designated five times a day Muslims must turn toward Mecca and pray to Allah.

There was a man whose left hand had been cut off, whom I felt compassion for. After an inquiry, I learned that this man had been found guilty of stealing with that hand, and his punishment was having his hand cut off. The locals explained to me that they still occasionally have hangings on the third Thursday of the month. The legal system is based on the government's official interpretation of Islamic law, and all citizens are required to be Muslims.

I couldn't help wondering, *Is this what it was like during Jesus's time?* On my own, I ventured throughout the city, absorbing the ambience of the culture, people and structures. This experience triggered my imagination of a time and place during Jesus's life. As I meandered into a beautiful, ancient building, I envisioned a young Jesus sitting in the temple courts amongst the teachers, listening and asking questions.

On account of my ignorance, I was unaware that I was in a holy mosque, a place where Muslims worship, study and discuss Islam. Within minutes, I was chased out; to enter you must remove your footwear and wear appropriate clothing. This was my first experience of being exposed to a religion that was so different from my Christian religion. This was definitely a new, strange culture, and to me, it seemed archaic even though the hotel was very modern. After returning to the hotel, I went for a swim. The outdoor temperature rises so high in Dubai that it is the only place in the world, that I know of, where cold water is pumped into the lap swimming pool to maintain a comfortable temperature.

We blasted off from Dubai and jetted to Hong Kong. We executed the Hong Kong Checkerboard approach and I remember being totally amazed, overwhelmed and enlightened (more on that in an upcoming chapter). The sensation is that of flying into a mountain in order to see an airport runway. We were now halfway around the world. Hong Kong is 13 hours ahead of New York City.

Before I stepped onto Hong Kong soil, I heard that voice, "This may be our last day, so we better have the most fun of our lives in Hong Kong."

Hong Kong is a bustling Asian city with a touch of Western influence. The currency is the Hong Kong dollar, which was pegged to the US dollar. At that time, Hong Kong was one of the best places in the world for shopping, particularly for electronics. I bartered a great price on a large Delsey suitcase.

In Hong Kong, there were always loads of people in the streets. It was not uncommon to see families with small children walking the streets late at night, and it wasn't uncommon for two or three families to share one apartment. And to think I had it tough when I shared a bedroom with my brother while growing up.

Hong Kong was fun, and after eating and shopping we always ended up at Ned Kelly's Last Stand, one of Hong Kong's oldest bars. This establishment served Australian Foster's beer on tap, and the live band always closed with that most famous Frank Sinatra song, "New York, New York." All humans—white or yellow, man or woman, native or foreign—joined together to dance and sing that blockbuster song as we closed the pub. I felt that Hong Kong was a New-York-City wannabe. It became one of my favorite international layover cities.

We blasted off from Hong Kong to Tokyo, a truly Asian city with a strange currency called the Yen. That mysterious voice followed me, "This may be our last day, so we better have the most fun of our lives in Tokyo." Japan has a long history of a monoethnic culture. The women were pretty, but they all looked the same: five-foot, slim, Caucasian black hair and dark eyes. They bowed to men. Yes, Japanese tradition calls for a woman to fully devote herself to the needs and success of her husband. Contrary to the USA, it is not uncommon for Japanese women to hold open the door for a man, refill his sake cup at dinner, serve the man his food first and, yes, bow to him.

In Hong Kong, I stayed in an executive high-level suite facing the Kowloon Bay. In Tokyo, the hotel was constructed with small matchbox rooms facing a Koi Pond. The bathroom door had to be closed if you wanted to use the closet door.

This tight configuration presents a problem for captain Not-Y, who sleeps naked. As the human male ages, just a few Sapporo beers can trigger your bladder to pee at 3 a.m. Captain Not-Y arose from a dead sleep to rid himself of unwanted liquids. He opened the bathroom door, stumbled in and closed the door behind him. However, he was not in the bathroom. He had opened the door to the corridor and was now totally naked, and locked out of his room. And he still had to pee.

Well, there were various stories of the reactions of a few shocked Japanese guests and the obliging hotel staff of that naked, six-foot, and fairly well-built white guy, a Flying Tiger pilot. I'm not saying don't go to Tokyo, drink beer, and sleep naked. I'm merely trying to suggest that you clearly identify which door to utilize to pee in those minuscule hotel rooms.

We departed Tokyo for Anchorage. Tokyo is 18 hours ahead of Anchorage. When it is 3:00 a.m. in Anchorage, it is 9:00 p.m. in Tokyo on the same calendar day. What I experienced on this particular eight-hour flight occurs during certain times of the year when the jet stream winds are just right. As the jumbo jet traveled through so many time zones, I observed the beauty of Mother Nature's sun rise and set during the same flight—a very short day, I said to myself. A screwed-up circadian rhythm and maximum jet lag, my human body was telling me.

Jet lag causes the human body to become disoriented, foggy and sleepy at the wrong times of the day. After flying through 18 time zones, my body clock told me it was one time of day, and the outside environment told me it was another.

Flying jets through time zones wreaks havoc on sleep. During this trip, around the world in ten days, my body traveled through so many time zones that my circadian rhythm never had a chance to readjust to a normal rhythm cycle. The circadian rhythm influences the body's sleep-wake cycles, hormone releases, eating habits and digestion, body temperature and other important bodily functions. The brain uses the input of sunlight through the eyes to reset the biological clock; however, if you travel through so many time zones, your clock is confused about when it is morning or night.

The human body generally prefers five 90-minute sleep cycles per night. Pilots sometimes sleep in blocks of five hours now and three hours later, or five hours now and a 90-minute nap twice within 24 hours. Pilots have a general rule that if you have not slept at least five hours straight within the last 24 hours, you are considered fatigued, and you should not operate a jet airplane or other sophisticated machines. Many plane crashes have been attributed to pilot fatigue. Sleep loss affects your attention, working memory and cognitive functions.

This was stolen from Lindberg to describe my situation. "Halfway through the flight, fatigue was Lindberg's most dangerous adversary. He fought back with every trick he knew: he left the side windows out in order to keep the flow of cold air on his face and studied his Mercator chart to refocus his mind on his navigation duties. Numb with exhaustion, he began to lose track of time and found himself in the state we call 'eye-open sleep.' Only the fear of death enabled him to fight off his exhaustion. He was so tired that at one point he began to see apparitions in the rear of the fuselage." [27]

How did Charles do it? On the previous two nights and one day prior to his famous trip across the Atlantic Ocean, Charles had slept only a few hours. In conjunction with prior sleep deprivation, he flew solo for 33.5 hours from New York to Paris at the age of 25.

At age 26, I had little knowledge of jet lag or why I was feeling so strange on this around-the-world flight. I, too, was trying to fight back fatigue with whatever tricks I knew. I, too, was exhausted and felt that I was in the state of "eye-open sleep." I, too, began to see apparitions, but mine were more of me lying down in the Hilton hotel bed in Anchorage, Alaska, and sleeping for 30 days. However, I was not alone; there were two other pilots with me. At times, two pilots would cover for the other pilot, so that the really fatigued pilot could take a short nap. Even just 30 minutes, or preferably 90-minute nap, tricks the human brain into believing it is rejuvenated like Superman, allowing you to perform your flight duties as normal. This is not the case; you cannot perform at your best without proper sleep.

Anchorage is an American city, and I was excited and relieved to land there. Although once again, I heard, "This may be our last day, so we better have the most fun of our lives in Anchorage." My immediate goal was to rack up the most sleep of my life in Anchorage. At least that was my initial goal.

Anchorage was one of my favorite layover cities. Even with the US dollar as the currency and English as the language, it seemed like a foreign place that was not Western, European, Middle Eastern or Asian. A salmon burger was less expensive than a hamburger. Milk was more expensive than beer. In winter, there are only a few hours of daylight and that was if there was not a snowstorm. In summer, it never really turns dark; the sky dims for a few hours. Just a few blocks from the hotel you can fish for salmon and watch whales in the bay. Walk a little farther out of town you can often see roaming deer. And for the brave-hearted who strolls a little farther, certain times of the year you'll see bears.

After Anchorage, it was on to Chicago. With the howling wind blowing from Lake Michigan, Chicago was colder than Anchorage. And to think just a few days earlier, I was in Dubai, where it so hot that the water in the swimming pools needs to be cooled. The least favorite part of my job is doing a preflight walk-around of a 228-foot, B-747 jumbo jet at 4:00 a.m. in winter in Chicago.

From there, we flew into JFK—back to New York. At age 26, I flew around the world in ten days. Life is great! Only in America can you leave home at 18 with a driver's license and return at age 26 with a pilot's license and fly around the world.

After this 10-day around-the-world trip, I reflected on the experiences and memories that I had collected. "This may be our last day, so we better have the most fun of our lives, in every city we layover," was the new reoccurring theme etched in my memory. This was the philosophy of the Flying Tiger pilots. The values, beliefs and worldview of our pilots are that this could be our last day, so we are justified in having the most fun of our lives with our pilot peers wherever we are. This was our culture that bonded us; as Siamese twins joined in womb we were joined by philosophy.

The time spent together on these flight trips built a strong spirit of good friendship, loyalty and mutual trust among members of our pilot group. Not only did I love my job, but I loved the camaraderie of the people I worked with. A high level of camaraderie among pilots on and off the jet not only makes it fun to fly together, but it is likely those flights will operate safer. Working together is more enjoyable when you get along with your co-workers. After a few days of time off, I yearned to go back to work.

The Gouge. Exercise helps the human body recover from jet lag. After a long flight, I swim, run, or walk to help readjust my circadian rhythm.

Fasting helps reset your circadian rhythm when traveling. It helps the body's internal clock reset, with the help of breakfast as the first meal at the destination. While traveling in the dry, high-altitude environment of jet airplanes, it is common to experience digestive issues. Fasting helps the gut relax to help avoid gastric reflux and bloating. What worked best for me was to have a small meal at the beginning of the flight and fast or intermittingly fast through the remainder of the flight. The key to fasting is to know your body. Know when you start to feel the effects of not having anything to eat or drink for a while.

If there is enough time, grab a 30- or 90-minute nap or try to indulge in a 20-minute meditation session. To avoid fatigue during long-duty days, I have conferred with my first officer pilot and meditated in the cockpit. A 20-minute meditation session can give you a refreshing positive energy boost to help your pilot motor skills perform better and help you continue with your flight schedule.

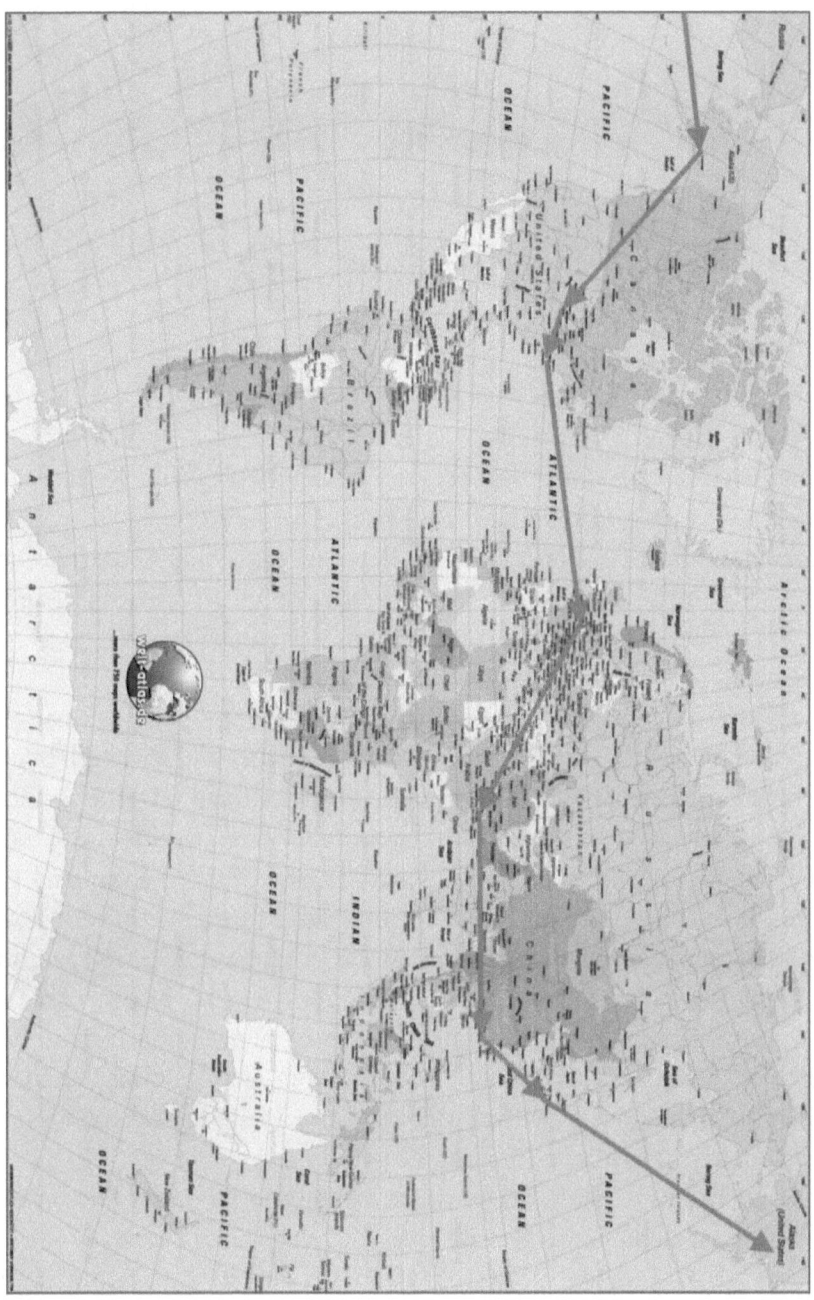

16

The Whale B-747

The largest airplane in the world.

Some aviators called the jumbo jet Boeing B-747 "the Whale," and others called it "the Queen of the Skies," because the B-747 was the largest aircraft in the world for many decades. Three flight crewmembers were required to operate the aircraft—a captain, a first officer, and a second officer (I was the second officer, sometimes referred to as the flight engineer).

The B-747 was known for being the first wide-body airliner, the largest and heaviest airliner, and the first to use fuel-efficient high bypass turbofan engines. The B-747 opened up international travel to millions of people and allowed shipment of commercial cargo worldwide. The B-747 had a wingspan of over 195 feet, was over 230 feet long, and was over 63 feet high. The max takeoff gross weight on the 200 model was 820,000 pounds; the max landing gross weight was 635,000 pounds, enabling the B-747 to carry over 500 people on board, or over 250,000 pounds of cargo freight. Operating these humongous jumbo jets all over the world made those pilots, including me, feel godlike at times. Operating "the Queen of the Skies" gave me a false self-centered image of a cool big-time pilot with a massive ego.

The B-747 is so big that it could carry up to 80 cars. "The Whale" is so big that some passengers are airborne longer than others. When the 230-foot B-747 rotates for takeoff, the passengers sitting up front in the first-class section become airborne before the passenger in the back in the economy section. Upon landing, the passengers in the back touchdown onto planet Earth before the passengers in the front of the plane. One could argue that one of the reasons first-class tickets cost more than economy-class tickets is that first-class passengers are paying for a longer flight. It is so massive; it was the largest plane in the world for decades.

At most airlines, pilots fly either cargo or passengers on the main deck on all their flights. Most passenger flights carry some cargo in the belly of the plane. At Tigers, the pilots flew cargo and passenger flights; therefore, I had to be prepared to operate of flight that carried up to a quarter million pounds of cargo freight or up to 500 passengers. With the B-747 I have operated flights with 515 people on board and flights with 256,000 pounds of freight on board. The B-747 could fly at a speed of over 500 knots and a distance of over 7,000 nautical miles (over 8,000 statute miles). The basic 747-100 model entered service with Pan America in 1970. The 200-model version was developed shortly after, allowing higher aircraft weights, longer range and more powerful engines. Initially, the 747-100 model was equipped with 4 Pratt and Whitney JF9D turbo fan engines that produced 48,000 pounds of thrust. The later 200 model produced 54,000 pounds of thrust. At Flying Tigers, we operated 21 B-747 jets, including the 100 and 200 models. Nineteen of the B-747s were cargo-configured versions and two were passenger-configured. We flew people and freight all over the world. Over 1,990 Boeing B-747 100/200 jets were built through 1991.[28] Other B-747 model versions are still in service today.

World Travels

The Tiger pilot group was a unique bunch.

After landing in a city—any city—anywhere in the world, the philosophy was simple: "Let's have the greatest time of our lives because this could be our last day," (or night) on planet Earth. As mentioned early, this philosophy developed strong camaraderie among our pilot group.

After a day or two in that city, we would start up the Boeing (the B-747 or the Whale), and take it to another city, and another city, and eventually to Gotham City. We imagined that Batman's Gotham City was supposed to be New York. Because we were based at John F. Kennedy International Airport in New York City, flying the plane to Gotham City was like flying the plane home, even though very few pilots lived near their base.

Tiger pilots lived all over the US and other countries, and they commuted to and from home to JFK to fly the B-747. Home! Yes, halfway through a typical 12-day trip, I wanted to go home to recuperate and take a time off from the fun. After being home just a few days, I craved to go back to work with the other Tiger pilots to fly somewhere in this world and have fun or, in other words, to make more fantastic memories.

In the B-747, I have flown around the world east-bound and west-bound. I have flown over the North Pole from Anchorage, Alaska (ANC-PANC) to London, England (LHR-EGLL) and back to Anchorage. I've flown that route a few times. I have flown to Bahrain (BAH-QBBI) to deliver Desert Storm war supplies. I've flown from Naha, Okinawa, Japan (OKA-ROAH) to U-Tapao, Thailand (UTP-VTBU) with 498 Marines for war-game exercises.

I've flown from Brussels, Belgium (BRU-EBBR) to Dubai, United Arab Emirates (DXB-OMDB) with zoo animals, including a few four-month-old baby tigers that were invited into the cockpit for photo opportunities.

I've flown from Anchorage (ANC-PANC) to Tokyo, Japan (NRT-RJAA) with 256 pregnant female cows.

Many of those B-747 flights had an aircraft takeoff weight of 820,000 pounds and a landing weight of 630,000 pounds, including 200,000 to 250,000 pounds of cargo freight.

Ever since my early childhood days, from those first bike riding experiences, my lifelong dream has been to travel. My airline career was the treatment for my addictive travel bug. My dreams of traveling all over the world to interesting places, to meet interesting people, had come true. These are some of the cities I visited when touring around the world: Brussels, Belgium (BRU); Berlin, Germany (TXL); Frankfurt, Germany (FRA); Cologne-Bonn, Germany (CGN); Munich, Germany (MUC); Stuttgart, Germany (STR); London, England (LHR); Prestwick, Scotland (PIK); Amsterdam, Netherlands (AMS); Paris, France (CDG); Basil, Switzerland (BSL); Zurich, Switzerland (ZRH); Milan, Italy (MXP); Guadalajara, Mexico (GDL); Mexico City, Mexico (MEX); Toluca, Mexico (TLC); Panama City, Panama (PTY); Dubai, United Arab Emirates (DXB); Anchorage, Alaska (ANC); Guam, Mariana (UAM); Taipei, Taiwan (TPE); Tokyo, Japan (NRT); Seoul, South Korea (ICN); Okinawa, Japan (DNA); Manaus, Brazil (MAO); Rio De Janeiro, Brazil (GIG); San Juan, Puerto Rico (SJU); Sidney, Australia (SYD); Singapore (SIN); and Hong Kong (HKG).

Hong Kong Checkerboard Approach

Oh, yeah, Hong Kong and the famous Hong Kong Checkerboard Approach. Every pilot has a famous approach-to-landing airport story. The approach is usually famous because of the challenges the pilot must overcome. Some pilots have died flying dangerous approaches and were not able to tell their stories. Because of the risks presented to the flying pilot, the Hong Kong Checkerboard approach was one of the most famous approaches known to international pilots for many years. The pilot must bring their "A-game" into the cockpit to successfully fly this approach.

An Instrument Landing System (ILS) approach terminates at a runway centerline, plus or minus 30 degrees. An Instrument Guidance System (IGS) approach is a variation of the ILS approach. However, the IGS approach terminates off the runway centerline.

The Kai Tak International Airport in Hong Kong had an IGS approach to runway 13, famously known as the Hong Kong Checkerboard Approach, one of the most unusual and dangerous airport approaches in the world. The *"Checkerboard"* approach was necessary for aircraft due to the surrounding terrain.

The airport was located between the Victoria Harbor Bay and Hong Kong city limits, and the runway was surrounded by city buildings and mountains. So basically, the captain would fly the B-747, guided by the IGS runway 13 approach, toward a large checkerboard pattern, which was colored in a red-and-white pattern and was located on a hill surrounded by buildings. While flying this approach, if you flew with bad visibility and you could identify the checkerboard at a predetermined distance, then the real fun—or challenge—began. Once the visual reference point of the checkerboard was established, the captain would have to look right about 40 degrees off the nose of the heavy jumbo jet to spot runway 13. If the pilot did not see the checkerboard or runway, then the pilot would have to execute a missed approach go around, and try again—or land someplace else.

If the pilot could spot the runway, then the captain had many tasks to accomplish in quick order—make a big turn to line up with the runway 13, lower the landing gear, set flaps for landing, correct for crosswinds if needed, adjust pitch and thrust. Many flight control adjustments and readjustments were made within a very short flight distance and time. The pilot needs to quickly react to changing flight forces, like a football quarterback's quick reaction to a blitzing defense during a designed long-pass play. Just like during a flight emergency, all of the human body sensors are enhanced to maximum alertness for best performance to execute this approach successfully.

Arriving on runway 13 required that the aircraft fly on autopilot until the pilot saw a checkerboard painted on a hill, then pilots took manual control, performing a right-hand turn at low altitude to reach the runway. The jet would enter the final right turn at a height of about 650 feet (200 meters) and exit it at a height of 140 feet (43 meters) to line up with the runway. This maneuver has become widely known in the piloting community as the "Hong Kong Turn" or "Checkerboard Turn." There are buildings up to six stories high in the area and during good-weather flights I remember clearly seeing televisions on in apartments, as we passed by. This approach required the pilot's best performance of flight skills and pilot ability. If the pilot landed long, the jet could fall into Victoria Harbor Bay (which has happened). If the pilot landed short or off-center line, he would crash into the airport's property or city buildings (which also has happened).

Later that night, international pilots from countries all over the world would gather at the "Someplace Else" establishment and tell their "Checkerboard" approach experience. It always amazes me, the interpretation of a similar experience and the different ways of telling a similar story, varies widely per international pilot. Some pilots did not succeed flying the approach and were unable to tell their story. It is better to live and tell the story.

For many years, the Hong Kong's Kai Tak Airport had the reputation as one of the most dangerous and challenging approaches in the world. In short, the Hong Kong checkerboard approach is like flying toward a mountain in order to see a runway. Because of many crashes and mishaps, the Kai Tak Airport and its challenging strange checkerboard approach was replaced in 1998 with the new Chep Lap Kak International Airport. Some of the most dangerous airports in the world today are: Madeira Airport, Portugal; Lukla Airport, Nepal; Courchevel International Airport, France; Princess Juliana International Airport, St. Maarten; and Narsarsuaq Airport,

Greenland. Some of the most challenging airports in the USA are: Aspen-Pitkin County Airport, Colorado; Laughlin/Bullhead International Airport, Arizona; Yellowstone Regional Airport, Wyoming; Ronald Reagan Washington National Airport, Washington, DC; LaGuardia Airport, New York; and San Diego International Airport, California.

Benefits of Airline Pilots

St Patrick's day in two separate cities, countries and continents

One of the perks granted airline pilots is jump-seat privileges, wherein a pilot can get a free flight. It is one of the most valuable privileges an airline pilot has earned. Pilots utilize the jump-seat privilege to commute to work and to go on pleasure trips, like to Australia. There is an actual seat, sometimes two, depending on the size of the jet, in the cockpit for individuals other than passengers or other flight crew not operating the aircraft. Most of the time, the jump-seating pilot is offered a cabin seat if the plane is not 100% full of paying passengers. Most airlines have mutual agreements allowing pilots from other airlines to jump seats on their planes. There is a professional protocol outlining procedures and etiquette for pilots to adhere to. The most important part of the entire process is for the requesting jump seater to always request the captain's permission beforehand, and to say thank you for the ride afterward.

In March of 1988, screw scheduling—I mean *crew scheduling*—called to tell me they were buying my next 10-day trip from me. They weren't trying to screw me. They wanted to use my trip to train a new B-747 second officer. The result? I would earn my wages for the 10-days but I would not have to work.

Great. I thought, *What should I do with my time off? Travel. Maybe I'll go to Sydney, Australia to celebrate St. Patrick's Day.* For the record, I am a half-breed; my father's side of my heritage is full Irish. After obtaining an Australian visa and money, I packed and left. I jump-seated on our Tiger's B-747 from New York City via Los Angeles and Hawaii to Australia.

In Sydney, Australia, I met many locals and some non-locals. The Australians are very friendly, easygoing people. Australians like Americans.

To me, their accent and sense of humor is strange, but I loved the country and the people. There is a huge community of Irish and Irish-Australians living in Sydney. Every day of my time spent there seemed to build up to their grand St. Patrick's Day celebration. Being half-Irish myself, and meeting so many Irish descendants, made the build-up to the big day all the more special.

After I celebrated St. Patrick's Day in Sydney, I needed more. I jump-seated to New York City (via Los Angeles) to land just in time to celebrate St. Patrick's Day again, but in New York City. This parade is the oldest and largest St. Patrick's Day Parade in the world. The first parade was held on March 17, 1762, and approximately 150,000 people marched in the parade in the view of about 2 million spectators.

This double celebration was so cool, I felt so special! My father and his people would be so proud of me celebrating Ireland's biggest holiday, twice. That year, I celebrated St. Patrick's Day in two separate cities, countries and continents. I may be the only human to have accomplished this special feat. That year, during workdays and during my days off, I racked up some of the best travel experiences of my life. These extensive travel accomplishments boosted my self-image that I was a cool, big-time pilot with a massive ego. Life is great! What could go wrong?

Witnessing Tragedy in Dallas

At the end of August 1988, I jump-seated down to Dallas, Texas, to visit friends at my old apartment complex. This is the place I had lived during my 100-day employment with Atlantic Southeast Airlines. On August 31, around 9 a.m., friend Wanda Wanther knocked on my door. "There's been a plane crash at the airport. Let's go," she said.

Wanda was the first non-pilot person I met in Dallas. Like me, she is a transplant from a northern state living in Texas. Like me, she had a varied schedule; sometimes she worked weekends and had days off during the week. Her apartment door is located six feet from my apartment door. We became good friends. She is a few years younger than me. She is energetic with a bouncy gate and usually carries an addictive, happy smile. I have seen her in her uniform looking serious, professional and conservative. She has another side to her. I have seen her after drinking a few margaritas, playing water volleyball, topless. On that day, Wanda was having so much fun, like the fun a 13-year-old girl has on her birthday, that she did not realize her top fell off. Wanda is a Delta Flight attendant. The bond between flight attendants and pilots are similar to the bond between nurses and doctors.

Wanda and I arrived at the Dallas/Fort Worth airport within minutes and approached the airport perimeter fence adjacent to runway 18L. There was the crashed B 727-232 jet (Delta Airlines flight #1141, Aircraft #N473DA).

Firefighters were still extinguishing the fires, and the survivors were emerging from the dark, smoky and acrid clouds and making their way to emergency vehicles. Two of the four flight attendants and 12 of the 101 passengers died.

Seeing this crash was emotional, and it affected us in both personal and professional ways—aviation was our professional career. *We make our money above planet Earth, and it is serious business.* In fact, sometimes pilots are only permitted to talk about their job while doing their job.

How did that crash happen?

FAA regulations require flight crewmembers to maintain a strict, sterile cockpit, meaning that once the aircraft starts moving, pilots are not to engage in any conversation unrelated to flight operations. This applies to any operation on the airport property and all flight operations up to 10,000 feet in altitude. This sterile cockpit also applies to the last 1,000 feet of any climb or descent.

The investigation of this crash found that while taxiing to runway 18L, the flight crew was talking extensively about things having nothing to do with the operations of that flight.

The investigation found two main causes for the crash—the crew's failure to extend the flaps and slats to proper takeoff configuration was attributed to inadequate cockpit discipline. The other problem was the plane's takeoff configuration warning horn, designed to alert the crew if the engines are throttled to takeoff thrust without the flaps and slats being correctly set, was not operating correctly.

The airplane did not gain sufficient speed to climb in a flaps-and-slats-retracted configuration, causing a loss of lift. The continued high angle of attack combined with a lack of lift resulted in a configuration where disturbed air flowing over the wings disrupted the airflow into the engines, causing compressor stall. Failing to gain altitude, the jet struck an antenna array 1,000 feet beyond the runway—and crashed.

The flight lasted only about 22 seconds from liftoff to impact.[29]

We had arrived at the crash site shortly after the crash. We were both affected emotionally. There I witnessed injured people, crying people, fire, smoke, and plane pieces and I absorbed the stench of death. Compassion flowed out of me for the victims and their families. Wanda cried, as did many of the people around us. The crying became contagious to others, but I did not catch it. The feeling of compassion was very strong within me, but so was the paranoid feeling that a crash could happen to me on the B-747. This plane crash motivated me to increase my studying, planning and preflighting in order to be the best at my job. Yes, I was back in the books studying again.

Little did I know at the time, that one day I would command the B-727.

On a side note, my previous English girlfriend Debbie Loveyearner traveled from Liverpool to Long Island to visit me. We had a good time together, but after a week, she concluded that I was not ready to settle down. She left disappointed and went home. It would take another special woman, at a later time, to make that happen.

Boeing B-747 versus Tesla

The B-747 can carry 80 cars

15 lengths by 32 widths

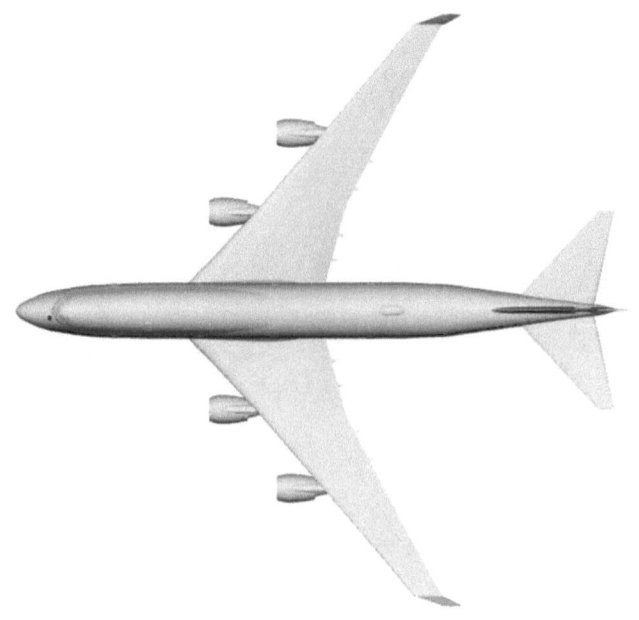

1 Embraer EMB-110 vs 2 Cessna C-150s

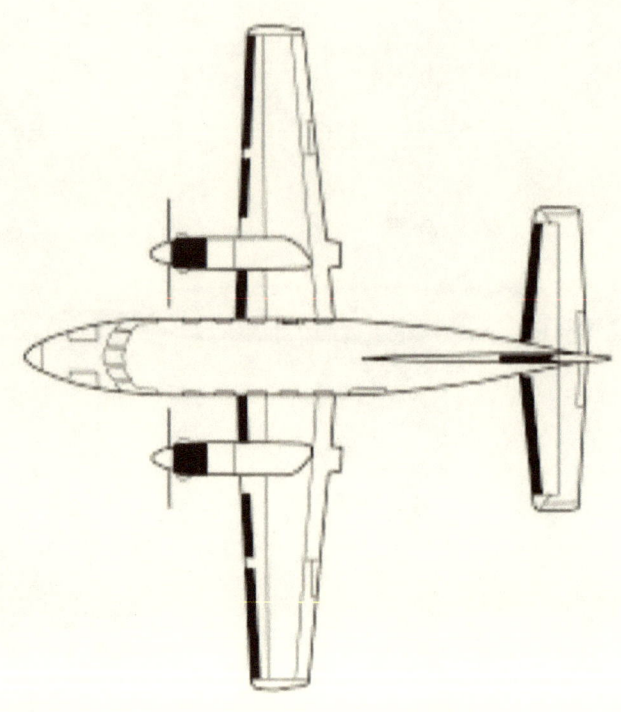

1 Boeing B-747 vs 5 Embraer EMB-110s

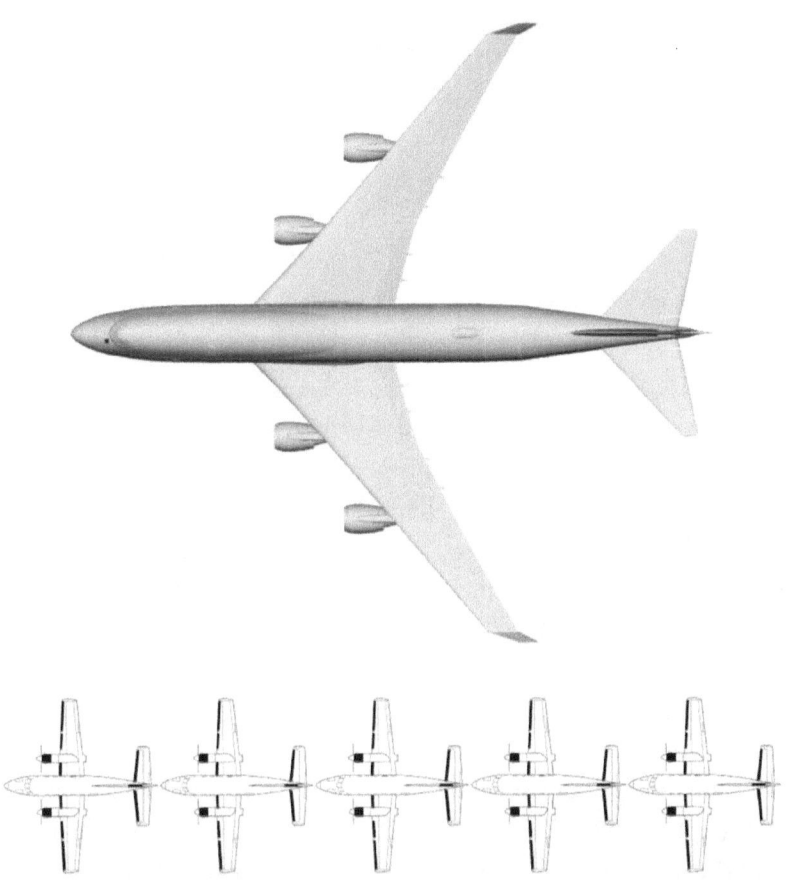

17

MEMORABLE FLIGHTS

When you get up there, don't forget to land.

There is a risk in flying planes. And 1989 was a year full of memorable events. That year, there were memorable flights and life changes that had a big effect on me, one way or another. Things happened that affected my work life and non-work life. There are times when it is a challenge to leave work at the office, or in my case, leave the flight bag in the cockpit, and go play. Separating business life from personal life may be difficult, but everyone needs some "me" time and/or family/friend time. The influence of work life on personal life may not be within your power to control. A major life-changing event triggered changes within me in 1989. It actually started in December 1988.

Airline merger talks started in December of 1988, when 17-year-old Federal Express Inc. (known today as FedEx®) announced that it would acquire the 43-year-old Tiger International, Inc. Federal Express offered $880 million on December 17.

I did not know it at the time, but my days with Flying Tigers were numbered.

Four days after first reading about the merger announcement, on December 21, 1988, a Pan Am B-747-100 was about a half hour into a scheduled flight from London's Heathrow airport to New York JFK Airport when an explosion occurred in the forward cargo compartment. The B-747 is the jet on which I was currently a flight crewmember. The plane was flying over Lockerbie, Scotland, when it tore apart and plummeted to earth. All 16 crewmembers and 243 passengers died. Eleven people on the ground were also killed. It was hard to imagine such an awful accident—but it was no accident. It would later be determined that two Libyan nationals had planted a bomb on the plane. This B-747 explosion reminded me that no matter how much studying, planning and preflighting pilots do before a flight, sometimes what happens to your jet is out of your hands. My life is on the line when I depart planet Earth.

Over the coming holidays, Bernadette and I shared our engagement news while spending Christmas Day with my father's side of the family and 54 relatives. New Year's Day was spent with my mother's side of the family and 27 relatives.

It is difficult, especially in this day and age, to separate work thoughts from play thoughts. It is good to have a balance of family pleasure and business work, but sometimes work-related events can influence that balance. Things that happen in your work industry can unavoidably sideline play in favor of work-related thoughts and emotions.

On February 19, 1989, a Flying Tiger B-747-200F aircraft, tail number N807FT, flight number 66, enroute from Singapore to Kuala Lumpur, Malaysia, crashed shortly before landing. These were fellow pilots at my company, and I had operated aircraft number N807FT beforehand. During a previous Anchorage layover, I had dinner and drinks with one of the flight 66 pilots. This crash hit home—these were my comrades, my company and my plane. The crew descended below the glide path and crashed into a hill after receiving ambiguous instructions from air traffic control. All four crewmembers were killed. Pilots study pilot accident reports, to learn the mistakes those pilots made and to make the necessary adjustment to avoid making similar mistakes on future flights. As always, there were several contributing factors to this jet crash and several lessons to learn—lessons that inspired me to become a better pilot.

The Gouge. Practice and always strive to maintain situational awareness and to participate in crew resource management. If you feel uncomfortable with the flight situation, even if you are not the captain, speak up assertively. Crew Resource Management (CRM) is the effective use of all available resources for flight crew personnel to assure safe and efficient flight operations, reduce error, avoid stress and increase efficiency. The primary goal of CRM is enhanced situational awareness, self-awareness, leadership, assertiveness, decision-making, flexibility, adaptability, event and mission analysis, and communication. CRM aims to foster a climate or culture where authority may be respectfully questioned.[30]

If something does not feel right, then speak up and remedy the situation.

Just five days later, on February 24, 1989, Flight UA811 was on a scheduled international trip from Honolulu, Hawaii to Auckland, New Zealand. This is another B-747 jumbo jet, a jet flying over the same Pacific Ocean, the same ocean I had flown over many times. About 16 minutes after takeoff, the United Airlines B-747-100 aircraft was climbing at about 22,000 feet when the forward cargo door on the right side blew out. The resulting explosion and decompression led to the loss of parts of the fuselage and the cabin interior, including a number of seats and passengers. Some of the ejected debris damaged the two right-side engines, and the crew had to shut them down. The crew was able to return to Honolulu and land about 14 minutes after the decompression. All 18 crewmembers survived, but 9 of the 337 passengers were killed. An investigation discovered the decompression occurred because of flaws in the electrical and cargo door latching systems. Afterward, an airworthiness directive was issued for all planes of that type, the type of planes I flew, to prevent the cargo door from blowing out. The flight crew, through good use of CRM skills, succeeded in landing the plane without further loss of life.

The Gouge. Develop, enhance, practice and utilize CRM skills.

On July 19, 1989, a United Airlines DC-10 crashed near Sioux City, Iowa, as a result of a hydraulic system failure: 111 of the 298 passengers were killed. The crew performed an emergency landing in a corn field after an engine failure severed all the hydraulic fluid lines. A microscopic flaw in an engine part caused it to fail, and debris severed hydraulic lines. The odds of survival were one in a billion. The captain struggled to fly the plane with abnormal flight controls. The captain utilized and assigned duties to the first officer, the second officer and an off-duty flight instructor pilot to help manipulate the thrust levers and flight controls, to stabilize and control the severely damaged jet. The amazing skills and ingenuity of these pilots enable them to get the plane on the ground and save 187 lives. This is an excellent example of the use of CRM. The captain excelled at enhanced situational awareness, leadership, assertiveness, decision making, flexibility and adaptability. The captain utilized all resources, human and non-human, available to land the plane and save lives.

It was not a banner year for the airline industry.

As pilots, we study and discuss what happened. We learn from the pilots who are able to deal with catastrophes and save lives, as was the case in Honolulu and Sioux City. But there are some situations, like Lockerbie, where there's just nothing to be done.

After completing a flight trip, I try to temporarily forget these events and all work-related business so that I can concentrate on other business and on personal life. I attempt to leave the job in the plane. I attempt to separate above-ground stress from on-the-ground stress.

On August 5, 1989, I operated flight number 766 aircraft number N822FT from Columbus, OH (LCK) to New York City, NY (JFK) carrying 145 thousand pounds of freight. This was my last flight as a Flying Tiger airline pilot. The official merger had been completed the day before, and my next flight would be as a pilot for Federal Express. I think it's worth noting that "merger" was a kind, gentle word that didn't capture the confusion and uncertainty among pilots and workers from both companies. It was us and them. Us: The Flying Tigers, had about 1,000 pilots, and they called us the Silver Pilots. Them: The Federal Express had about 1,100 pilots, and we called them the Purple Pilots. How would the pilot lists be merged, and what would be my new *seniority* number? Normally, airline pilot mergers are stressful, and I should have been more concerned, but I had just bought a house and was about to get married in Ireland (we'll get to that story soon).

I purchased a furnished three-bedroom, two-bath home located at mile marker 105 on a canal adjacent to the John Pennekamp Coral Reef State Park, in Key Largo. I thought it would be a perfect house for my new soon-to-be wife and me to live in.

Key Largo in Monroe County is located around 100 miles north of Key West and 50 miles south of Miami International Airport. Key Largo is located in the sub-tropical zone; temperatures ranged a high of 60°F in the winter and a low of 80°F in the summer with very little humidity. From my residence in Key Largo, I would commute to work at JFK International Airport and then fly all over the world. Typically, on a monthly basis, I would drive to Miami International airport, jump-seat to JFK, fly a 12-day trip around the world, jump-seat back to Miami and drive home.

My father always made a big deal of my commute versus his commute in conversations to his friends. This was an especially hot topic for him at the time because he had just completed the mandatory 10-year US Census form. My father commuted an average of 16 ground miles with an average commute time of one hour from Long Island to New York City five days a week. His son (*moi*), drove one hour from Key Largo to Miami airport and then jump-seated two-and-a-half hours of air time to JFK airport for a total distance of 1,300 miles, once a month. He commuted 16 miles each way five times a week while I commuted 1,300 miles each way once a month. Here is just one example of how some pilot's lifestyles are very different from those of non-pilots.

Two memorable flights occurred on August 17, 1989. Bernadette, my future lovely wife, was on one flight and I was on the other. Bernadette boarded an Aer Lingus jumbo jet B-747 flight to fly from JFK International Airport with a quick scheduled stop in Shannon International Airport and then on to Dublin International Airport, Ireland. At the last minute, I obtained the jump seat on a Pan Am B-747 jumbo jet flight to fly from JFK International Airport to Shannon International Airport, Ireland. While riding in the cockpit, the captain transmitted an air-to-air message to the Aer Lingus captain to inform Bernadette to depart at Shannon International Airport. It was not difficult for the flight attendant to locate Bernadette—she was the gorgeous blonde carrying a wedding dress and sitting in seat 6A. During the plane ride across "the pond," the Pan Am pilots and a few flight attendants were jokingly trying to talk me out of getting married.

"Frank, what do you mean you don't like to fight? Why are you getting married, then?" The overabundance of joking was in good spirits. In the end, like just before I exited the completed flight, they were happy for me and wished me a happy married life.

Upon meeting at Shannon Airport, we rented a car and drove 17 miles on the wrong side of the road to her parents' house.

The Gouge. If you are ever planning a trip to Ireland, do not rent a large automobile with an automatic transmission—instead, rent a small, midsized automobile with a manual shift because most of the roads are very narrow, winding and hilly. Gasoline is very expensive in Ireland, and manual transmissions always get better mileage than automatics.

Twenty-five friends and relatives traveled to Castlecomer, Ireland, where Bernadette and I were married during a short, 12-hour wedding. We held a second reception in New York City as well. After a ten-day honeymoon, traveling all over the west of Ireland, we departed for the USA.

We flew from Shannon International Airport Ireland to John F. Kennedy International Airport to attend the 100-person New York wedding ceremony and reception. I know: I always was a pain in the butt.

Not only did I have to get married in a foreign country, but I had to have two ceremonies and receptions—one in her country and one in mine.

After the New York reception, not many of my relatives wanted to fly on commercial airplanes anymore. Maybe because at the reception they met my pilot colleagues: John of American Airlines, Mark of Trans World Airlines, Bill of Continental Airlines, Bob of USAir, and Robert of United Airlines. My five pilot friends, and probably me as well, painted a picture of wild, fun-filled, young amateurs. Most ground people are not afforded the opportunity to witness the calm professionalism of air people (pilots) performing in the cockpit. Pilots sometimes project only fun on the ground but we are serious in the air. You get the picture—I think?

A few days later, we drove home to our furnished home in Key Largo, Florida, to live happily ever after. Mr. and Mrs. Donohue moved into their new home in Key Largo, mile marker 105. Shortly thereafter, Bernadette revealed to me that she was with child. Our conception of this child was dated a few days after the wedding—hence, a honeymoon baby was on the way. During this time, I was so happy, it was as if I were floating on a friendly cloud in heaven.

Throughout this book, you may have ascertained that the greatest thing to do in our world is to fly planes above planet Earth. Stories are told here of my bonding with my airplane, like "Crazy Glue" bonding your fingertip to a material item. For the record, I am stating that the greatest thing to do in our world is to fall in love with a partner, get married, and raise children together. The lovable bond with your immediate family is far greater than the bond with an air machine, even a jumbo jet air machine like the Boeing B-747.

Almost Died on a Layover

Passed out and Choking in Frankfurt, Germany

The year started out really badly, with plane crashes, and then I married the loveliest woman, who was with child. Life was fantastic. Life seemed like those storybook tales, "And they lived happily ever after" … until I almost died.

Shortly after the Berlin Wall came down in November 1989, Captain Jean, First Officer Bob, and I flew from JFK New York to Dover, Delaware, and then on to Frankfurt, Germany. We had a three-day layover in Frankfurt and decided to turn it into a little vacation. One of the many benefits of an international airline pilot is that you fly to many cities all over the world. Not only does the pilot have the opportunity to tour the layover city, but the pilot can visit other cities during off times. Traveling all over the world was one of the reasons I wanted to be a pilot. That night, we went out to eat Schweinshaxe (pork with cabbage and potatoes) and of course, German beer. The next day, the three of us took a Pan Am jump seat to Berlin. We crossed the dilapidated Berlin Wall into East Berlin. We spent the night in West Berlin, and the next day, we took a jump seat to Stuttgart, Germany. After a day in Stuttgart, we took the midnight train back to Frankfurt and went to get a late-night snack—a near-fatal mistake.

I ate a Bratwurst sausage, drank some milk and went to sleep.

Dreams are funny things. They have several levels of awareness. At times, you may be unaware that you have dreamed. Occasionally a dream may be recalled in sharp detail, and other times it is vague. You may experience a dream that is so lucid that you think the events are real—it's so vivid that you cannot initially distinguish between the reality of the dream and the reality of the awake life. In your dream, you see, hear, feel and touch. The effects or feelings that we experience in our dreams can persist after we are awake and can seem as real as anything in the awake life.

In this dream, I had to piss but the bathroom was miles away, and I was so tired that I began to crawl and eventually stopped to fall back asleep. But there was something ferociously alive in my stomach and it was trying to escape by trying to squeeze through my throat. It was too big to get through. As I tried to open my mouth, my tongue tasted its nastiness. Just then, my breathing system stopped and I started to panic for air. "It won't get out." "I cannot breathe." "I do not want to die."

"What is this nasty creature?"

I had had some bad milk and some good alcohol, and I woke up on the bathroom floor around 4:00 a.m., choking on my own vomit. When choking, you cut off the airway to your trachea. If you vomit and choke on the big chunks, you can die from suffocation. The choking actually woke me up. As my eyes started to blink open, I crawled up to the top of the toilet bowl to let the creature escape. After getting a strong whiff of that terrible stench, I realized that I was transitioning from a nightmare dream to the reality of awake life—*somewhere, sometime, somehow*. I stood up on my own two feet, turned the bright bathroom light on and stared at myself in the mirror. Next, I splashed my unusually pale face with cold, refreshing water, took some Lomotil (an oral anti-diarrheal drug), drank a bottle of warm water, and thanked God I did not die at age 28.

Rock guitarist Jimi Hendrix died at age 27 in London in 1970 from choking on his own vomit after drinking wine and taking too many sleeping pills. All I consumed was some bad milk, a little good beer, and a German bratwurst sausage. Thank you, thank you, and thank you. I did not die.

The Gouge. If you ever suspect that you may vomit in your sleep, do not sleep on your back, staring at the ceiling. If you do vomit while sleeping in this position, there is nowhere for the vomit to go, and you might choke and die. Sleep on your side so that it will all drain out of your mouth as you sleep. For those planning on traveling around the world, take Lomotil, Imodium or a similar oral anti-diarrheal drug with you, in case those foreign fluids or solids give you diarrhea.

Screwing with Flight Attendants at 35,000 feet.

On one particular 10-day trip we transported almost a quarter-million pounds of cargo freight and over 500 passengers. We flew flight number 1021 aircraft number N813FT from Keflavik International airport (BIKF) to Anchorage, Alaska (PANC) carrying 239,590 pounds of freight. Our max takeoff gross weight that day was 819,731 pounds. On the next flight, we carried over 500 passengers.

The year ended on a fun note. There are numerous secretive pilot stories that require the listener to display their pilot's license before the story is told with the confidence that the federal officials will not get wind of the details. Many of these stories are treated with the same level of confidentiality as between doctor and patient, or sometimes, more appropriately, a priest and confessor. Here is a pilot story I can tell you without the requirement of a pilot license. Here is an example of how we turned work into fun. Keep in mind, the gouge here is to find the fun in your job.

The memorable flight occurred near the end of 1989. Back then, and even today, very few airlines transported more than 500 people on a jet. I have joined that rare class of pilots who have flown with more than 500 souls on board. Captain Billy, First Officer Larry, and I flew flight number 2121 in a B-747-100, aircraft number N890, from Anchorage, Alaska (PANC) to Kadena Air Base, Okinawa Japan (RODN). We carried 492 passengers and 17 crewmembers for a total of 509 people on board.

Passengers? On a cargo plane?

Yes, Flying Tigers operated 21 B-747 jumbo jets. Of those, 19 were configured for transporting cargo, and two were configured for transporting passengers. The two-passenger airplanes were used for charter flights—mainly for military personnel. Therefore, I had to be prepared to operate a flight that carried up to a quarter-million pounds of cargo freight or up to 500 passengers.

One of the main differences between the two types of flights, is that passenger flights require that we maintain comfortable temperatures throughout the various zones of the jet (cargo doesn't tend to complain so much). Usually, if one of the 14 flight attendants enters the cockpit and complains that zone three is too cold, it usually means that a passenger complained of the cold, and I would adjust the temperature accordingly. However, if another flight attendant came into our office (and that's what the cockpit is—an office) and informed us that it was too hot in zone five, that usually indicated that she was busy working hard and sweating. Most of the time, I ignored this request. In fact, this coming and going and the running commentary—"It's too cold in zone two. It's too hot in zone five"—became a distraction to my other duties.

The Captain, First Officer and I devised a fantastic scheme.

I labeled an inactive switch (we called it the Dummy Switch) the "TEMP. SW." Whenever one of the working girls came in to complain about how hot it was in zone "XYZ," I authorized my special flight-operation permission to adjust the temperature herself using that special "TEMP. SW." I made her promise to keep this a special secret between us because the Captain would be angry if he found out. In fact, the Captain was discreetly laughing all the way to Japan. We had our laughs and they were happy to adjust the "TEMP. SW" up or down as often as they wished. This flight was a great memory flight and an example of how to turn work into fun.

18

First Jet

We make our money above planet Earth and it is serious business.

Silver versus Purple

Have you ever belonged to one group and that group had to join a completely different group? Maybe you belonged to a team and your team was forced to merge with another. Imagine being employed with a company for many years and then another company buys your company and changes everything. You may have strong emotional connections with your group, team or company, and you may not want to merge with a different group of people. This upcoming merger of our two contrasting pilot groups into one group caused me apprehension about what lay ahead for Frank the pilot.

Every airline and its pilot group has a distinct culture.

The FedEx® pilot crew (the Purple Pilots) and the Flying Tiger crew (the Silver Pilots) were the two most distinctive pilot groups that ever existed. However, the challenge in 1989 was to merge, to become one culture, like two completely different families being joined together by their children's wedding.

A physician and medical consultant hired by FedEx to evaluate the two pilot groups unofficially said that the Purple Pilots were like "the church choir" and that the Silver Pilots were like "the Hells Angels club." Most of the Purple Pilots were novices to the airline industry. The Purple Pilot group only had a 15-year history in the airline business. Most of the Silver Pilots were much more experienced and the company itself had a 45-year history.

The Purple Pilots were a non-union group and consisted of mostly ex-military pilots—mainly Navy, Air Force and some Marines. They were regimented and individualistic.

The Purple Pilots were used to abiding by the company requests—follow the general or colonel and don't ask questions. One pilot stated to me, "Whatever Fred Smith says is okay by me." Another pilot remarked, "If Fred wants a domicile in Anchorage, he will get one."

Up to this point, most of the work rules for the Purple Pilots was dictated by the company and not negotiated, like most of the other airline pilot groups. The Silver Pilots were an ALPA Union group and consisted of a varied group of mostly civilian pilots. They were fun, friendly and group-oriented.

"When we land in XYZ city, let's have the best time of our life together because it could be our last day." I was a Silver Pilot and that was our attitude.

The Silver Pilots were dubious of company intentions. If the company wanted an Anchorage, Alaska domicile, then the pilot union group would investigate and negotiate.

"What do they (the company) want, and what do we (the pilot group) want?"

The majority of the Purple Pilots were based near their headquarters in Memphis, Tennessee, and flew domestically. In the 1980s, you could buy a really big house in Memphis and drive to work on the average pay of a Purple Pilot. The majority of the Silver Pilots flew internationally and lived all over the United States. Most Silver Pilots lived where they wanted to and commuted by plane to their home bases to begin work. I initially commuted from Key Largo to John F. Kennedy International Airport and temporarily lived in Memphis for one year (1991). The standard of living—and the cost—was higher in New York and California than it was in Tennessee.

Most of the Purple Captain Pilots promoted the use of the aircraft autopilot to direct the jet's flight path, even during the departure and approach phase of flight. You'd hear suggestions like this from Purple Pilots: "Practice using the autopilot so that you will be proficient at it if the weather gets bad." One time, when I was flying with a Purple Pilot, I had disconnected the autopilot to practice some hand-flying; that captain said, "What are you doing? Put that autopilot back on." Most of the Silver Captain pilots promoted the use of hand-flying during departure and approach. Our belief was this: "Practice hand-flying so that if the autopilot fails, you will be proficient at hand-flying the aircraft." I am in the camp that pilots should disconnect the autopilot and other automation at least once a week, to practice hand-flying the jet in order to keep their pilot skills sharp.

The Purple Pilots did not have probation for new hires. So, if a friend of a friend got hired, and if he or she was a bad pilot or had a bad character, then that pilot stayed and did not get fired. The Silver Pilots had a one-year probation period for all new hires. So, if a hiring mistake was made, the company could fire that pilot and not suffer from the poor hiring decision.

While on layovers, the Purple Pilots generally paid their own way, except that, because the Second Officer carried the coffee jug, the Captain and First Officer would take turns tipping the limo driver on behalf of the Second Officer.

All Silver Pilots did their own tipping to the limo drivers; however, the Captain gave an extra tip to the limo driver for providing attitude-adjustment beverages for the crew while being transported to the layover hotel.

It was not uncommon for the Captain to buy dinner for the crew.

One time in Taipei, Taiwan (TPE), the limo driver did not have cold beer for the crew. The Captain uncharacteristically scolded the driver. It was the first time I saw a grown man cry. Driving a limo in Taipei in the 1980s was a good-paying job, and the driver feared that he might lose it. Besides, it was a 45-minute drive to the hotel. Well, the driver stopped, we purchased beer, the driver kept his job—and he earned a tip. The Captain and First Officer always bought drinks and sometimes meals for the Second Officer because the Second Officer was on probation and could not afford to buy drinks.

These are just a few examples of how extremely distinctive these two pilot groups were—and we had to merge and get along.

FedEx

Fred Smith, the founder and chief executive officer of Federal Express (renamed FedEx in 1994) first got the idea of developing a new logistics system while living in New Haven, Connecticut, during his college years. While Fred Smith was a charter pilot at Tweed New Haven

Airport, he observed the logistical challenge of flying large computer parts around every time a computer broke down. While at Yale University, Fred wrote a term paper on the idea of using a hub-and-spoke overnight logistics system to solve the challenge of moving cargo. His professor was not impressed with the idea and issued him an average grade on his term paper.[31]

After serving in the US Marine Corps, Fred continued to develop his idea of a new cargo delivery service. In 1971, Fred incorporated Federal Express. Using $4 million of his own money and $80 million from investors, he started developing his idea. On April 17, 1973, Federal Express officially began operations with the launch of 14 Falcon aircraft based at Memphis International Airport, and delivered 186 packages to 25 US cities. In less than two years, Federal Express made its first monthly profit of $20,000 by delivering over 13,000 packages per night.

In 1978, Federal Express was listed on the New York Stock Exchange under the ticker symbol FDX, and by the end of 1980, two years after the passage of the Airline Deregulation Act of 1978, Federal Express became the nation's leading cargo carrier.

By 1983, Federal Express became the first US corporation to achieve annual revenues of $1 billion in less than 10 years. In 1986, Federal Express's volume exceeded 1 million packages per night. In 1990, Federal Express became the first service company to win the "Malcolm Baldrige National Quality Award." In 1994, Federal Express changed its name to FedEx and launched its worldwide website: fedex.com.[32]

FedEx continually expanded the size of the company through growth and acquisitions. In fiscal year 2022, FedEx delivered more than 8.5 million packages per day and more than 50 million pounds of goods to the United States and to more than 220 countries worldwide, utilizing approximately 5,500 pilots. FedEx produces over $85 billion of revenue per year.

Little did I know at the time, that flying for FedEx was like finding a precious gem within the airline industry. The cargo business is more profitable with less competition than the passenger business. There were tremendous career growth opportunities for pilots at my company during my 30-plus years of service. Today, FedEx operates the largest fleet of wide-body jets.

On September 6, 1990, I operated flight number 116, aircraft number N621FE from Oakland, CA (OAK) to Saint Louis, MO (STL) carrying 342 passengers and 17 flight crewmembers. This was my last flight as a second officer on the whale, the "Queen of the Skies." In over three years I had accumulated 1,500 hours as a Flight Engineer on the jumbo Boeing B-747 jet. Part of me felt sentimental on leaving the second officer position on the B-747, while another part of me was excited going to the new first officer position on the B-727. A second officer is more of a systems operator and monitor, like Spock on the Starship Enterprise; whereas a first officer commands the flight controls to fly the plane, like Kirk.

The Flying Tiger's pilot philosophy and culture cemented me to an unbreakable pilot camaraderie with our pilot group, like the blood bond connecting immediate family members. There were many rumors and falsehoods spread among Silver Pilots about the Purple Pilots; just as the Purple Pilots had their gossip about the Silver Pilots.

Several pilots from each side started to dislike each other. There was a strong love for our Silver Pilot group and a growing dislike for the other Purple Pilot group, mainly because that group is different. There is a natural fear of people who are different from us, especially when we do not know anything about them. Each group assumed that the pilots from the other group would not fit into their social group, and they felt threatened that those other pilots would change their group. People are wired to see other people outside their group as enemies. Our brains' negative bias toward outsiders evolved as a survival mechanism. For self-preservation, the primitive parts of our brains are wired to separate friends from foes. People may hate what they don't understand. People reject those who think differently and look different from us.

As mentioned above, I did have a feeling of apprehension toward flying with a new group of pilots and their distinctive pilot culture. The feeling is like a freshman student entering high school or college without knowing anyone or anything about anyone there. My concerns were: *Are these rumors about them true? How difficult will it be to fly with these guys? Will they take the fun out of flying?*

Most of the B-727 captains I would be flying with initially would be Purple Pilots.

On December 13, 1990, I upgraded to Boeing B-727 First Officer pilot position. The B-727 jet was the first jet airplane I ever flew. I was 29 years old.

An airplane's engine or engines move the airplane by pulling it through the atmosphere, or by displacing air from in front to behind the airplane. The two forms of propulsion—the means to displace air—are propellers and jets. Propellers are small airfoils, carefully shaped to generate lift, yet instead of directing lift vertically like wings, props direct the lift horizontally. Jets generate propulsion by pulling in air, combining it with fuel, igniting the mixture, and using the resulting explosion to push the airplane forward.[33]

A turboprop plane has a turbine engine that turns a traditional aircraft propeller and **the jet plane does not.** Turboprops have a propeller on the outside of the engine while jets have fan blades inside the engine housing. Jets produce thrust through the discharge of gas instead of powering a driveshaft linked to a propeller. This allows jets to fly faster and at higher altitudes. Turboprops are more efficient at slower speeds whereas jets become more efficient at higher speeds. Props are better for shorter regional routes, while the jets are better for long-haul flights. Jets dominate the majority of medium- and long-distance flights around the world. Most jets are built with more sophisticated systems and instruments. Jets can fly higher, farther and faster than turboprops or propeller planes. I prefer jets.

B-727

The Boeing B-727-100 jet aircraft was developed in 1965, shortly after the 727-200 jet version was offered. The 200 model was basically the 100 model with the fuselage stretched 20 feet, allowing increased passenger and freight capacity.

The B-727-200 entered service with Northwest Airlines in December 1967, and 1,831 B-727s of all model versions were built from 1967 through 1984. The B-727 had a max gross takeoff weight of more than 200,000 pounds. It could carry more than 200 people or more than 50,000 pounds of freight. The wingspan of the B-727 stretched more than 100 feet, and its length measured more than 150 feet. It stood more than 34 feet high. The B-727 included three turbo fan engines. Each engine produced more than 16,000 pounds of thrust, enabling it to fly a distance of more than 2,000 nautical miles (2,300 statute miles) and a speed of more than 500 knots (575 mph).[34] The jet is so fast that with favorable tailwinds the jet could fly 600 mph. The next time you are on the highway driving at the speed of 60 mph, just think to yourself, *Frank the pilot is flying ten times faster.* Three crewmembers were required for the B-727—a Captain, a First Officer, and a Flight Engineer. I was the First Officer.

The first officer or co-pilot has many duties from preflight planning to landing the aircraft. The first officer assists the captain during flight and works with the captain to complete the many checklists involved with flying the jet. Generally, when the captain is flying the plane (called the flying pilot) the first officer (called the non-flying pilot) is communicating on the radio, assisting the flying pilot with navigation and monitoring flight instruments. Generally, flight segments (called legs) are split, and these roles are reversed when the first officer is the flying pilot. The captain decides when and who is the flying pilot and the captain has the full authority to take the flight controls at any time.

The first officer assists and helps make the captain's job easier, so that the captain can maximize his level of situational awareness. During an emergency, the first officer's primary job is to fly the jet and let the captain manage the cockpit. If the captain should die or become incapacitated in flight, the first officer will have to land the jet. Every captain is different and prefers certain things to be done in a certain way. The first officer must evolve into Gumby, the animated character in an old American television show that ended in 1988. Gumby was made of clay and was flexible and stretchable. Do whatever the captain says. The first officer's main priority is to keep the captain out of trouble. In turn, good captains mentor good first officers to become good future captains.

The Gouge. The first officer's first job is to keep the captain out of trouble. Be like Gumby. Be flexible. Do everything and anything to assist the captain. The first officer's second job is to fly the jet. Prepare for every flight and learn from every captain.

The transition and training, from B-747 second officer to B-727 first officer were a challenge for me. I loved learning, but I hated being tested. At Flying Tigers, everything seemed fun, even training seemed fun. At FedEx, training seemed so serious. Prior to this, I guess I was too young to be scared of training. Feeling and thinking, *What is going on inside me?* Prior to the B-727 practical exam, I became nervous and worried that I may not make it through the B-727 flight training program, which went at a very fast pace and was challenging, especially to me, since this was my first jet flying experience. Jets are so much faster than propeller planes. The jet pilot must ramp up their scan and reaction skills to prevent falling behind the plane. The jet pilot's high level of scanning instruments, interpreting flight information and reacting with flight control inputs is like an IndyCar race driver or the best professional quarterback facing a blitzing defense.

The B-727 training program consisted of a few weeks of ground school followed with a written test and an oral test, and then a few weeks of simulator training followed with an oral test and a multiple simulator flight test. I particularly remember the challenging, non-precision Memphis LOC 27 approach, complicated with its steep, short descent and a strong crosswind component. After the simulator training, there is inflight training with several instructor pilots followed by a flight check ride. From start to finish, the flight training program encompassed several months of non-stop studying.

By the skin of my teeth, I graduated as a B-727 first officer. However, I soon found out that my airline jet flying training had just begun. Over the course of the next six years, the captains I flew with mentored me. With all the knowledge and experience that oozed out of these captains, I decided to start my own notebook to record the valuable lessons I was learning from them. Some captains would take the time to teach, while other captains just demonstrated valuable flight knowledge and techniques. Each captain had their own flight personality and pilot style.

The Gouge. If you ask, they will tell. It may take years for a pilot to learn something that a captain can teach a first officer in minutes. If you ask a captain a pilot/flight question, 9 out of 10 times, the captain pilot is honored to teach to the first officer pilot. Most captains are honored to share and teach their knowledge and skills to an inquisitive first officer. Keep a notebook and record what you have learned as a first officer, for one day you will be the captain mentoring first officers.

Most of the B-727 captains that I was paired with initially were Purple Pilots, and I was apprehensive about what the cockpit atmosphere would be. One time, I met my captain, a Purple Pilot, at 1:00 a.m. in the hotel lobby to start a seven-day flight trip. This quiet guy was from Texas and spoke with a strong, slow Southern accent; I, from Long Island, was different from him in every way. *This Redneck probably hates Yankees like me*, was my initial thought. At times, I doubted that we were speaking the same American English. My first impression was, *How am I ever going to get along with this person for seven days?* After fighting off the pre-judgment syndrome and opening a conversation with a few one-liners, we discovered things we had in common. We discovered we had a similar sense of humor. Excluding those first few hours, we got along great during the entire seven-day flight trip. The pilot rumors swirling about the Purple Pilots did not come to fruition for me. To begin with, both pilot groups had flying and the safety of flight operations in common. Once I broke through the initial unfamiliarity barrier, I had discovered there is always something outside of flying those two distinct pilots have in common.

Getting along with your co-worker helps make working together more fun, less work and safer. Additionally, I had to accept that person and we had to quickly gel as a team; the safety of the flight depended on it. Later in this book I will expand on why pilots need to gel as a team for the safety of flight.

The Gouge. Do not dislike your co-worker. Learn to get along and work as a team. Don't judge a book by its cover; at least read the first chapter. (By the way, thank you for getting this far reading my words.) Don't let that first impression, that the other person may be so different from you, dictate how you will get along. Accept that person and start gelling as a team; the safety of the flight may depend on it.

The B-727 aircraft was a fun plane to fly. It was like a high-speed go-cart.

"If you could see it, you could land on it," was the motto of B-727 pilots. The motto meant if you could see the landing runway from level altitude, then you were capable of descending at a steep rate, slowing down and landing.

While on my European vacation, I recall a particular fun trip from Paris to Basil. The company would put me on a business class flight to Europe, I would fly around Europe for a week and then the company would put me on a business class flight to return home. Even though this was a work trip, I called it my European vacation.

We flew high-speed climbs out of Paris, France (CDG), climbing at a speed of 350 knots or more, up to 600 mph in cruise flight, and then flew high-speed descents of 350 knots or more into Basel, Switzerland (BSL). We would fly at that pace until we were around 30 miles from the field and about 3,000 feet above ground and then slow the aircraft down to stabilize before touchdown. We had fun!

This is how it was done.

From cruise flight, at the very last moment, just before the site of the Basil airport would pass under the jet's nose, I started the descent. Thinking, *If I can see the airport from a cruise flight then I will be able to make the adjustments to land at the airport.* I pulled the thrust levers to idle, extended the speed brake to deploy the wing flight spoilers and pushed the yoke forward. This commanded the jet to be piloted at a high rate of descent within a short forward distance. At around 30 miles from the Basil runway and about 3,000 feet above ground I would transition from flying super-fast to slowing down to land. As I pulled back on the yoke, the jet's attitude rose and the airspeed began to decrease. As the airspeed fell below 250 knots, I extended the landing gear, retracted the speed brake, and began to extend all flaps within flap speed limitations. The thrust levers were still at idle as I pulled the control yoke back further. This action directs the jet to an attitude to just below the stall attitude. With the gear and flaps extended and the engines producing only idle thrust, the jet was drastically slowing down and dropping out of the sky like a boulder.

The goal is to simultaneously slow down quickly to the final approach while descending at a high rate in order to join the appropriate glide path. The ILS information is used to confirm the visual cues to join the approach glide path and course. The challenging part is to time advancing the thrust levels while reducing the jet's attitude in anticipation of the ILS instrument indicating the jet is about to join the proper glide path. Lowering the jet's attitude and increasing the thrust levers reduces the drag force and increases the thrust force. Anticipation and timing of these flight actions must occur before the jet joins the appropriate approach glide path. The pilot must stay a step ahead of the flight forces of momentum. My blood pressure, heart rate, breathing rate, scan rate, data interpretation rate, motor skills and flight skills are operating at its maximum efficiency level. At this moment and time, I am operating the jet as the best pilot I could be.

By ten feet above the runway, I ensure the jet is on target airspeed, all checklists are complete, the thrust levers are out of the idle position, and the jet is stabilized on final approach. I land the B-727 jet. We taxi to our parking spot, set the parking brake and shut down the engines. Someone would say, "Last one out buys the first round."

We had a requirement to be stabilized on final approach. This would mean the flaps would be fully extended, the final checklist would be complete, the landing gear would be down, and we would have the on-approach airspeed and engine out of idle before touchdown. Our goal was to have all this done by 10 feet above the ground, to allow for some margin of error.

No one flies like this today. Today the requirement is to be stabilized on final approach by 500 feet above the ground during good weather and 1,000 feet above the ground during bad weather. In the USA, all planes are restricted to the maximum airspeed of 250 knots below 10,000 feet.

While piloting a jet airplane, my body is operating at a heightened state of physical and mental alertness. I experience a maximum adrenaline rush from landing the jet, especially during certain challenging landings like this one. It is rewarding and a fantastic feeling! It feels like a quarterback throwing the winning touchdown during the Super Bowl or standing on the podium to receive an Olympic gold medal.

These approaches and flying fast was the most fun part of flying the B-727 and sometimes challenging. I was not the only pilot that flew fast like this, but somehow, I was given a new call sign "Fast Frank." Maybe because back then, I always flew fast, and also, according to the pilots from the South, I talked fast.

There were many other challenging airports.

Flying into Vnukovo International Airport, Moscow (VKO-UUWW) in 1986 was challenging. Russia uses a metric system in aviation. On the B-727, the altimeter is calibrated in feet, so we had to use a conversion card for determining the altitude in feet, before dialing in the altitude to the autopilot. Altimeter's settings were converted from *inches of mercury to hectopascals.*

Flying out of Milano Malpensa Airport, Italy (MXP-LIMC) was sometimes challenging—at times you would have to climb in circles to gain enough altitude to cross the beautiful Swiss Alps. Pilots must disregard the visual illusion that a climb can be made to clear the mountains in lieu of the pre-calculated climb performance of what the jet can actually do. It is more enjoyable to fly *over* the Swiss Alps than to fly *into* them.

Flying the arrivals and departures in and out of Paris, Charles De Gaulle Airport (CDG-LFPG) was challenging using the B-727's old navigation technology, especially when the French controllers spoke English to us but spoke French to the French pilots. Instead of always saying "Bonjour," sometimes I would just say "Bon Jovi" (you know the guy who wrote the song, "You Give Love a Bad Name").

Flying into Guadalajara (GDL-MMGL) and Toluca, Mexico (TLC-MMTO) could be challenging at times; you had to tell the controllers what you wanted to do and not ask them what you wanted to do; the language confusion could result in a clearance to fly into a mountain. *We make our money above planet Earth and it is serious business.*

Pilots beware!

Thinking about the serious business of flying a big jet, I wrote the poem "Half Awake or Half Asleep."

Half Awake or Half Asleep

Are you half awake?
No, I feel half asleep.
I love it when I'm half awake,
I kick the autopilot off for flight's sake.
I can smoothly pitch and bank,
I aviate like the number one rank.
All radio transmissions and receptions I can make,
Executing all motor and decision skills without one mistake.
Watch me, watch me, I bet you a steak,
I am the best pilot, and a smooth landing I can make.
I wish I could always live and fly half awake.
Flying in daytime when half awake is a piece of cake.

I can be dangerous when I'm half asleep,
My performance is not the best when I cannot leap.
I may be off by ten degrees, ten knots, or a hundred feet,
Deviating from standards with a lack of enthusiasm to meet.
I may just turn the autopilot on at 500 feet,
And off after the airplane and runway meet.
Candy, soda or coffee, whatever it takes to not count sheep,
I must successfully fly the plane and my job I must keep.
I don't enjoy flying above the ground much when I'm half asleep,
But half asleep is better than being underground six-feet deep.

Coffee

Pilots beware! *Candy, soda or coffee, whatever it takes to not count sheep* or whatever it takes to stay awake. Coffee. Ah the smell of roasting coffee beans. Whether those beans come from Arabica, Excelsa, Liberica, or Robusta plants, it all smells wonderful to me. Sometimes just the enticing aroma awakens me and brightens my day.

Ah, the taste of fresh coffee. To sit in French Café in Paris and sip of French roast coffee or stand in an Italian bar in Milan and sip an Italian espresso coffee with Sambuca is one of my favorite pastimes. I love the taste of coffee. I drink coffee for comfort, social and health benefits, and for the energy boost. The caffeine from coffee increases adrenaline in the body and gives me a boost. The caffeine manipulates my dopamine production and makes me feel good. Drinking coffee creates a pleasurable, enjoyable experience for me. However, as an airline pilot, at times I have to use coffee as a work tool.

As an airline pilot, I cannot always drink coffee whenever I want for pleasure. The caffeine in coffee is a useful tool for pilots. Pilots have to manage their energy level while flying planes. There are numerous times I would prefer having a cup of coffee midway through a flight with my crew meal. However, I need to postpone the consumption of that coffee to a more appropriate time that will be most beneficial to my body's performance.

Sometimes, I will drink coffee prior to takeoff, especially during a demanding takeoff like the standard instrument departure from Paris Charles-De-Gaulle airport (LFPG). Most of the time I use the coffee tool just prior to top-of-descent. The positive effects from the caffeine of coffee helps the human body and all the senses stay alert. The maximum caffeine benefit kicks in about 20 minutes after consumption. From an altitude of 35,000 feet, pilots usually start their descent around 25 minutes prior to estimated touchdown. The use of this tool is more common to me for challenging approaches and landings, especially difficult ones like the Hong Kong checkerboard approach (VHHH) or the Bogota, Columbia (SKBO) landing.

There's a Catch-22 to drinking coffee prior to the approach to landing. The dilemma is to drink enough coffee caffeine to keep alert to execute a challenging approach and landing, but not drink so much that will prevent falling asleep at the layover hotel. Consuming too much caffeine will disrupt the body's pattern of sleep. This is the balancing act that pilots must play; be awake for the landing yet stay tired enough to go to sleep afterward.

Allow me to digress for a moment with this funny coffee story that did not turn out so funny. During the first year of our second son's life, I was flying the same trip—leave Norfolk airport (KORF) around 9:00 p.m., fly to Richmond airport (KRIC) and then on to Newark airport (KEWR). Spend a few hours in Newark airport, fly to Richmond and then on to Norfolk, arriving at around 6:00 a.m. The scheduled crew rest was in a Norfolk hotel, which I did in our home in Virginia Beach. Between night flying during my workdays and night baby feeding during my off days, I became addicted to caffeine. The nightly cup of coffee in Newark started the addiction. At home, I started making espresso with a 3-Cup Stovetop Moka pot that I had received as a holiday gift from my sister. There was no need for me to read directions. All I had to do was put the coffee bean grains into the pot, brew and drink. After several weeks I would brew two pots during the day and have two coffees in Newark at night.

Through a casual conversation with my sister, I relayed, "I feel jittery, shaky and tired. I think it is from that espresso maker you gave me."

She asked, "How are you making the coffee?"

"I just put the coffee bean grains into the pot, brew and drink."

Dumbfounded, she remarked, "You drink the whole cup?"

Nonchalantly, I admitted, "Of course, sometimes I drink two cups."

My sister shockingly responded, "One cup makes three espresso servings."

Apparently, a 3-cup Moka pot makes over 6 ounces of espresso coffee, which is equivalent to three 2-ounce espresso shots of approximately 105 mg of caffeine per shot. Little did I know, until I did the math, I was consuming over 315 mg of caffeine per day and sometimes over 630. After some research, I discovered that the American soldiers stationed in Italy during WWII would dilute a shot of espresso with hot water to emulate the American cup of coffee they were familiar with. This is known today as an "Americano" coffee. My conception of a cup of coffee is three times stronger than the "Americano."

The coffee caffeine addiction cycle suckered me within its detrimental spell. The increased caffeine consumption was affecting my sleep. I was able to fall asleep, but I was missing the benefits of deep sleep. That sleep deficit started building up fast. The next day after a sleep cycle, I felt worse, so I would consume caffeine as soon as I got get out of bed to feel better. Sleeplessness wasn't my only developing problem, either. I had become restless, anxious, jumpy, and irritable. I would consume two cups, or the equivalent of six shots of espresso. This cycle was continuing day after day. When I attempted to stop trying to take caffeine, I would get tired, depressed and get splitting headaches as blood vessels in my brain dilated. These negative effects forced me to run back to caffeine, even when I wanted to stop.

It took several weeks of motivated discipline to wean myself off coffee. My caffeine withdrawal symptoms lasted several days after that last cup of coffee. The lesson I learned is that I had to manage my coffee consumption like I manage a work tool.

After that health scare, I made changes. Now, on days off from work I sometimes restrict the quantity. If I drink a cup of coffee every day, my body will build up a tolerance and I may eventually require up to six cups of regular coffee a day to obtain the benefit of the caffeine needed for flight operations. By restricting my daily use to two cups a day, or fewer, during my days off, I am able to extract the maximum benefits of one cup of coffee prior to my takeoff or approach landing. The other change I made is that, in my flight bag, I carry healthy snacks like nuts and raisins, dark chocolate and oatmeal. After a long flight, at the top of the descent, I would often choose to eat half a bar of dark chocolate instead of drinking a cup of coffee for a boost for the approach and landing phase.

The Gouge. Pilots beware! The use of caffeine must be managed appropriately whether it is in the form of coffee, tea, soda or candy.

A Quick Lesson in Flight

What makes planes fly? Before we take my last trip in the B-727 as a first officer, allow me to summarize. If you hum a song during this section, try "Under Pressure," the classic rock song by David Bowie and Queen.

Inventors Hon von Ohain of Germany in 1939, and Frank Whittle of Great Britain in 1941, built the first jet engines. The simplest gas turbine engine for aircraft was the turbo jet. A turbo jet engine is like a horizontal container—a can. The can is open at both ends and includes several sections inside. Air is sucked in through the intake and compressed. Then, the air is heated and burned with fuel in the combustion chamber. The air moves through the turbine rotor, developing power to operate the compressor, and then the air exits through the engine tailpipe to create propulsion. The difference between the inlet pressure and the exit pressure is the thrust force that moves (pushes) the engine and the aircraft to which it is attached.

Yes—pressure. It's the pressure differential of the engine that makes a plane move forward.

Newton's First Law of Motion: "A body at rest remains at rest unless it is acted upon by an outside force."

Newton's Second Law: "A change in motion is proportional to the force applied."

$F=Ma$.

Force = Mass (wt.) x Acceleration.

However, thrust alone from a turbo jet won't get you to cruising altitude of 35,000 feet.

If the captain of the jet aircraft pushes the thrust levers full forward to obtain maximum thrust (and did nothing else), the jet would just race down the runway and run off the end.

What else does the pilot need? Do you hear a song playing?

Pressure.

You need airfoil pressure to give the plane lift.

The basic description of what makes a jet, or any airplane fly, is the pressure differential between the upper surface of an airfoil wing and the lower surface.

An aircraft's wing is flat on the lower surface and curved on the upper. Air moving across the top of the wing takes longer to travel from leading edge to the back of the wing than the air that is moving underneath the wing. Bernoulli's Theorem states that "the sum of the pressure energy and potential energy and kinetic energy is constant through a tube." If velocity decreases, then the pressure must increase. This pressure differential between the lower part and the upper part of the wing is called Lift Force. Lift pushes the wing, which is attached to the jet, upward.

There are four forces involved—lift force, gravity force, drag force and thrust force. But it all comes down, basically, to pressure. It is engine pressure differential and wing pressure differential that move the jet from Point A to Point B. While the jet is accelerating down the runway, the captain pulls the aircraft's flight control yoke (at the appropriate moment) to change the wing surface to create the correct-wing pressure differential and lift the jet into the air.

Obviously, there are a lot more complicated things going on in a jet, but that is the basics—pressure.

And sometimes pilot pressure. There is an increase of pilot pressure and stress during company-union contract negotiations. Anger and animosity have erupted between the company and its pilots during over-extended union work-rule negotiations.

Pilot Union

Why do you need a union anyway? If a company takes care of its *people*—the workers—and the workers provide a good *product* or *service*, then the company will make a good *profit*, and everyone will be happy—right?

Well, it is the inherent nature of most companies to squeeze more hours out of its employees and to try and get them to do the work for less pay. The owners and stockholders want to make more money so they can buy bigger yachts than the next guys. The more money and power they get, the happier they will be—right?

This is not personal between us and them; it is just business. In "pursuit of happiness" and seeking shorter hours and higher pay, printers were the first to go on strike in New York in 1794. Cabinetmakers struck in 1796, carpenters in Philadelphia in 1797, and shoemakers in 1799.[35]

In the early years of the 19th century, efforts by unions to improve working conditions and pay through negotiations or strikes became more frequent. By the 1820s, various unions were formed in an effort to reduce the working day from 12 to 10 hours. Unions popped up all over—the National Labor Union in 1866; the Knights of Labor in 1869; the American Federation of Labor in (AFL) in 1886; and the Committee for Industrial Organization (CIO) in 1935. The AFL and CIO merged in 1955.[36]

The Airline Pilots Association Union (ALPA) was formed in 1931.

As a major cargo and package delivery business, FedEx placed a priority on customer service. The company established a People-Service-Profit (PSP) philosophy. However, taking care of the people was not working for the pilots. The profits were piling up, but the pilots felt left out.

Since FedEx started in 1972, and over the course of 26 years, FedEx had increased pilot working hours, working duty, days of work and pilot medical costs. At the same time, it had eliminated profit-sharing plans, refused pay increases, shifted FedEx cargo and FedEx pilot flight time to other air carriers and feeder aircraft, fired pilots, and reneged on many promises.

Pilots cannot legally negotiate without representation (a union), and therefore, what you get is what the company wants to give you, and that can and did change any time at the whim of the company. There were times when the pilot crew force united and obtained increases to their employment package or decreased the degradation process, but it wasn't until 1999 with the FedEx Pilots Association Union and over 90% of pilot unity did the FedEx pilots get a legal contract, including significant increases to their employment packages.

Obtaining the first pilot contract was not easy, and to get it, pilot unity was paramount. In February of 1999, 87% of the voting FedEx pilots ratified the first pilot contract at FedEx. This was a five-year contract and the first contract obtained by the FedEx pilots in FedEx's 25-year history. This wasn't the best contract, but it was a legal contract and a good start. How did the pilots finally get a contract? First, and most importantly, it took pilot unity of more than 90% of membership.[37] It was good business for FedEx to sign the contract with the pilots. As Michael Corleone tells Sonny, "It's not personal; it's strictly business" (*The Godfather*).

On October 17, 2006, the pilots voted to ratify the new four-year contract. This was the second pilot contract acquired by the pilots with FedEx. A third pilot contract was ratified October 20, 2015 and today they are working on a fourth contract.

The Gouge. Do not let non-flight stress, like contract negotiations, enter the cockpit. Pilots must learn to compartmentalize, keeping non-flight issues separate from flying issues while flying the jet. Leave all other non-flight issues on the ground or at home.

Is it fair for the airline company to require a pilot to fly eight hours per day, six days per week? Probably not. Is it fair for an airline pilot to only fly three takeoffs and three landings every 90 days? Probably not. With a union representing a pilot group, a middle-ground can be negotiated. The new negotiated contract will define new responsibilities and authorities of the company and the pilot. For instance, the pilot contract with the company defines the pilot's responsibilities and authorities on travel to and from work.

The B-727 flight schedules enabled me to travel to many interesting places and meet many interesting people. On my last B-727 trip to Europe as first officer, I spent the day in Rome before heading to Basil, Switzerland, where my trip would begin. On the Rome stopover, I saw Pope John Paul II for my second and third time. The second time, while in St. Peter's Basilica, at a distance of six feet, stood the Pope. With that holy-ghostly look, white face and white-gray hair, the Pope looked into my eyes and blessed me. His gaze was so powerful it felt as if he were looking into my soul. The Pope's brief, spiritual stare, froze me into a standstill that seemed to last forever, although the encounter lasted only a few moments—*I'll never forget and always remember.* To date, this is one of the top ten experiences of my life.

For a precious moment in time, I stood face to face, heart to heart and soul to soul with the holiest person on planet Earth. Without one word spoken between the Pope and me, I felt the immediate formation of an obedient bond between me and God. Guilt of sins and wrongdoings evaporated from me as I transformed into a person who only wanted to love; love God, love myself and love everyone. There was this newly acquired self-belief that I would never sin or do harm to anyone ever again. For the record, like you, I am human and that did not happen. Humans are not perfect. Humans make mistakes.

Later that day, I was present for Pope John Paul's afternoon blessing in Saint Peter's Square. After a day in Rome, I boarded the night train that would take me to Basil, where I would start my eight-day European vacation flight trip. This is just one example of the travel benefits I savored as an international airline pilot.

19

CAPTAIN'S RESPONSIBILITIES

That's why the captain gets paid the big bucks.

The Role of Captain

As a B-727 First Officer pilot, I logged over 2,200 hours of multi-engine jet flight time and made about 900 landings. Although I had achieved command authority as a Captain on the Cessna C-402 airplane at Midnite Express, the Boeing B-727 aircraft was the first jet that I had obtained command authority as a Captain.

On May 28, 1997, I added to my Airline Transport Pilot license the B-727 Aircraft Rating. The Federal Aviation Rules define the responsibility and authority of an airline captain (FAR 91.3 and FAR 121.537).

➢ The pilot in command of an aircraft is directly responsible for, and is the final authority as to, the operation of that aircraft.

➢ In an inflight emergency requiring immediate action, the pilot in command may deviate from any rule of this part to the extent required to meet that emergency.

➢ Each pilot in command who deviates from a rule under paragraph "B" of this section shall, upon the request of the Administrator, send a written report of that deviation to the Administrator.[38]

An airline captain has the ultimate responsibility for the safety of the airplane and the crew. The captain, by authority of the United States Federal Aviation Administration, is the person legally in charge of the aircraft and its flight safety and operation. When the captain signs the

Flight Plan Release, he accepts responsibility for the preflight planning and safe conduct of the flight between the two airports listed on the Flight Plan Release. His signature indicates he is in compliance with Airport Familiarization (FAR 121.443), Special Airports and Area Qualification (FAR 121.697), and Pilot Route Certification (FAR 121.697 a.4).[39]

The Captain is responsible for everything:

The Captain is responsible for ensuring that the aircraft is loaded properly and is capable of taking off from the runway of intent. If there is no computer-generated flight plan release, the Captain is responsible for preparing a manual release. The Captain must be familiar with weather characteristics, navigation facilities, communication procedures, types of terrain and obstruction hazards, minimum safe flight levels, pertinent air traffic control procedures (including terminal area, arrival and departure, holding), all types of instrument approach procedures and the physical layout of the airport in the terminal area, including congested areas and obstructions.

The Captain has to ensure that the flight can be accomplished safely and in compliance with the FARs and any company policies and procedures. The Captain is responsible for immediately notifying the company in the event of any aircraft damage or injury to any person on board.

During the flight, the Captain is in command of the aircraft and crew and is responsible for the safety of all crewmembers, jump seaters, passengers, cargo and the airplane itself.

The Captain is responsible for preflight planning, any delay, and release of the flight. The Captain is responsible for monitoring the accuracy of radio communications, monitoring engine and system operations, alerting the other crewmembers of malfunctions, maintaining adequate watch for traffic and maintaining situational awareness. The Captain is responsible for the proper operation of the flight including compliance with all checklists. The Captain is responsible for the operational security of the aircraft, law enforcement officers (FFDO) on board, cockpit security (in particular, the cockpit door) and document security. The Captain is responsible for inflight security decisions that affect the safety of the aircraft and crew.

If at any time the First Officer screws up, then the Captain must physically take control of the airplane. The Captain is responsible to see that all discrepancies that may affect the air-worthiness of the aircraft are reported to maintenance and recorded in the aircraft maintenance log. The proper exercise of the Captain's authority is the basis for flight deck leadership and is critical to safe, legal, reliable and efficient flight operations. Therefore, my priority is to operate each flight in a safe and legal manner, and my secondary goal is to operate each flight in a reliable and efficient manner.

In order to meet all of these responsibilities, the Captain is permitted to break any rule or regulation to ensure safe flight operations and the safety of all humans on board. However, he may have to justify his actions. Did you watch the movie or read the book on Sully Sullenburger's *Miracle on the Hudson*? Sully lost both of his only two operating engines and decided to land the jet in the Hudson Bay. All lives on board were saved; however, *afterward* Sully the captain questioned himself, "Did I do everything right?" *Afterward,* during the flight emergency investigation, many questioned whether he had other, better choices of where to land. Initially, some investigators indicated that one of the engines were still workable and could have been restarted. The final conclusions were that Sully did make and execute the correct decisions. The movie realistically depicted *the afterward* of flight emergencies or flight abnormalities of my entire pilot career. In this book, Frank the Pilot is providing you with a fascinating view into the mind of an airline pilot. *Afterward,* I will say to myself, *Did I do everything right?* The investigators may say, "Why did you do it that way?" and "You should have done it this way." Remember the C-402 gear up, almost career-ending emergency, discussed earlier in this book? The *afterward* creates enormous stress on the pilot-in-command.

Afterward, the captain may have to justify his actions and decisions; otherwise, the pilot can find himself (or herself) in major trouble with the FAA, which can void the pilot's license. The federal government always has the choice to prosecute the pilot on the following regulation. "*No pilot may operate an aircraft in a careless or reckless manner as to endanger the life or property of another*" (FAR regulation 91.13 and FAR regulation 121.537.f).[40] The interpretation of careless and reckless can be very subjective in the eyes of the federal judges.

Captain Briefings

Most Captains usually take the first leg, meaning the Captain is the flying pilot and the First Officer is the non-flying pilot, to set an example. I take a different approach. I usually give the first leg away to the First Officer unless I am required for weather reasons to fly the first leg. I do this for two reasons. One, because 75% of all accidents happen on the first day of two crewmembers flying together for the first time, with the Captain being the flying pilot on the first leg. By giving this first leg to the First Officer where he's the flying pilot, it breaks the chain in that statistic. The second reason is that I want to see, on the first leg, "What do I have?" By that I mean, what is the caliber of my First Officer? Is he a really good pilot, is he an average pilot, or is he a substandard pilot whom I have to keep an extra-close eye on?

This may seem like overkill, but here is an example of a full brief I would give to my First Officer before we start the jet engines.

"Hi, 'Super John Doe' co-pilot, I am Frank Donohue, your Captain."

Security Brief: "Do you have your pilot's license, medical certificate, passport and visa? Are you a federal flight deck officer (FFDO)?"

If he is an FFDO:

"Your mission is to protect the flight deck from any specific threats. I will continue to command the aircraft." The rest of this briefing is detailed, extensive and confidential.

Then, I will discuss the departure and arrival security threats of the day: terrorist threats, special terrain, minimum equipment list items, configuration deviation list items, weather, fatigue, stresses, any abnormalities for the flight, etc. If there are any passengers jump-seating or air cargo attendants, "give them a full briefing using the appropriate briefing card." Even though the Captain is responsible for the passenger jump-seat brief, the captain can delegate this task to the First Officer.

Weather Brief: this covers if the weather is good enough to take off in. Using information received from the airport's Automatic Terminal Information service, the Captain will have a discussion (called the ATIS brief) on the winds, visibility, cloud ceiling, temperature, dew point, barometric altimeter setting, the runway in use and the possible use of engine and wing anti-ice for takeoff. Will we need to spray the aircraft with de-icing and anti-ice fluid before takeoff? Is there snow on the taxiways and runways? Is there a possibility of wind shear? Are there any other special items for consideration? What are the takeoff and landing runways? If we take off and have an emergency, can we come back and land, or do we have to go to another airport?

Departure Brief: How will we depart from the airport? What direction and altitude will we fly and when will we turn and climb? Each airport issues specific instructions through a Pre-Departure Clearance to flight crews on detailing how to depart that airport. I will say things like this to the First Officer: "Let's discuss the Pre-Departure Clearance (the PDC brief) and perform a route check to make sure that the route loaded in the flight management system (FMS) is the same route we have been cleared to fly on the PDC. We are flight number 1409, aircraft number 749, cleared on XYZ route, and will use transponder squawk code 954."

Flight Operations Manual Brief (the FOM Brief): Airline companies have a Flight Operations Manual for their specific air operation that list specific operating policies and procedures for their airline and their flight crews.

For the FOM Brief, I will say: "We will operate using standard flight operating procedures. You (or I) will fly the first leg. We will take off from runway 36."

I will brief noteworthy items on the airport facilities diagram, the airport operations diagram, and the airport parking diagram.

Takeoff Brief: If I am flying the first leg, then I will do the Takeoff Brief:

- The terrain function selected for takeoff to avoid local mountains or buildings; or the radar function selected for takeoff to avoid thunderstorm weather.
- The takeoff constraints that we have to comply with for the takeoff, such as what airspeed, heading, and altitude we will fly and when.
- Whether we will take off in heading mode or flight management system navigation mode.
- What specific engines are on the jet, the start-up time limitations and the warm-up time limitations. (In very cold weather, you may need longer engine warm-up times.)

> If we will take off using maximum engine takeoff thrust, or a degraded, reduced engine takeoff thrust. (A degraded takeoff thrust puts less stress on the engine components, therefore reducing the chance of an engine failure on takeoff and helping prolong the useful life of the engines.)

> The navigation and communication equipment and frequencies we need for this takeoff. I will brief in the event of an emergency, like an engine fire or failure, what altitude and heading we will fly, and which runway we plan to land on.

"At the minimum, in an emergency, we want to do the emergency checklist items, get the landing gear down, and land. Safety and legality are mandatory; our goal is also to be reliable and efficient, but it's optional. Any questions? Let's execute good crew resource management (CRM) and do the Before-Start checklist."

Debriefing

It's ironic, but the debriefing after the flight is complete is usually much shorter than the pre-briefing. Debriefing: "Did we operate safely and legally? Do you have any questions? What do you think we did right or wrong and how could we have done it better? Were there opportunities for improvement such as being more reliable and more efficient?"

The Gouge. First officers think like a captain because one day they will be a captain. Learn something on every flight from each captain. Captains customize your briefings and have a short backup phrase to cover everything. My short backup statement is: "*At the minimum, in an emergency, we want to do the emergency checklist items, get the landing gear down, and land. Safety and legality are mandatory; our goal is also to be reliable and efficient, but it's optional.*" At the minimum, in an emergency, do the emergency checklist items, get the landing gear down, and land. First and always, of the highest priority be safe. Second, if possible, be legal. Other optional and secondary goals are to be reliable and efficient.

Severe Turbulence

On a trip from Norfolk to Indianapolis, I encountered severe turbulence that resulted in a landing gear problem.

Throughout this book, I want you to learn about various weather phenomena in our atmosphere that affect pilots commanding planes and affects you as flying passengers sitting in the back. During the first missed approach in the C-402 in Atlanta, you read about fog. During the hailstorm pounding on the EMB 110, you read about thunderstorms. Turbulence can affect your ride in the back and affect the level of controllability pilots may have on the plane.

Turbulence is non-smooth air, air that is irregular with rapid changes in direction and strength. Turbulence causes the aircraft to bounce around: yawing, pitching, and or rolling. There is wake turbulence encountered when the plane is following or crossing behind another airplane. This is more common when a small plane is landing or taking off behind a large plane. There is mechanical turbulence encountered when there is friction between air and the ground's irregular terrain or man-made obstacles. There is thermal turbulence encountered when there is unequal heating or cooling of air masses. There is frontal turbulence encountered when warm/cold fronts collide with cold/warm fronts. There is wind shear turbulence with a story on that later. There is clear air turbulence (CAT).

CAT is severe turbulence that occurs at altitudes of 18,000 feet or higher, either in cloud-free conditions or within clouds. Previously, this unknown turbulent phenomenon was later labeled CAT because initial encounters by pilots occurred in areas of the atmosphere that was clear of clouds without any warning to pilots. CAT is one of the most unpredictable of all weather phenomena that are of significance to pilots and to you, the passenger.

The level of intensity of turbulence is classified as light, moderate, severe or extreme. In extreme turbulence, the airplane is violently tossed about and practically impossible to control. Extreme turbulence may cause structural damage. Unrestrained crew and passengers are especially vulnerable to getting hurt. Flight crew and passengers should fasten their seat belts at all practicable times because some turbulence can be extreme and unpredictable like CAT.

It was a beautiful, clear, calm night; there wasn't a cloud in the sky. At times, flying can be very easy to do and very pleasant, like taking a walk in the park. It was five minutes before top of descent with no perceived dangers or threats detected. Then wham! CAT violently attacked us! One of the most unpredictable of all weather phenomena, clear air turbulence had overpowered my jet and my ability to fully command her. Like a homerun baseball bat connecting with a toy model plane, we were slammed. Our plane was tossed and half rolled. The autopilot kicked off. "*I have the jet,*" I said as I clutched the yoke with two hands and I tried to control the pitching, banking and rolling of the jet. Yank and bank!

Before the invention of iPads, most pilots, like me, would carry a Jeppesen notebook with personally custom secret pilot stuff. In my book I had pictures of my sons and a picture of the USA airport weather reporting map, the B-727 limitations and emergency procedures, the weather minimums for landing and takeoffs, weather acronym definitions, pilot work-hour duty limits, notes on certain airports and a bunch of other pilot stuff to help me perform the best at my job. This book was about 6 x 9 x 1/2 inches and weighed about half a pound.

My Jepp book, which had been sitting comfortably on the top of the cockpit dashboard, rose like a ghost and stayed suspended in midair for several seconds. Just an arm's length away, I captured my Jepp book floating before my eyes. I thought and felt, *OMG, are the wings going to crack and fall off?* It is highly unlikely that the wings would break off, but my brain briefly conjured up these images. There was not much available time to see and feel these brief flashes of dangerous events; I had to command my ship to survive.

ANC, aviate—I had to fly the jet; navigate—I knew we were 120 miles southeast of Indy heading toward Indy; communicate—I needed to tell ATC my intentions. My right hand transferred to the thrust levers in order to slow the jet down to the B-727 turbulent maneuverable airspeed. I commanded to the first officer, "Tell ATC we are in extreme severe turbulence and want to start down now."

I chose to fly the maneuvering speed because it is the maximum speed at which a pilot can make full or abrupt movements of the flight controls without causing structural failure of the jet. This speed provides certain stall and limit load factor protection.

We started a steep descent. The jet descended very fast and within a few moments, we were 10,000 feet lower and the severe clear air turbulence subsided.

The first officer, second officer and I had thankfully expressed our thoughts, emotions and feelings. We exchanged all the "I can't believe" and "I thought" such and such was going to happen. Eventually, we settled with the jet and everything about us and with us seemed normal again. That feeling re-emerged within me, I felt like a cool, big-time pilot with a massive ego once again.

As we approached the Indie airport environment, all was great, and all was smooth, we were back to flying being as easy and pleasant as walking in the park. One emergency during one flight was usually enough for a pilot, but not tonight. As we nonchalantly descended on final approach, I requested, "Gear down before landing checklist." Joe put the gear lever down, and the gear unsafe warning light illuminated.

Landing gear problem—Déjà vu! Remember the C-402 gear-up, almost career-ending, emergency landing in Mobile, Alabama? The B-727 is much bigger than a C-402, and the B-727 has more metal and more fuel onboard. This could end in a catastrophe. That feeling left me in a flash; I no longer felt like a cool, big-time pilot with a massive ego.

Unlike the emergency in the Cessna C-402 in Mobile, Alabama, I was not alone. I had two other pilots with me, to help me during this potentially severe landing gear emergency. However, I was still the captain, the pilot-in-command, and I had to make some decisions. The first command I made was to execute the go-around maneuver. Then, I explained to the ATC our situation and our intentions. Taking into account my prior landing gear malfunction experience, I requested a flyby in front of the ATC tower. I wanted ATC to view the position of the landing gear. We executed the "gear unsafe warning indicator light" checklist and aviated the plane for a flyby in front of the tower. This time, unlike in Mobile, the tower stated that in their opinion all landing gears seemed to be down in their normal landing positions. We flew the jet back around the pattern to make our final landing.

After all checklist has been completed, I said "Gear down before landing checklist." I discussed with the other two pilots that I will attempt to make a very smooth landing and gently lower the nose gear onto the runway payment. If it seemed to us that one of the landing gears was not down and locked, then we can execute a go-around again. We had enough fuel to go back up in the air and rethink a new strategy if in fact one of the landing gears was not locked down.

50 feet, 40, 30, 20, 10 … the main landing wheels embraced the runway ever so gently, like holding a newborn baby. I eased the nose to make contact with the runway concrete. The weight of the jet against the runway stood at the proper height. All three landing gears were in the down-and-locked position and we landed safely. The first officer said, "Whew! You handled that perfectly, Frank." The second officer said, "Nice job! Thank God we're safe on the ground!" My pride and self-esteem did not need those compliments, but it is still feels good when one, or in this case two, of your pilot peers acknowledge a job well done. Those words from my flight crew made me feel like a cool, big-time pilot with a massive ego, once again.

The severe turbulence that slammed us earlier had jolted some microswitches and indicators of the landing gear system of our precious jet. We were all thankful that it was just a bad light indicator and not an actual unsafe gear extension emergency. For the second time within an hour, we exchanged our thankful feelings, thoughts and emotions. We were doubly thankful that we had arrived on planet Earth safely.

The Gouge. Flight crew and passengers should fasten their seat belts at all practicable times in flight because some turbulence can be extreme and unpredictable like CAT. Encountering severe turbulence without a fastened seat belt could cause bodily harm and possible death to people onboard planes. Wear your seat belt!

20

PILOT'S LIFE AND KEEPING THEIR JOBS

Keeping is harder than getting.

It's easier to get it than to keep it. Airline pilots spend more time keeping their jobs, than obtaining their jobs. Becoming a pilot involves arduous training, dedication and years of building flight experience. Once a pilot is working for an airline, their time is consumed with keeping that pilot job. It may take years to secure that highly regarded airline pilot position, but it will take the remainder of your flight career to keep that job. Keeping is more challenging than getting.

Airline Pilot's Life

After six years of hard work, I finally made it. I secured that airline pilot job. Now I had to keep it. Commanding and controlling a powerful transport machine, like a jet, gives the pilot an overwhelming feeling of self-accomplishment. When piloting a jet airplane at 35,000 feet above planet Earth, you acquire a different perspective; planet Earth looks smaller when you're looking down at it from seven miles above it. I have traveled to over 50 international cities and most American cities. I have flown around the world eastbound and around the world westbound. I have flown from Tokyo to Anchorage, and while flying through 13 time zones I have seen Mother Nature's beautiful sunrise and sunset during the same flight.

The office view from 35,000 feet is the best in the world, and every day it's different. I have viewed amazing sights through the cockpit windows. I have seen the Aurora Borealis, shooting stars, meteor showers, comets, beautiful and ferocious thunderstorms, volcanoes, every cloud type, every precipitation type, and all forms of terrain: sea, land, mountains, valleys, deserts, lakes, cities, farms and several wonders of the world.

I have flown from Anchorage over the North Pole to London and have observed the optical illusion of the Sun moving around planet Earth and depicting noon at various points around our planet. Through my extensive travels, numerous times, I have been wowed by this wonderful planet Earth, so full of energy and awe.

Over my 30-year career as an airline pilot, I've met thousands of other wonderful people throughout my travels. I have flown with over one thousand pilots, many of whom may differ from me in ethnicity, religion, social class, social groups, culture, cuisine preference, social habits, musical taste and values. Topography and manmade structures change throughout this planet Earth, but people are generally the same worldwide. Physically, humans may appear very different from the outside, but 99.9% of our DNA is identical. We are beautiful, complex, wonderfully made humans.

There is a strong pilot camaraderie that develops during those flight experiences and times spent together during layovers. Personally, what I enjoy most is aviating with professional pilots from very diverse backgrounds from all over the USA. Often, I would meet the other pilot for the preflight crew brief, a man or a woman from any background from anywhere in the USA, and one hour later, we were safely operating the jet as a team from departure airport to destination airport. Sometimes, we fly together as a flight crew for the first time on an eight-hour flight across the ocean to a foreign country, and the crew will be together for a 10-day trip. Meet a co-worker for the first time and work together for a day or 10 days—I am unaware of any other profession on planet Earth that operates like this.

There is nothing better than getting paid to do what you love! And captains get paid well, allowing you to live a good life. Pilots receive health, life, vision and dental insurance, a retirement plan, paid vacation, travel benefits and a uniform allowance. Airline pilots get a lot of time off, usually at least 12 days per month. Pilots travel a lot, and pilots can fly overseas to experience other cultures. However, there are responsibilities that come with all those rights and benefits.

A pilot's contract is negotiated between the pilot group and the airline company with which a pilot must comply. The pilot's contract contains written legal language that spells out pilot pay provisions, travel expenses, relocation expenses, vacation, training, hours of service, seniority, scheduling, crew rest, retirement and so forth. As an airline pilot, I was a member of the Air Line Pilots Association. ALPA, with over 60,000 members, was begun in the 1930s to protect the safety interests of airline pilots and passengers in the USA and around the world. ALPA has a Code of Ethics that pilots live by, addressing our duty, responsibilities, conduct of affairs, our professionalism and passengers' safety. The pilot contract spells out the rules on seniority. A pilot's seniority number is the most important number of the pilot's life and career.

Seniority

When hired at a major airline, the new pilot is assigned a *seniority number*. In my class of 24 new-hire pilots, the oldest person in the class was assigned the next pilot seniority number. Then, in descending order, the youngest person was assigned the last pilot seniority number. Every year, the seniority list is adjusted to account for pilots who are newly hired, retired or deceased. This results in active pilots acquiring a new, lower seniority number every year, thereby increasing a pilot's overall seniority. *Your seniority number is the most important number in airline life* because bidding on flight schedules, aircraft equipment, domiciles, training dates and vacation days is based solely on seniority. Seniority number 1 gets first choice. Seniority number 5,024 gets whatever is left over.

If you're going to make a mistake bidding, then make the mistake early in your airline career, so that you won't make the same mistake twice. Early in my airline career, I mistakenly bid (in pilot language, "I failed bidding") and was awarded a McDonnell Douglas DC-8 pilot position. This was a huge mistake because at the time I had a pilot position on the Boeing B-747. The result was that I had actually downgraded myself from a bigger jumbo jet plane to a smaller jet plane without upgrading my pilot position. This mistake resulted in me going to DC-8 training and operating the DC-8 for several months. I love to learn, but I hate being tested. After just getting comfortable with the B-747, I had to go to Los Angeles and learn a new jet. My life was deconstructed for approximately six months—two months of training and four months of operating the DC-8. As soon as a new bid was posted for the B-747, I quickly bid off the DC-8 and back on to the B-747.

The Gouge. Learn the rules of your work life. It's okay to make a mistake, especially early in your career, but learn from that mistake and don't make that same mistake again. One can usually recover from a mistake early in their career, but a mistake in the later stages of a career may be unrecoverable.

Work Schedule

Pilots have variable work schedules, with varied work days followed by varied days off, which may include vacation and or training days. Airline pilots may fly up to an average of 80 hours per month and work twice as many hours performing other pilot duties.

Here is an example of a typical pilot schedule. It starts with the arrival of the monthly bid pack schedule. A pilot, according to his seniority, will bid (designate first through last choice) the flight schedules he wishes to fly the following month. Pilots bid preferences vary for multiple reasons, including days off, city layovers, easy versus hard trips (physically), number of flight legs and layover cities, vacation days and training days. During the later years of my career, I preferred to fly north to Canada during the summer months and fly south to Puerto Ricco or Panama during the winter months. Most commuter pilots prefer a one departure 12-day trip, like the trips I bid on the B-747 in my earlier years, or two 5-day trips with 9 days off in between, like the trips I bid on the B-727 and AB-300 during most of my flight career. The most popular domestic passenger flight schedule is 3 days on, 4 days off (senior pilots get weekends off, junior pilots work weekends). For pilots who live within driving distance of their pilot base (the place where trips start and terminate), they may fly any of the above combinations or one- or two-days trips here and there. As a wide-body captain, during the later years of my career I bid the easy-on-the-body trips: day flights less than 90 minutes flying north in the summer and south in the winter.

Then there are pilots on reserve trips, for which a pilot is compensated whether he flies or not. It is almost like paid time off, but the phone can ring at any moment, and the pilot must be prepared to fly with an hour's notice. These reserve trips usually vary from one to six days in length. A reserve pilot usually flies a trip to cover for another pilot for a variety of reasons, like a last-minute sick call or weather-related duty time limits.

After the pilot obtains his bid award, spelling out his flight schedule for the month, the pilot may be able to adjust that schedule by trading trips, dropping trips, swapping trips or picking up additional flight trips. The commuting pilot will arrange or book jump seats or purchase dead-head commercial flights to commute to work according to the new monthly schedule.

For over 20 years, I was very fortunate to bid flight schedules that consisted of me flying to and from my hometown airport. For that privilege, I sacrificed flying large jets around the world for flying smaller jets from home. Flying from home for less pay was more than worth the extra precious time I had with my family. Monthly flight schedules change all the time per the needs of the industry, and pilot preferences change all the time for multiple reasons.

How Do Pilots Keep Their Jobs?

American baseball is a bat-and-ball game played between two opposing teams who take turns batting and fielding. While fielding, all nine baseball players play defense together as a single team unit. When at bat, the individual player plays offense solo against the opposing team of nine players. If a batter receives three strikes while at bat, it leads to an "out" and the player is removed from the game. The player is removed from the offensive portion of the game; thus, the phrase "Three strikes and you're out." In the real world, that can mean that a company or an organization has a policy stating that if a person commits three offenses, then that person is punished very severely, even if the initial offenses were not very serious.

How does a pilot keep their job? First of all, the pilot must show up for work. At my company if you're late for work or miss a trip, on the first infraction the pilot will get a letter of reprimand.

Strike one.

If you're late for work the second time, the pilot would be penalized with loss of pay for thirty days.

Strike two.

If this pilot is unfortunate to be late for a flight trip a third time, then that pilot will be terminated.

Strike three.

"Three strikes and you're out!" This three-strike rule extends throughout the pilot's entire career. Three times late for your flight trip show time throughout your entire career and you will be fired. "Three strikes and you're out."

The business model at the cargo-carrying FedEx is different from the business model of the passenger-carrying airlines. The passenger airlines business model works like this: the passenger pays for an airline ticket anywhere from one hour to a year in advance. The customer has paid in advance for transport service from the departure airport to the destination airport with the scheduled times that the customer prefers the airline to abide by. However, there are times when your flight gets postponed or canceled, or the passenger may even be rebooked on another airline. The original ticket price may stay the same or increase, and rarely is the passenger given a full refund. The cargo-business model at my company works like this: the customer requests a package to be shipped from destination to departure, and the customer can choose the level of priority.

For instance, the customer may want their package delivered by 8:30 a.m. the following day, or by 10:30 a.m. the second business day. After the package is delivered, the customer is charged for the service and must pay. If the package is not delivered by the time of the level of service that the customer has requested, with a few exceptions, then that package delivery service is free. Except under a few circumstances, if your package is late, then the customer will not be charged. My company will go through great effort to make sure that your package arrives on time and will not be free. My company positions spare planes and standby pilots throughout the entire transportation system, to recover freight from those flights that cannot deliver the freight for whatever reason (e.g., maintenance issue and crewmember issues are the most common).

There were many times in my career when I have been rerouted to recover freight. For instance, I was on a flight from Norfolk, Virginia (ORF) to Indianapolis, Indiana (IND) and during cruise flight the aircraft dispatcher requested me to land in Richmond, Virginia (RIC) and pick up freight to bring to IND. Maybe the RIC plane broke down, maybe an RIC crewmember had a last-minute emergency or maybe a lot of extra freight showed up at the last minute. For whatever reason, if there was space available on my jet, then I was going land in RIC to put additional freight on and take it to IND.

We do not want your package to arrive late and free. That is why the "Three-strikes and you are out" rule applies throughout the pilot's entire career at my company. Oftentimes, the pilot endures great stress just to get to work on time. So much time, money and effort were invested to accumulate that fantastic airline pilot job, and at times, there is so much effort to keep that job. Imagine the stress on a pilot who could be fired just for being late three times throughout their entire career. Again, we make our money above planet Earth, and it is serious business.

There are different variations of being late. For instance, at a pilot's base like Memphis, the pilot must check in via the company's on-facility computer before show time, which is usually one hour before flight departure. Airlines have many trips in which the company pays the pilot to commute and start their flight trip in a different city or different country. If the pilot did not live at his base, then he could commute from his home airport to the city in which the flight trip starts. Let's say the pilot lives in Virginia Beach, Virginia, the pilot base is Memphis, Tennessee, and the flight trip starts in Paris, France. The pilot is authorized to commute from Virginia Beach to Paris without going to Memphis, which is great for the commuting pilot. However, there are company rules with which the pilot must comply. At my airline, domestically, you have to be within 100 nautical miles of the airport where the flight trip starts eight hours before show time.

Internationally, the pilot must be within 100 miles of the airport 12 hours before show time. So, a prudent pilot will not depend on one airline flight to get him to that airport eight hours or twelve hours before show time. The prudent commuting pilot must have backup flights to get to Paris. For example, if the pilot books a flight on an airline and that flight gets canceled for maintenance, weather, lack of crewmembers or for any other reason, what is the backup flight or flights to get the pilot into position eight hours or twelve hours before show time? After working so hard to achieve that airline pilot position, the pilot does not want to get fired because he was late for a trip three times, especially if he depended on other people to get him to work without a backup plan. Many times, I have positioned myself at my start work airport the night before the show time of the trip.

No Show – Strike One

One summer night, I was flying from ORF to MEM and back to ORF, Monday through Friday. Pilots call this "hub turning"—fly one leg *into* a major hub and fly another leg *out*. Usually, there is a change of jet and crewmembers on the MEM outbound leg. I was operating a work schedule of five trips turning in and out of MEM (my pilot base), and back and forth to ORF (my home base). The trip consisted of a departure from MEM around 4 a.m., fly to ORF, layover for about 14 hours and fly back to MEM arriving around midnight where the trip ended. Four hours later, I would start and operate the same trip: MEM to ORF to MEM. I lived in Virginia Beach, approximately 15 miles from ORF airport, so these trips helped me to spend more precious time with my family, coach 12 years of basketball and soccer, and help with my son's baseball and football teams.

After I arrived in MEM, I would get a sleep room to catch a nap. The goal was to get three hours of sleep, which is two human body sleep cycles, but usually at best I would end up only getting 2 1/2. Humans usually sleep in cycles of 90 minutes. In Memphis, we had 100 small sleep rooms, about 10 x 10 feet, just big enough for a bed, a chair, a small table and a phone connected to a sophisticated wakeup call system. There were two ladies who ran the sleep room operation. A pilot would check in with these ladies, give them their name and a requested wakeup call time. One lady would give the pilot a key to a sleep room, and the other lady would enter the wakeup call time with the room number into the sleep room telephone computer system. The plan was to go to sleep, and a phone call would wake the pilot up, who would then return the key, check in for their trip and go fly.

Each key had a little ring, and attached to the ring was a small round silver metal disk with the room number insignia on the front. On one particular Wednesday at midnight, I checked in for a sleep room and received the key with the number 6 on it. At least I *thought* it was room number 6. The key fit into the door lock keyhole and I turned the doorknob to open. I did not realize that I had not actually unlocked the door. The door was not locked. I opened the door, crawled into bed and entered a really deep, much-needed sleep, like a self-induced comatose sleep.

Let me tell you, when I awoke on my own without a wakeup call, I felt like Superman. I felt well rested with Superman powers and ready to conquer the world. As I was returning my key, one of the ladies said, "Crew scheduling is looking for you, give them a call." I straggled into the huge, almost empty crew trip planning room. The 300-plus pilots had vanished. "Where did they go?" I said to myself. I quick-eyed my watch and was shocked to see the digital numbers displaying 5:36 a.m. I had missed my trip! I was a No-Show! Strike one! The lounge was nearly empty because everyone had already left to go fly. My stress level (the *bad* type of stress) was at its peak.

I called crew scheduling and they demanded, "Where were you?" I explained I was in the sleep room and never received a wakeup call. They said we attempted to call and locate you. We tried room 9, 19 and 29. I defended myself with the, "I was in room 6." With crew scheduling, pilots are normally considered guilty unless overwhelmingly proven innocent with direct, detailed indisputable evidence. I returned to the head honchos running the sleep room operation to have them talk to crew scheduling. One lady claimed I was room 6, and the other lady claimed I was a room 9. Either way, crew scheduling had put me down for No Show. Strike one of my career on account of missing a trip.

Not only did I miss my flight trip, but I would be docked $1/12^{th}$ my monthly salary, which was the value of the trip that I did not fly. Also, I had to go find a hotel and pay for the room. I had to find a place to stay until four o'clock the next morning, when my next trip would start.

Before I left the crew lounge to go to the hotel, I shot off an email to my chief pilot, explaining the circumstances. The next day—or should I say, later that same day—after accumulating more much-needed sleep, I called my chief pilot in Memphis. I was expecting that he would call me in, reprimand me and have me sign a bad "No-Show" letter for my file. I was very fortunate; I had never caused the company any trouble before, and I had never been late or missed a trip before. My chief pilot told me that I would not have to come in to the office, that I would not get a reprimand and that I would not get a bad letter for my file. There is a file on every pilot; some files are thin and some are thick. There was no ill intent on my end, and there was a lot of confusion on the other end as to what room I was actually in.

Depending on which way one looks at that small metal disk with the room number 6 insignia, one could argue that the room is 9, not 6. Why room 6 was not locked prior to my entry was undetermined. The room should have been locked, and if I had had the incorrect key, then I should not have been able to enter that room and fall into a long, deep recuperating sleep. Additionally, it was obvious to my chief pilot that I was in position for my flight trip, only 200 feet from check in, but was unable to check in because I was in a deep sleep and the sophisticated computer wakeup call system did not wake me up.

My stress level subsided, and I was happy that I did not get an official "strike one" with a negative letter. However, I was unhappy that I lost the pay for that trip, I had to pay for a hotel room and I was a No-Show coach for my son's soccer practice that day. The next time I returned to the Memphis sleep room, I noticed that all keys with a number 6 or 9 had a horizontal line added, so no one could confuse them again. Also, I purchased a miniature alarm clock (this was before the smartphone era) as a backup for me to wake up and check in for my trip.

The Gouge. Lesson learned—have a backup. Even though hundreds of pilots before me trusted those sleep-room ladies to wake them up in time to check in for their trips, my trust in them faltered. Now I have a backup with my own miniature alarm clock set five minutes after the scheduled sleep room wakeup call is scheduled.

While working on keeping that pilot job, the Feds are involved too. The pilot must stay legal. There are Federal Aviation Regulations (the FARs) that stipulate such regulations as: the pilot must pass a 1st-class medical exam and a simulated check ride every six months, and pass an inflight check ride every year. Today, the Federal Aviation Administration (FAA) requires nine-month versus six-month simulator check rides at most airlines. Plus, an unannounced FAA or company inflight check ride may occur at any time.

There's also ongoing studying, to prepare for possible emergencies and to learn ever-changing aircraft systems technology. In addition, if a pilot flies too fast or turns to the wrong heading or levels off at the wrong altitude or does anything that is considered careless or reckless by the FAA, then the pilot can be heavily fined or even lose his license and his job. The interpolation of careless and reckless is very subjective in the eyes of the

FAA. As a captain, many times I have said, "*It's on me, it's my ATP; if I get violated, I can lose my license.*" Pilots are the most regulated professionals in the United States. We earn our money above planet Earth, and it is serious business; it is so serious that the Feds regulate us.

Pilots have many responsibilities when we take our customers or packages on that journey with us. One of those responsibilities is our health. Pilots must stay healthy. To ensure airline pilots are in their best shape, to perform at that high level, pilots must pass an FAA flight physical every six months. Eyes, ears, nose and throat are tested, along with the pilot's mental state, and the neurologic and cardiovascular systems. Pilots have to pass a urine test, a cholesterol test, a blood pressure test and obesity test. Pilots must also pass an electrocardiogram (ECG) annually.

Failed Medical Exam

One time during the required medical exam, I was lying on the flight surgeon's bed (a flight surgeon is a pilot's doctor authorized to perform FAA pilot medical exams) with all the ECG wires hooked up, and I experienced a shocker. As the doctor was interpreting the ECG graph exam results, he half shook his head, squeezed his lips together and squinted. *What is wrong with me?* Danced through my head. The unwanted feeling is kind of like going to the auto repair shop and the mechanic saying there is a problem with your engine, you need a new engine and we currently have a special on new engines. However, it is my heart that may have a problem. My stress level shot through the roof as all fears entered my thoughts within seconds. Shortly after, which seemed like an eternity, the medical doctor assured me that the unfavorable reading was probably due to a few wires not making correct contact with my body. He adjusted a few wires, reran the exam which produced a more favorable result, and faxed the results to FAA Oklahoma City headquarters. I gave a sigh of relief as all the stress immediately dissipated.

Weeks later, I received a letter from the FAA stating that my first-class medical certificate will be revoked unless I can provide a new favorable ECG exam within 30 days. A bad feeling rose, and my stress level erupted. With the letter in hand, I expeditiously revisited my flight surgeon. The doctor calmed me with an explanation that my ECG exam was good and the problem was with the fax machine connection with the FAA in Oklahoma City. Apparently, the FAA installed new software and there was a glitch in reading the ECG exams correctly with older FAX machine models. My doctor had just installed a newer model fax machine and re-sent my ECG exam. He assured me that all would be fine. The nearly uncontrollable stress within me subsided.

If you fail the flight physical, you cannot fly jets; if you cannot fly jets, you cannot make money, and that is a very bad thing when you are also responsible for feeding and supporting yourself and your dependents. Have you ever feared losing your job? How would you put food on the table? Are you responsible for feeding hungry mouths in addition to your own? It is not a pleasant feeling.

Also, the federal government has a list of the medications and prescriptions that would disqualify a pilot from flying planes. It is an unreleased list that is summed up in the Code of Federal Regulations. Pilots are prohibited from performing crewmember duties while using any medication that affects their faculties in any way that might impinge on safety. The Federal Aviation Administration must approve all medications for pilots. And if the pilot does not disclose the medication that they are taking, then the pilot has committed a very serious federal crime.

I liked my job; I liked getting paid and I knew the importance of passing that physical. And I couldn't start preparing for that physical or electrocardiogram two days before and be successful. It had to be ongoing. So, for the last 36 years, maintaining good health was a very important goal to keeping my pilot's job and to help me perform at my best, aviating jets. In the process of developing a healthy body and mind, I developed what I call "Ten Healthy Tips." These health tips, published in my second book *Ten Health Tips* helped me keep healthy and pass medical exams throughout my flight career. These tips are not just for pilots. Everyone may benefit. Here are my health tips:

Ten Healthy Tips

I. *Do not smoke or consume illegal drugs or abuse legal drugs.*
II. *Drink at least three glasses of pure water per day.*

III. Eat at least five portions of fruits and/or vegetables per day.
IV. Eat foods from the good list and avoid foods from the bad list.
V. Do not consume foods or drinks that contain man-made sugars or sugar derivatives or caffeine.
VI. Fast on Fridays, or at the minimum, one day per month.
VII. Get a minimum of eight hours of sound quality sleep per night.
VIII. Meditate at least 15 minutes per day.
IX. Exercise a minimum of 20–30 minutes, at least three or four times a week.
X. Do not consume more than two alcoholic drinks per day.

All humans are different, but striving for good health and longevity are desirable goals. Most of us want to feel better and have our bodies and minds at optimum performance. There is no strategy that is suitable for everyone. These tips, or rules if you want to call them that, are my guidelines that have helped me throughout my airline flight career. Remember, I had to pass a flight exam every six months and command a sophisticated powerful wide-body heavy jet airplane.

I share these reflections on a host of health issues in the hope it helps motivate and provide you with a flight plan to improve your health. My thinking is that if just one healthy tip helps just one person in some way, then I am happily rewarded and my lifelong goal to help mankind has been achieved.

The Gouge. Take action now to help improve the physical and mental well-being of the only body you have. Develop your own personalized list of health guidelines to help you stay healthy throughout your lifetime and to help you perform the best at your job.

Pilots must continue to train. Most airlines today have an FAA-approved Advance Qualification Program (AQP) that includes online training and tests. Usually, at least once or twice a year there is online computer training requirements on new systems, new procedures, refresher courses on aviation subject matters, and a lot of other pilot stuff.

This FAA-required training can usually be accessed from any mobile device or computer, without having to travel to the pilot's home-based classroom. These training modules and tests are usually low stress; however, if you do not complete the required training by the due date, then the pilot's status changes to non-qualified, meaning the pilot is not qualified to fly planes on flight trips. If the pilot fails or does not complete the training, then the pilot cannot fly jets; if the pilot cannot fly jets, then the pilot will not get paid, and that is a very bad thing.

The Gouge. Sometimes using two computers simultaneously helps streamline online training. Use one computer to read and answer the questions, and the other computer to research the answers. Does that make sense?

Pilots must take flight tests in a real plane and a simulator plane. Captains have to pass an inflight line check at least once a year that consists of two flight legs. On one flight leg, the captain is the flying pilot, and on the other flight leg, the captain is the non-flying pilot. Usually, the out-of-the-ordinary happens on line-check rides.

These inflight line checks should be considered low stress tests; after all, the pilot is just flying the plane like any other day. However, when someone is looking over your shoulder at every decision and execution the pilot makes throughout the flight, it is unavoidable to block out the stress that grows before and during. The stress causes the pilot to sometimes make mistakes that he would not normally make, if it were not a test check on the pilot's performance. If the pilot fails this flight line check, then the pilot will be grounded and sent back to training, or shall I say, retraining. If the pilot fails the recheck, then the pilot may be demoted or fired, and that is a very bad thing.

The Gouge. Like that private pilot practical exam I took with Jack, try to ignore the check pilot and pretend he is not there.

Pilots must study. Pilots are always studying to prepare for a flight, prepare for possible emergencies, prepare for a simulator check ride, to learn changing jet aircraft systems technology or to learn a new jet airplane. Every six months, federal law requires pilots to take a simulator check ride, although today many airlines have obtained AQP approval from the FAA to do these simulator check rides every nine months. I call this "yank and bank" school because during the simulator check ride, the pilot is manually pitching and turning the plane much more often than during a normal flight trip. During an actual flight, there is far less pitching and turning, and most of those actions are done smoothly with the use of the autopilot.

There is a two-hour oral test followed by a four-hour flight simulator test. The oral test consists of answering numerous questions on jet systems, jet limitations, emergency mandatory memory checklist, federal aviation law, various jet operations and procedures, and many more things related to the safe, legal and efficient operation of the jet airplane.

This simulator flight check ride consists of multiple complicated emergency and abnormal tasks that pilots rarely and hopefully never encounter, but if you should encounter such an emergency, you would be prepared and be able to survive. One example of such an emergency was Sully Sullenberger's miracle on the Hudson. If you fail this flight check ride, you could be out of a job, so there is great pressure to perform to the flight standards as required by federal law.

The preparation for and the actual check ride creates high levels of stress for the pilot test-taker. The pilot must ratchet up their memory brain functions to retrieve knowledge and demonstrate their pilot skills. The pilot spends hours of study time preparing for these check rides. The pilot is tested on normal every day procedures, abnormal procedures and emergency procedures.

For example, occasionally, I, the captain, would be tested on the preflight walk-around procedures of the exterior of the plane. The first officer normally does the preflight walk around, but the captain is responsible for everything and is required to know that task. The walk-around task ensures that all doors are closed, there are no fluid leaks, and the flight controls are clean and unbroken. The pilot checks that the plane and its components are secure, undamaged and unobstructed. Even though this is a normal procedure for the first officer and atypical for the captain, the captain is tested on the procedures. The security of their pilot job is on the line.

The Gouge. Every pilot makes mistakes, sometimes at the very beginning of the check ride. Ignore these mistakes and continue. Don't let a few small mistakes affect your performance so that you create even bigger mistakes. Most check airmen who conduct the test are looking at the big picture of the pilot's performance.

Do not let the check airman rush you. Slow down, and go through the entire checklist. Go slow, be quiet and think. Gather information, assess the situation, prioritize the emergencies and delegate responsibility. Decide when to say, "I have the jet and the radios, you work the checklist." Aviate, navigate, communicate and configurate. During check ride, do the "C"s: the checklist, the required call outs, the status of the circuit breakers, when and how to configurate the jet, what are the conditions of the airport, use crew resource management, clear the electronic computer to reflect the updated status of the airplane, and comply with the airplane reference handbook and minimum equipment list manual. During the check ride certain emergencies require confirmation of one pilot to the other, like pulling the engine fire handle, fire agent switch, fuel lever cutoff, thrust movement and circuit breaker pull/reset. Slow the jet down and use the autopilot as much as possible, but be prepared to hand-fly the jet. If normally you fly the plane at 250 knots to the marker, then during the simulator check ride, slow down and fly 210 knots to the marker.

If an airline pilot upgrades to a captain position or upgrades to another jet airplane, then that pilot will have to go to flight school and train for several months. The pilot must pass a written test or computer online test, at least one oral test, several simulator flight tests and several inflight tests. If you should fail any of these tests, it is possible to lose your job or be demoted. Pilots are the most regulated professionals in the USA, and airline flight standards in the USA are very high.

Pilots must study and prepare for their flight trips. Flying is not like a car, where you can just jump in and drive; pilots must prepare before they fly a plane. If the pilot flies regularly between two domestic cities, like Memphis and Nashville routinely, then there's not much studying to do beforehand. Check the weather, airport NOTAMs, like any possible construction going on at the airport, and the mechanical safety readiness of the jet you're going to fly. However, if a pilot is going to fly to an international airport or a challenging domestic airport, then there is much more to prepare for. One of my trips consisted of commuting to Dublin, Ireland, then from Dublin to Stanstead, England to Paris, France and to Madrid, Spain. Each of those cities and countries have their own flight rules with which pilots must comply.

For instance, in Dublin, there is a special climb departure performance procedure to comply with. At 2,000 feet, the pilot automatically switches communications frequencies to the next ATC controller without be told to do so. (Normally, ATC instructs the pilot when to change communication frequencies and who to converse with.) In Stanstead, using reverse thrusters to help the jet to slow down on the runway after landing is not permitted. Utilizing the Auxiliary Power Unit (APU) is not permitted except in extreme temperatures. The captain self-parks the jet using a sophisticated light guidance system. In Paris, reverse thrusters are permitted upon landing. The pilot must exit the runway after landing expeditiously and then slow the jet to normal taxi speed. Paris has one-way roundabout taxiways. Their arrival procedures are very complicated, requiring the use of three separate arrival diagrams. In Madrid, there are various arrival speed constraints to comply with: 270 knots below flight level 250, 230 kts below flight level 100, 200 kts at 15 miles and 160 kts at 5 miles from the airport. Madrid's airport is so huge, that depending on your parking gate and runway in use, the pilot may need three airport diagrams to taxi around the gigantic 7,500-acre airfield.

These are just a few examples of many differences that each of the international airports and countries has. Pilot beware, you'd better study beforehand to avoid a violation resulting in a fine, or worse, loss of pilot license, or even worse, an accident resulting in jet damage or loss of life.

Pilots have many soft and hard skills. A pilot must wear many hats. A captain must be a lawyer to interpolate and comply with all the FAA flight rules and regulations, an accountant for the paperwork, a weatherman to interpolate the weather, a negotiator to work with the airline dispatcher and mechanic, a mathematician to add the numbers up, a physicist and a scientist. A pilot must have the ability to understand technical information in order to know how their jet works.

A pilot must be social with good communication skills to build teamwork and manage the crew. Sometimes, the captain must be like a parent or a sibling to the first officer, especially when mentoring new first officers. A captain may ask the first officer for input, "What do you think?" But the captain decides and commands, "This is what we are going to do." To many people, the captain is looked upon as a god; the captain knows all, answers all, and can solve all problems. The captain is also responsible for everything.

Stress Management

From getting to work, inflight job performance, passing medical exams, passing pilot check rides and other tests, and abiding by all the federal rules and regulations, pilots are forced to endure very high stress levels at times. Bad weather, jet maintenance issues, abnormal and emergency flight situations as well as many other variables can ramp up a pilot's stress level.

Stress is a very natural, important part of life and is an unavoidable consequence of life. Stress has physical and emotional effects on us, and can create positive or negative feelings. Eustress (good stress) helps keep us alert, motivates us to face challenges and drives us to solve problems. Distress (bad stress), on the other hand, is unpleasant, can seriously impair performance, and can lead to serious physical and mental illness if not controlled. The effects of distress can hinder a pilot from performing at his best and prevent him from passing those required FAA medicals.

It is very important for pilots to manage a healthy stress level. There are many techniques to help maintain a healthy level of stress. For me, my order of priority to manage pilot stress is to: first obtain quality sleep; then eat well-balanced, nutritious meals; then exercise, and finally, prepare for my flight or tests.

The Gouge. Take action now to adopt techniques to help you manage a healthy stress level. Through my years of extensive flight experience, I have learned to continually be grateful for every moment of flying. Commanding airplanes in the atmosphere above planet Earth is precious, valuable and unpredictable. Enjoy every moment of flight because you do not know when your last moment of flying will be.

As you have read before, there may be around 1.1 million doctors and 1.3 million lawyers in the USA, but there are only around 160,000 airline pilots in the USA. We are an elite group of professionals. Our jobs involve serious business. You can't just pull over to a cloud and check the oil. Flying for a living is a cool, elite and a prestigious professional career. Even though becoming a pilot and maintaining pilot status is very hard work, an airline career has been great for me and I recommend it for you. However, this is not to convince you to be a pilot, but rather to help you achieve and maintain your career goals.

The Gouge. Getting there is part of the battle, staying there is most of the battle. Make a flight plan for life—how to acquire that ultimate career position and how to keep the position.

21

FLYING THE BIG METAL

Wind shear can kill you.

As a FedEx B-727 Airline Captain I logged over 4,000 pilot flight hours and made over 1,400 landings. In 2009, I transitioned from the narrow-body Boeing B-727 jet aircraft to the wide-body heavy Air Bus A-300/310 jet aircraft. This new Air Bus airplane rating was added to my

Air Transport Pilot (ATP) license. With the promotion to the Air Bus 300 jet, I had achieved the top of the career ladder in my aviation field—a senior wide-body heavy-jet aircraft major airline captain pilot.

As a senior wide-body A-300 pilot, I flew trips that operated in northern cities in the summer and southern cities in the winter: to Canada in the summer and to Puerto Rico or Panama City in the winter. Occasionally, I flew trips to Europe for what I called mini work vacations. The majority of the time, I flew short, five-day trips with double deadheads like: commute to Milwaukie, Wisconsin (MKE), fly for four days leaving MKE each morning to fly 50 minutes to Indianapolis, Indiana, and return to MKE each evening, and then commute home at the end of the week. A pilot flying two short legs is compensated the same as a pilot flying two long legs (like four hours each way) at my airline. So, it is not fair to judge a pilot's flight experience on just total flight hours without considering total landings. A flight from Memphis, Tennessee to Guangzhou, China yields around 17 hours of flight time with one landing, and the flight from MKE to IND yields around 50 minutes of flight time with one landing. Senior pilots have the privilege to choose to fly the long-haul flights or the short-haul flights.

During the later years of my flight career, I started treating my flight schedules as a marathon race versus the sprint race in the earlier stages. The marathon was my perspective of taking care of the body to finish the race, to finish my flight career with good health.

Over 25 years, something within me had changed. My pilot personality changed from aggressive *"Fast Frank"* (captain on the B-727) to the laid-back, easy-going Frank (captain on the A-300). Very few pilots still called me *"Fast Frank."* With all the increasing oversight on pilots on each flight segment, I had evolved into an easy-going pilot, making conservative, safe pilot decisions, flying by the book and staying out of trouble. This was my effort in an attempt to finish my airline flight career with no major pilot violations. This evolution within me created this statement that I briefed to every first officer before the start of each flight: *"Safety and legality are mandatory, our goal is to be efficient and reliable but it is optional."*

The A-300 is technologically different from the B-727, different like transitioning from driving an old Honda Civic to a new Tesla. The Air

Bus A-300/310 jet is the largest and heaviest airplane I have had the privilege to command. In fact, when an aircraft is capable of takeoff weights of more the 255,000 pounds, then the FAA certifies that aircraft weight class as "heavy." Any aircraft that is classified as a "heavy" must use the word *heavy* when communicating with air traffic control on or near the airports. The use of the word *heavy* alerts pilots and controllers of the additional wake turbulence produced by these larger, heavier airliners. Therefore, I would now have to include "heavy" with my call sign:

"Kennedy departure FedEx 1340 Heavy climbing out of 2,000 feet cleared to 5,000 feet."

Other pilots would say, "He is flying the big metal." The next time you are at a big airport, transporting to or from the runway, view all the various airplane types and sizes. The really big jets are the big metal jets. When inquired what plane he flies, a pilot would say, "He's flying the big metal." The Airbus A-300, which is similar in size to the Boeing B-767, could carry about 275 passengers plus flight attendants and pilots. However, the plane I flew was configured with 22 LD3 containers in both the forward and aft belly cargo holds in order to carry a total payload of over 120,000 pounds of freight. The Airbus A-300 could carry a total of about 275 people (assuming each person weighs 200 pounds and is carrying a 100-pound bag—then that equals a total weight of only 82,500 pounds).

Some of our cargo AB-300 is configured with up to eight passenger jump seats. There were numerous flights where I was flying cargo and passengers on the same flight. Many passenger airlines carry passengers on the main deck, and cargo in the belly of the plane on the same flight. Cargo pilots and passenger pilots both carry passengers and cargo on their jets, it is just that the ratios of cargo to passengers are different.

To command a jet with 275 people on board is a great feat, and so is commanding a jet with 100,000 pounds of cargo freight.

But it's a different, great feat.

The Airbus A-300 had a gross takeoff weight of more than 375,000 pounds, a wingspan of more than 147 feet, a length of more than 177 feet, and a height of more than 54 feet. The Airbus A-300 could fly more than 4,000 nautical miles (4,600 statute miles) at a speed of around 480 knots (550 mph). Our Airbus jets were configured with Pratt

&Whitney's PW400 or JT9 engines or General Electric's CF-6 engines. The CF-6 engines produced 61,500 pounds of thrust per engine. The AB-300 aircraft entered service with Lufthansa Airlines in April 1983.[41] The Airbus A-300 only required two flight crewmembers—a Captain and a First Officer—and I was the Captain.

All aircraft have individual unique flying characteristics, or personalities defined by pilots. While the B-727 was sleek and fast, the A-300 was hulky and slow. The A-300 had a huge mass and when velocity is added, the wide-body jet produced a huge momentum. Technically speaking, momentum equals mass times velocity. The bigger the plane and the faster a plane moves, the more momentum the plane produces. Piloting wide-body heavy jets, the big metal, requires planning and anticipation. From the pilot's view, when the jet was commanded to turn, the cockpit would turn and a few seconds later the rest of the jet would follow.

For instance, the A-300 is so big that the nose wheel gear and main gear are located 13 feet and 47 feet behind the pilot, respectively. Therefore, as the commanding pilot enters a turn, while taxing onto the runway, from the pilot's point of view, he will have to overshoot the runway centerline to compensate for the aft position of the nose gear. The position in the captain's seat must actually pass the runway centerline before the pilot begins to turn, in order to align the jet properly onto the runway centerline.

Originally, our company purchased 25 brand-new Airbuses from the French. The A-300 were new, modern jets, and the B-727 were old, ancient jets. The phase quickly spread among the first previous B-727 pilots who flew these new jets, "It looks nice and smells nice but it flies like a dog." The B-727 is fast, maneuverable and flies like a high-speed go-cart. The A-300 is less maneuverable and flies like a cruise ship. The A-300 is slower than the B-727, hence the phrase, "She flies like a dog," and hence, the new call sign for the A-300 became "Fifi."

Air and space travel changes

One glorious day while I was commanding Fifi with 99,000 pounds of cargo at 33,000 feet, I started to indulge in recollecting enjoyable events of my past flight career. I was reminiscing about the time I watched on television the first space shuttle launch (Columbia STS-1). It was April 12, 1981. I had just completed my third student pilot flight lesson, and I went to the RAF Lakenheath Dorms and turned on the television.

Even though I had memories of the first US landing on the moon, this memory of the first manned space shuttle launch impressed me greatly.

Remember, I decided to be a pilot right then and right there.

When I was a Cessna C-172 Certified Flight Instructor, I had witnessed the Space Shuttle Challenger (STS-51L) blow up while piloting a Cessna C-172 at 4,000 feet—less than 80 miles from the disaster.

When I was a Boeing B-747 Second Officer, Bernadette and I observed the Space Shuttle Discovery (STS-31) launch from our car parked on Highway 95 near Coco Beach, Florida. When I was a Boeing B-727 Captain on a layover in an Orlando, Florida hotel, I watched the night launch of Space Shuttle Discovery (STS-103). Finally, as an Airbus 300 Captain on July 21, 2011, I watched on television the final space shuttle mission STS-135 (Atlantis) land at the NASA's Kennedy Space Center in Florida. Atlantis had completed its final 13-day mission, delivering 8,000 pounds of cargo to the International Space Station. At the time I contemplated, *When will be my last day of delivering cargo?* During the 30 years I had been aviating airplanes *above* planet Earth, US astronauts had flown space shuttles above the *atmosphere* of planet Earth.

The Columbia, Challenger, Discovery, Atlantis, and Endeavor space shuttle missions carried people and cargo into orbit; launched, recovered and repaired satellites; conducted research; conducted space walks; and built the International Space Station. The only thing constant in life is change. Our space program is changing to something bigger and better.

From here on, NASA wants rockets and capsules produced by multiple civilian companies to carry important supplies, experiments, equipment and astronauts to the International Space Station. In 2012, SpaceX became the first privately funded company to send a spacecraft there. In 2015, SpaceX achieved the first vertical takeoff and vertical propulsive landing for an orbital rocket, and two years later they were the first to reuse an orbital rocket. The development of reusing orbital rockets is a major advancement toward increasing space launches and reducing the cost to launch. In 2020, they sent astronauts to the ISS.

SpaceX has flown and re-flown their Falcon-9 series rockets over a hundred times. Elon Musk, with the SpaceX team, figured out how to reuse rockets, which drastically reduced the cost of launching. Can you just imagine that after every airline jet flight, the engines had to be changed? In the past, that's how our space program operated with rockets. Now we can launch into space and reuse those rockets, just like an airline reuses the same jet engines on each flight segment. The reuse of rockets allows SpaceX to drive down the cost of space launches. Just like the airline industry, the space industry is and will continue to go through major changes.

Shortly after 1926, when Weston Air Express began year-round overland passenger service, other companies began entering the airline business. The same is happening in the space business today, with Boeing, Orbital Sciences, United Launch Alliance, Richard Branson's Virgin Galactic, Paul Allen's Vulcan airspace, Jeff Bezos's Blue Origin, Sierra Nevada Corporation and many others entering the space industry.

From 1986 to 2021, there have been 35 years of airline changes. In 1987, Weston, the oldest continuous operating airline in United States, merged with Delta. In 1991, Pan Am declared bankruptcy. Delta airlines bought most of Pan Am's European routes, and on December 4, 1991, the once-mighty Pan Am ceased operations.

In 1986, Pan Am had been the first major airline from which I sought employment as a pilot, and now it no longer existed.

My second choice, Eastern Airlines, also went out of business in 1991.

Trans World Airlines (TWA) bought Ozark Airlines in 1986 and American Airlines bought later TWA in 2001. Airline "mergers"—there's that word again—had been going on for years. American Airlines purchased Air California in 1987. USAir bought Pacific Southwest Airlines in 1987 and Piedmont Airlines in 1989. American merged with USAIR in 2013. Northwest Airlines (NWA) bought Republic Airlines in 1986. Delta Airlines (DL) bought Western Airlines in 1987 and Northwest Airlines in 2010. Continental Airlines bought New York Air and Texas International Airlines in 1986 and Peoples Express Airlines in 1987. United Airlines (UA) bought Continental Airlines (CO) in 2011. Southwest Airlines (WN) bought Muse Air in 1985 and Air Trans

Airways (ATA) in 2011. Air Trans Airways had previously bought Value Jet Airlines in 1997. Braniff Airlines came and went out of business three times—1982, 1990, and 1992.

In 1986, the major airlines in the US were Pan Am, Eastern, TWA, USAir, American, Northwest, United, and Delta. There were a number of small cargo airlines like Flying Tigers, Federal Express, DHL, Emery, UPS, Kalita, Airborne, Zantop and others. Within the last 32 years, there have been countless airline mergers, buyouts, bankruptcies and corporate restructurings.

In the US today, the four big major airlines are American, Delta, United, and Southwest. The other mainline passenger airlines are Alaska Airlines, Allegiant Air, Frontier Airlines, Hawaiian Airlines, JetBlue Airways and Spirit Airlines. Breeze Airways and Avelo Airlines are two new startup airlines that entered the market in 2021. FedEx and UPS are virtually the only two US major cargo companies. The other freight companies are Atlas Air, DHL, Kalitta Air, Polar Air and Amazon Prime Air. Amazon is quickly building its own cargo transportation unit, primarily to have control of their own shipping. A similar scenario is happening in the space industry today. Blue Origin, SpaceX and Virgin Galactic are beginning to carry people on trips to space, while SpaceX carries people and cargo to the International Space Station.

What an industry!

How would a pilot know which airline company to get hired with in 1986 or even today? Who would have known that FedEx would evolve into a great major airline, financially sound, still growing, and one of the best airline companies for pilots? Which airlines companies will survive, and which airlines companies will be the best place for pilots in the future? Which space companies will survive, and which space companies will be the best place for astronauts in the future? Pilots are desperate whores for flying. They love flying so much that many would fly planes for free.

But we do need to eat.

Wind shear can kill you

Wind shear is a critical issue, and one with the potential to kill everyone on board. Here you will learn just what pilots face while flying and how they handle the situation. Passengers are understandably very interested in the things that happen in the cockpit that could affect their safety. *What can happen in the air that can endanger my life? How good are the pilots in the cockpit?* Passengers have ceded all control of their lives to those pilots upfront and want to be assured of the pilot's level of skill. *What happens up there, and how do pilots handle dangerous situations?*

Earlier in this book we talked about thunderstorms. Do you remember that flight in San Angelo when a severe thunderstorm spewed hailstones at our plane, causing it to bob about haphazardly like a wine cork in rough ocean waves? It is worth repeating that severe thunderstorms can produce funnel clouds, tornadoes and wind shear. Wind shear—a rapid change of wind direction and wind strengths with clouds of different levels moving in different directions—can develop from a variety of other meteorological conditions such as temperature inversions, land and sea breezes, frontal systems and strong surface winds. The updrafts and downdrafts can produce microbursts.

Russel and I blasted off from Norfolk (ORF), my hometown airport, and headed to Indianapolis (IND). We knew that it would be windy in Indy. Based on the weather forecasts, we were anticipating both the approach and landing to be challenging and turbulent. We both knew that I'd be flying this leg. Traditionally, captains fly the most challenging legs of a flight, especially in adverse weather conditions. Russel is short and bald, in great physical shape. He was married and divorced during his early 20s; now, at 55-years-old, he has a longtime girlfriend. He has no children, so stories of my children entertain Russel. He is a happy, positive guy.

We talked casually on a number of topics, but the bad weather in Indianapolis was never far from our minds.

"Russel," I began. "How's your golfing coming along?"

"Great! I have been taking private lessons from a pro, and it's paying great dividends. My golf swing and putting has improved tremendously. Just last week I almost had a hole in one."

"Good for you. You know I almost had a hole-in-one?"

"Really?" Russel replied, surprised. "I thought you were too busy these days with your kids to play golf."

"I missed the hole-in-one by only four strokes." Russel laughed out loud, temporarily making me forget my stress due to the weather.

"Frank," he continued. "What's going on with soccer now?" (He and I have flown together many times before so he knows I coach kids' soccer).

"After each soccer game," I told him, "We line up our players across from the other team to shake hands and say 'good game' or something to that effect. Well, on Saturday, we beat this other team really bad. During the after-game line up, one of our players said to each of the other team's players, 'You suck.' Apparently, the other team's coach and the referee did not approve. The referee approached me and inquired about player number 10."

"What did you do?" Russel asked. "I had the little smart-aleck rascal apologize to all the other players, and then I made him run around the perimeter of the soccer field three times." Russel laughed out loud again and I joined in. "What did you say to his parents?" Russel wanted to know.

"I did not tell his mother, fearing she would get all upset and blame the coach."

"Did you talk to the father?"

"No," I replied, "for the simple reason that I don't like talking to myself. Number 10 is my son."

"You're kidding me!" Russel said, trying not to laugh.

"No. This is what I have to deal with. They're kids and sometimes they're a challenge." Russel smirked, trying to restrain from laughing again. "It's not funny!" I blurted out, at which point we both laughed wildly. It was a joyful atmosphere in the cockpit, for the time being. We both acted cool, calm and professional to each other, but I knew he was just as concerned about the weather and the landing as I was.

About 100 miles southeast of Indianapolis, as we began our descent, all communications subsided so we could concentrate on how to execute a difficult task. The atmosphere of silence felt like a chess player contemplating the final move in order to declare check mate. The thrust levers are at idle, the jet is pitched down and we listen to the rush of the air as our jet blasted through the stillness. As we drew near to our approach, the Aviation Routine Weather Report (METAR) read: Pilot Raw data: KIND 161853Z AUTO 30025G35KT 3/4SM+TSRA RN BKN008 OVC012CB 18/15 A2970 RMK PRESFR OCNL LTGICCG WS020/18050K, which means the 16th day of the month, 00:23 local time, wind 300° (west) at 25 knots, peak gust 35 knots, visibility 3/4 statute miles, heavy thunderstorms, rain, broken skies at 800 feet, overcast skies at 1,200 feet with cumulonimbus clouds, temperature 18° Celsius, dew point 15° Celsius, the barometric pressure 29.70 in Hg and dropping rapidly, occasional lightning in the clouds and from cloud to ground, non-convective low-level wind shear at 2,000 feet above the ground, wind 180° (south) at 50 knots. The winds are expected to increase rapidly from 25 knots at the surface to 50 knots at 2,000 feet AGL.

This weather report also implied that winds would shift direction from 180° at 2,000 feet to 300° at the surface. There's no way to know how or where the wind will shift within the wind shear layer. A special caveat here. When the magnitude of wind shear is significant, say, above 45 knots, and is coupled with heavy convective rain showers (+TSRA), then hazardous conditions exist, which can cause dangerous downdrafts with the potential for microbursts.

The solemnness of the cockpit is interrupted occasionally by briefings and checklists. Approach and landing briefings are conducted before each approach and landing. In addition to the wind shear briefings, I emphasized that we needed to pay close attention to maintaining a minimum speed at or above the approach speed minus 10 knots above ground speed. Variations of temporary high spikes of airspeed are acceptable. Maintaining the proper jet attitude is a higher priority than airspeed fluctuations. I also briefed Russel that we would land with the final slats/flaps 15°/20° versus the typical 30°/40°. Using this lower flap setting would help maximize the climb gradient capability in case we have to climb out of a severe wind shear threat.

It was Thursday night—the fourth night flying this week—and I was tired. There was pilot pressure to land and get some sleep, land to move the freight, and land among the peer pressure of the 50 other arriving jets. The 30-plus years of experience had taught me not to succumb to these pressures to land and to make good captain decisions in these situations.

We entered the first air pocket passing through 2,000 feet. We started getting banged around from wind shifts and erratic rain. Positive and negative air energy from microbursts pushed and pulled us against our will.

A microburst is an intense downdraft of air that rushes toward the surface at high speed and spreads out in all directions on the ground, producing unstable vortices of circulating winds. There is a vertical component and a horizontal component of this erratic, powerful wind force. These dangerous microburst vortices can encompass an area up to 2,000 feet above the surface vertically and one to two miles horizontally. There could be a greater flow in one direction and a lesser flow in another. The downburst may be at an angle, and the strength of the downburst is exacerbated by precipitation. Microbursts usually last about 15 to 20 minutes and can generate winds of greater than 145 knots.[42]

During the approach, I had to contend with the change of wind speed that was increasing rapidly with height from the surface. At 2,000 feet, AGL the winds are at 180° and 50 knots, resulting in headwind component of around 32 knots and a crosswind component of 38 knots. To counter the winds, I had to steer the plane right of the runway heading to maintain the desired runway track. At this point, the plane's groundspeed will be abnormally low, and the crosswind is out of landing minimums for my jet. At the surface, the winds are at 300° and 25 knots; the headwind component is 8 knots, and the crosswind component is 24 knots. Before landing, I would have to steer the plane left of the runway heading to maintain the desired runway track. At this point, the plane's groundspeed was within normal limits and the crosswind was within the landing minimums for my jet. During this approach I would transition the jet from a right crosswind correction to a left crosswind correction, and the groundspeed component would decrease by about 24 knots. This big transition and large groundspeed change is a rare event not normally encountered during everyday approach to landings.

However, if the report is 300° at a peak gust of 35 knots at the surface, then the headwind component is 12 knots and the crosswind component is 33 knots, which is beyond the authorized landing minimums for my jet. If the crosswind is out of limits, then a normal go-around must be executed. If severe wind shear is detected during the approach, then the wind shear escape maneuver must be executed. These procedures to execute each of these maneuvers are different.

There were dangers I had to contend with. When the wind spreads out from a positive wind shear micro downburst, an oncoming airplane can experience increased headwind over its wings, which can cause the plane to unexpectedly lift into the air due to a sudden surge in airspeed. As the aircraft enters the microburst, it first encounters an increasing performance shear in the form of a strong headwind. During the approach, the pilot compensates for the positive shear; when the nose of the jet pitches up, the pilot pushes the yoke control down to maintain the desired glide path, and when the airspeed increases, the pilot reduces thrust to maintain the targeted speed. Without notice, a severe positive shear can shift to a severe negative shear producing a strong tailwind, forcing the jet's nose to pitch down and the airspeed to decrease.

During the approach, the pilot reacts to the negative shear; when the jet's nose pitches down, the pilot pulls the yoke control back to maintain the desired glide path, and when the airspeed decreases, the pilot increases thrust to maintain the targeted speed. During the approach in these conditions, constant changes to pitch and airspeed must be made. These were some of the dangers I had to battle with throughout the approach and landing phase.

During a microburst encounter, the most dangerous scenario occurs when a positive shear is followed by a negative shear at a low altitude, leaving the jet dangerously low and slow, potentially not being able to recover. As I was recovering my knowledge on possible wind shear during the landing phase, my brain's files brought up the unexpected flashback: On August 2, 1985, Flight 191, an L-1011 aircraft, crashed in Dallas/Fort Worth, resulting in 134 fatalities. The cause of that fatal crash was attributed to wind shear and microburst. The flashback briefly interrupted my thought process on the knowledge I would need for this approach and landing.

Overly aggressive pilot reactions with pitch and thrust could also leave the jet low and slow, resulting in a stall or ground contact. Thrust and pitch can affect the jet's airspeed or glide path, but pitch will affect the airspeed and attitude more quickly and effectively than thrust. This is why I contend that maintaining the proper jet attitude is of higher priority than airspeed fluctuations. To me, allowing temporary spikes of airspeed is an acceptable practice.

BAM! We were slammed by another shear of energy. The airspeed fluctuated between minus 10 knots and plus 15 knots. I was okay with the momentary plus 15-knot airspeed fluctuations. A pilot considers wind shear severe when the its energy affects the plane's flight with airspeed fluctuation changes of greater than 15 knots, or a vertical speed fluctuation change of greater than 500 feet per minute, or the aircraft's pitch altitude fluctuation change of greater than 5°.

Severe wind shear can displace an aircraft abruptly from its intended flight path, requiring substantial pilot control inputs to compensate. This is particularly dangerous during the most critical stages of flight at low altitude close to terrain where any loss of aircraft control by the pilot may make recovery difficult or impossible. While fighting the wind energy force, it is very important that the pilot does not over-control pitch and thrust adjustments.

At 1,000 feet, we heard the controller report, "Wind 280 at 35 knots, peak gust 50 knots." That computes to a 38-knot crosswind. Significantly, the crosswind limit on the AB-300 is 32 knots for a dry runway and 30 knots for a wet runway. Russel and I knew that during peak gust, the wind limit would exceed the crossing limit of the AB-300 and if that should happen just before touch down, we would have to execute the normal go-around procedure. A captain's decision would have to be made to come back to try another approach to landing or fly to an alternate airport with friendlier weather.

In our cockpit, as in most sophisticated jets, we have a wind shear warning indicator instrument, which includes a square-inch-size button that provides a level-one red-light illumination warning and a level-two oral warning of severe wind shear. The policy was that if the light flashed "wind shear" and you heard the oral warning "wind shear, wind shear" then the captain was required to execute the wind shear escape maneuver. If the light flashed "wind shear" and you did not get an oral warning, then the captain had the option of continuing the approach or executing the wind shear escape maneuver. My inner voice spoke to me to initiate the emergency wind shear escape procedure: *Thrust to takeoff go-around (TOGA), autopilot and auto-throttles disconnect, aircraft attitude 17.5' nose up, thrust levers push full up to firewall power, speed brake retract. Maintain configuration (do not move gear and or flaps) until clear of the wind shear.* With a normal go-around procedure, the flaps are retracted one detent, and the landing gear is retracted with a positive rate of climb during the procedure. My thoughts again seemed to scream out: *This is not normal, do not move the gear and flaps.* Also, *Trade excess airspeed for altitude. Do not crash!*

Severe wind shear and some microbursts can exceed the performance capability of all aircraft, and even the best of pilots would not be able to survive. Mother Nature is impervious to human intervention, and she must be respected. Pilots must adhere to the laws of aviation weather.

Jolted again by another positive shear of forceful energy, heavy convective rain combined with frightening wind pounded us. Our anxiety level rose. Fifi (the A-300) spoke to me; she creaked and cried, rattled and moaned.

Déjà vu.

Fifi's influence was unavoidable: *My wings may break off.* It is, of course, highly unlikely that that would happen, but my rattled brain nevertheless briefly transmitted these horrific thoughts.

Mother Nature and Fifi were crying out to us. The battle had begun between Mother Nature and us. Who would win? She would blast us with positive shears, and I would fight her back with my left hand clutched to pitch and bank controls, and my right hand clenched on the thrust control. I felt her rattle, shake and rumble, like a roller-coaster ride, but with unpredictable turns, climbs and descents. Imagine driving your ground transport machine with the strongest gusty winds blasting your vehicle, rattling, shaking and rumbling. However, you and your car are grounded to planet Earth's surface. Fifi and I had no ground to support us. The fluid nature of the atmosphere jigged us about like a ragdoll in the jaws of a hungry, feral cat. These forces of nature could attack us from any direction and move us anywhere. As my senses absorbed the input stimuli, my brain directed my life-saving hands to fight the forces of the weather we were battling, using my pitch and thrust. During a world-champion boxing match, each fighter will defend and attack each other with clutch-fisted hands. My opponent does not fight fair; she attacks me from different angles with different thrust forces, and I cannot see where she is coming from. I can only react, my hands directing pitch and power, my feet adjusting rudder inputs.

At 500 feet, the severe wind shear warning light flashed once! My heart rate and blood pressure ratcheted up a notch. The cockpit was completely devoid of human sounds, only the emergency noise of the rocking and creaking of this old ship fighting God's powerful wind were present. We heard no *wind shear, wind shear* oral warning. A supernatural wind arm locked my innocent jet, and rumbled us, as if the alien force were trying to wrestle Fifi and us to the earth. Mother Nature grasped our 150 x 175-foot, 300,000-pound air metal machine, rolled and tossed it. The drastic, unnatural movement stunned me like Dorothy from *The Wizard of Oz* as she was lifted into the air by an unforgiving tornado. We entered the dreaded microburst; a positive shear was shifting to a negative shear. She rocked us into a slight roll, pitched the jet's nose up and spiked the airspeed up. Within those nanoseconds of reacting in shock, the jet suddenly unrolled, drastically pitching down as the airspeed dropped like a boulder.

The light flashed again—this time it flashed twice! My reaction intensified. Once again, I was thinking, *If I have to perform a Wind Shear Go-Around, this is not normal; do not move the gear and flaps. Trade excess airspeed for altitude. Do not crash! Just the light!* There was no oral wind shear warning with the flashing light. Russel and I glanced at each other as if to confirm we saw the light but did not hear the oral *wind shear, wind shear* warning. I made the command decision to continue the approach. At around 100 feet, the tower blurted out the words, "Winds, 300 degrees at 30 knots." No gust. He did not report gust this time; therefore, with these winds, the crosswind component was 28 knots, within the legal design limitation of AB-300. The winds were just within our limits. I made the decision to continue and land.

The lashing of the heavy rain was so loud I could barely here Fifi say, "50 feet, 40 feet, 30 feet," at 20 feet above planet Earth; she was not finished with me. This weather phenomenon blasted one more gust of powerful swirling wind force at us, as if she had to get in one more backhanded hook punch. As the airspeed dropped, I held the jet landing pitch attitude to the desired setting, added a little thrust power, and then planted the beat-up jet smack onto the runway's wet pavement.

After taxing off the runway, I called for the "after landing" checklist. The euphoria started oozing out of me like blood from a severe gash. All of a sudden, I felt exhausted and hungry, yet proudly relieved. I felt the exhaustion an athlete feels after completing a triathlon; yet I also felt the relief a patient experiences when all the test results come back normal. On top of that, imagine all of a sudden, I realized I was hungry. The physical sense of hunger was pounding my stomach with moans and growls. Those feelings were temporarily put aside in order to contend with thoughts of my fellow pilots who flew that night.

Of the 50 inbound planes, 17 of those coming into Indianapolis executed a go-around, or wind shear escape maneuver, on that unforgettable, ferocious night. Sometimes it is the luck of the draw, when the microburst peak gust attacks the plane. At the moment of my "land or do not land" decision, the winds were within the landing limits of the A-300, and there was no severe wind shear.

Whew! We landed safely. I reached forward with my right hand, patted the dashboard and said to myself, *Nice job, Fifi, we did it!* There was an enormous feeling of the power of accomplishment, probably not unlike the feeling an Olympic gold medalist experiences during the award ceremony. It was a great feeling of accomplishment to touch down on planet Earth after that challenging landing. I was so glad that my jet and I fought off Mother Nature's microburst attack, allowing us to land safely. I am so happy that I did not encounter severe wind shear and that I did not have to test my pilot's best ability and the jet's integrity to escape and survive. Even the best of pilots in the best of airplanes cannot survive some severe wind shear.

The Gouge. Do not try to be a big-time cool pilot hero, because severe wind shear can kill everyone on board. Be safe and avoid the hazards of severe wind shear. Avoidance is the best defense against the hazards of severe wind shear, which is beyond the handling ability of commercial aircraft and even highly skilled pilots. *Safety first! It is better to tell an embarrassing story than to die and not be able to tell a story at all.*

Pitch control will affect the attitude, altitude and airspeed more quickly and effectively than thrust control. Maintaining proper airplane attitude is more important than occasional airspeed fluctuations.

Become familiar with the wind shear recovery procedures for your particular airplane. If during the approach phase the pilot encounters severe wind shear, then execute the wind shear escape maneuver; on my jet, it was: *thrust to takeoff go-around (TOGA), autopilot and autothrottles disconnect, aircraft attitude 17.5' nose up, thrust levers push full* up to firewall power, speed brake retract. Do not change configuration (do not move gear and or flaps) until clear of the wind shear. Trade excess airspeed for altitude. Do not crash!

Before the approach, tighten your seat belt and ensure all loose items are stowed away. Be honest with the passengers in the back. Transmit: "We will be encountering turbulent weather conditions; please stay seated and fasten your seat belts tightly."

We should fly together.
You should join Frank the Pilot as captain on the perfect flight.
Come on up here in the cockpit and come fly with me.

22

COME FLY WITH ME, FLIGHT 1340

Frank the pilot in action.

I thought you might like to go for a ride with me, up here in the cockpit.

The following flight happened—*sort of.*

I've changed a few details to protect all involved. I'm writing this book with the goal of showing you how a pilot's mind works and how my life was shaped by becoming a pilot. So, I thought you might like to go with me on one specific journey that ends, shall we say, in one of those "you never know" moments that shows just how critical preparation and training can be.

Just like life.

So, take a seat up here in the cockpit and buckle up.

Take Off

"FedEx 1340 heavy cleared to line up and wait runway 31 Left."

The transmission is from John F. Kennedy International Airport Air Traffic Control tower, and Charlie, the First Officer of 1340, responds.

"Roger. FedEx 1340 heavy cleared to line up and wait runway 31L."

I reach up above my right shoulder and turn on the taxi lights while simultaneously pressing both feet on the brake pedals of the Air Bus-300 wide-body heavy aircraft. I lower my right hand to turn and release the parking brake handle, and relax brake pedal pressure. The jet starts to roll, but with more than 90,000 pounds of cargo on board, I will have to advance the thrust levers to assist the movement of this 300,000-pound jet.

"Charlie, complete the before-takeoff checklist," I say.

"Takeoff configuration? Normal for takeoff. V speeds?" I scan the forward instrument panel. "Checked." Charlie does the same. "Checked. Radar?"

"On," I confirm. "Flight control panel?" I scan the flight control panel to double-check that the appropriate airspeed, altitude, heading and navigation controls are correctly set for takeoff. "Set." Charlie does the same. "Set," he states. He engages the ignition selector and turns on the runway turnoff and landing lights. "Ignition selector continuous relight. Before takeoff checklist to the line complete," he says. I scan left to confirm that final approach path to runway 31L is clear of arriving aircraft. Even if the control tower tells me it's clear, I want visual confirmation. "Clear left." Charlie looks right to view that the runway is clear of all obstacles—especially other aircraft. You can't be too careful. "Clear right." I look right and double-check. In our line of work, there is a lot of trust. This trust, however, must also be verified.

Kennedy Tower Controller tells me 31L is clear for me to enter, and my first officer tells me runway 31L from his viewpoint is clear to enter. I look left and right to double-check and confirm.

Trust but verify. If they are wrong and I do not catch the mistake, another aircraft could land on the one I'm piloting. On me. On us.

My day would change from good to bad.

All is clear as I taxi onto the unoccupied runway, 150 feet wide and over 14,500 feet (nearly three miles) long.

Pushing the rudder control pedals with my feet provides limited control of the jet's steering, but it is the steering tiller installed on all large jets and controlled by my left hand that will steer the nose wheel through the hydraulic system.

This AB-300 has a wingspan of 147 feet, a length of 177 feet, and a height of 54 feet. The nose wheel gear and main gear are located 13 feet and 47 feet behind me, respectively. Therefore, as I enter the turn onto the runway from my point of view, I will have to overshoot the runway centerline to compensate for the aft position of the nose gear. My position in the captain's seat must actually pass the runway center line before I begin to turn in order to align the jet with the center line. Just as I complete the turn and return the nose wheel steering tiller to the center position, the Kennedy Air Traffic Controller issues us a takeoff clearance. "Fed Ex 1340 Heavy, winds 010 degrees at 10 knots cleared for takeoff runway 31L."

Of course, as the airline captain of this flight, I have the authority to decline the takeoff clearance, but instead, I let Charlie respond. "FedEx 1340 Heavy cleared for takeoff runway 31L."

To my left is the Jamaica Bay and to my right is the airport, a sprawling facility with seven passenger terminals and ten cargo buildings. After pushing the thrust levers to 40% N1 position, I observe that the engines have stabilized.

"Set standard power." I give the command as I engage the takeoff go-around thrust levers. Each of the two General Electric CF-6 engines is capable of producing over 60,000 pounds of thrust at maximum power for takeoff. However, when conditions permit, it is best to takeoff with a reduced power setting, called Standard Power, in order to decrease stress on the engine and prolong engine life.

Charlie confirms the engines are stable at the desired thrust setting. "Standard power set," he confirms. The sound of the engine increases. The airframe vibrates, shakes and rumbles. You can feel the power building up. The airspeed gauge comes alive and tells me our increasing speed—10 knots, 20 knots, 20 knots. The jet rolls faster, and it's my decision whether to reject the takeoff or continue. I may reject the takeoff for just about any reason, like an unusual noise or vibration, a warning light or sound, any system failure, a tire failure, or even abnormally slow aircraft acceleration.

"Eighty knots." Charlie spits out the reading as I check the airspeed gauge. "Check," I say.

Above 80 knots, we are in the high-speed phase of the takeoff roll. Below this speed I may reject the takeoff for just about any abnormality. Now, I am in a more go-oriented decision mode and will only reject the takeoff for a serious situation that might prevent the jet from flying safely. Wind shear, engine fire or engine failure are good reasons to reject the takeoff at this speed.

"V1." Charlie eyeballs the airspeed indicator and scans the other instruments.

I remove my right hand from the thrust levers and grasp the control yoke where my left hand is located.

"Rotate," says Charlie.

The V1 speed is a numerical speed, which varies between aircraft types. V1 varies due to aircraft weight, runway length, wing flap setting, engine thrust used, runway surface contamination and other factors. The simplest definition is that V1 is the takeoff-decision speed. Before V1, if something bad happens, I have to choose to continue or abort the takeoff. After V1, if something bad happens, it is usually safer to continue the takeoff. Charlie observes positive rate of climb on the vertical speed indicator and altimeters.

We go. The aircraft is airborne—doing what it was designed to do.

"Positive rate," he says. "Gear up," I respond. Charlie retracts the landing gear lever to the up position. With my hands on the control wheel yoke and my feet on the rudder pedals, I turn the jet left toward Canarsie VOR as required for this standard instrument departure. We are quickly 1,500 feet above the ground.

"Flaps up." Charlie retracts the wing flaps from the takeoff position to the flight position. "Slats retract, after-takeoff checklist." Charlie retracts the slats and verifies that the ignition selector, slats and flaps, gear and spoilers are placed in the appropriate position with no warning lights illuminated.

"After-takeoff checklist complete to the line," he says.

"FedEx 1340 Heavy contact Departure Control on 125.87."

"Switching to departure on 125.87," he says.

"Kennedy departure FedEx 1340 Heavy climbing out of 2,000 feet cleared to 5,000 feet," Charlie says.

"1340 after Canarsie cleared direct to Robbinsville, cleared to 12,000 feet. Contact New York Center on 135.47."

Charlie reads back the clearance, dials 135.47 for the VHF frequency and sets 12,000 feet in the altitude select window. After verifying the correct altitude is set, I state the new altitude.

"12,000 feet."

"New York Center, 1340 cleared to 12,000 feet."

"1340, traffic at your two o'clock position descending to flight level 210. After Robbinsville, cleared as filed, climb to flight level 240, contact New York Center on 135.5."

Charlie reads back the clearance once again and sets 240 in the altitude select window, switching the VHF radio frequency to 135.5. I verify the correct altitude is set.

"Flight level 240."

I join Charlie in scanning for traffic in the sky.

Looking westbound, various shades of the dark and light blue sky is partially obscured by mostly white, puffy cumulus clouds.

There are rays of orange and pink from the dying sun coloring the ever-changing clouds. Far above us, a jet contrail crosses our view from the cockpit. It is the only man-made feature included in this beautiful scene, provided free of charge by Mother Nature.

We're heading westbound and chasing the sun, but she's outrunning us, and darkness is not far off. Although I have not identified the traffic, I fixate below on New York, a city of over 8 million diverse people. New York City has the most ethnicities of any city in the world; it is truly the melting pot of planet Earth.

I'm lucky to be up here, in the clouds. And it's beautiful.

"Altimeters 29.92."

We are climbing through 18,000 feet, I set the altimeter.

"29.92."

"After-takeoff checklist is complete."

The aeronautical airspace above 18,000 feet is classified as Class A airspace. All pilots flying in the United States set the altimeter to a standard pressure 29.92 inches of mercury. We reference altitudes as flight levels. Flight level FL 240 is the height of 24,000 feet above sea level.

Our cargo jet accommodates jump-seaters as passengers, so if it is not too turbulent, I check to ensure that Charlie has turned the seat-belt sign switch off. Additionally, I check that the runway turnoff and landing lights have been turned off and that our altimeters are within the variance of plus or minus 200 feet tolerance in order for us to enter the reduced vertical separation minimum airspace. I check that the aircraft temperature is suitable for the jump-seat passengers and the live chickens we're carrying. Finally, I check all systems: hydraulic, electric, pressurization, fuel, etc.

While monitoring the fuel, I catch one last glimpse of New York City, far below and disappearing fast.

John F. Kennedy Airport hands us off to Washington Center, meaning they have told us to switch our frequency to another Air Traffic

Control Center. Washington Center clears us to flight level 350 (35,000 feet), but I tell Charlie to relay to Washington Center that we are unable to climb to flight level 350 due to our weight.

It is usually more efficient to fly at the highest altitude, but because we are carrying over 90,000 pounds of cargo freight and over 60,000 pounds of fuel, we are too heavy to climb to flight level 350. Washington Center clears us to flight level 310. The autopilot is controlling the jet's flight path now, and through a system of electronics, hydraulics and computers, the jet levels off at flight level 310.

I know my plane, and she—Fifi—knows me. Fifi and I have spent many hours together. I know her so well that I am able to close my eyes and with my hands I am able to locate the various control buttons, knobs and switches to direct changes in how she moves. Experienced pilots are so familiar with their air machine that they are able to direct their eyes one way while moving their hands another. It's like driving your ground machine and looking forward while blindly reaching with your hand to adjust the radio station or air conditioner. However, there are over 100 Air Bus jets in our fleet, and each Fifi has its own personality. Sometimes, she is rebellious and disregards my commands, and I never know when she will act up. My plane is 99% reliable and compliant for me, but it is that 1% of the time when Fifi does her own thing that I must catch and correct her.

I keep my hands on the control yoke and on the auto-throttles just in case Fifi's autopilot does not do its job and levels off at an incorrect altitude. If the jet levels off below or above where it's supposed to be, the flight crew, particularly the captain, could get a Federal Aviation Administration (FAA) violation, including a monetary fine, a pilot license suspension, or worse—loss of pilot's license.

The jet levels off at flight level 310. I scan and monitor a few systems.

My mind runs through a series of questions.

Is the temperature for the chickens appropriate?

Is the temperature for the jump-seat passengers appropriate?

Are there any abnormalities with the engine, hydraulics, the electrical system, the fuel system, the pressurization system or other systems?

Is the flight management system and navigation system performing appropriately?

Do I need to make any adjustments?

I check our estimated time of arrival for Memphis and fuel on board. Time and fuel are important in this business. We want to be reliable, and that means delivering the cargo to the customers on time. Flying at a slower speed is more fuel efficient, but when we're running late, we must fly faster to arrive on time.

It's an ongoing balance between speed and fuel.

Changing Light

It is now nighttime—the sun won. The sun is always moving faster on its journey than we can fly.

The brain and eyes play tricks during nighttime flying, so I concentrate more on the cockpit instruments. On long nighttime flights, I keep the cockpit lights turned bright for optimal eyesight. Photopic vision, under bright light, helps detect color, details and far away objects.

But since we will be landing in Memphis soon, I turn all the cockpit and instrument lights from bright to dim to allow my scotopic vision to adapt to the dark. Scotopic vision works in low light and helps detect objects, particularly moving objects. However, detail and color are not so good. It may take up to 30 minutes for our eyes to fully adapt to optimum night vision, which we will need for landing.

"Look at that," says Charlie.

"Where?"

"Over there."

Again, Mother Nature provides first-class entertainment free of charge. Glowing shades of pale, yellowish-green rays are shooting up and dancing in the dark, eerie sky. A collision of electrically charged particles from the sun and gaseous particles from the Earth's atmosphere perform in the Aurora Borealis show, more commonly known as the Northern Lights.

"It's just energized ions and atoms colliding, or at least that's what they told us in school," Charlie explains.

You can explain it scientifically, but there is no explanation for the beauty that Mother Nature frequently displays.

Co-Pilot

My co-pilot, Charlie, is a healthy 6-footer. He's muscular, black-haired and brown-eyed. He's cleanly shaved with a military haircut. From the way his starched, short-sleeved white uniform shirt captures his physique, a woman could idolize his big biceps and presume he has a chiseled chest and a flat abdomen. One of the greatest benefits of my career is that I have the opportunity to fly with pilots of diverse personalities and backgrounds. There are unique and interesting features of Californians, Floridians, Kansans, New Yorkers and Texans.

"Charlie, how did you become a pilot?"

"I grew up in Texas on a small, not-so-profitable farm," says Charlie. "To supplement the household income, my father started a small air-crop-dusting business with one Air Tractor-502 Ag plane. My father took me with him many times and taught me the basic fundamentals of flying—climbs, descents, turns and straight and level. I entered the United States Navy and attended flight school at Pensacola. I learned to fly T-34 trainers at Corpus Christi and learned to fly T-45 Goshawks at Kingsville Naval Air Station. After receiving my wings, I was assigned to fly F-14 Tomcats."

I always enjoy getting to know who I'm working with so I ask, "Where did you go to school, Charlie?"

Charlie tells a story of being in high school and one evening after dinner his father presented him with some papers. "He told me, sign these papers. The US Navy will educate you, teach you to fly and pay you at the same time. It's a good deal.'" So, Charlie ended up attending the US Naval Academy in Annapolis, Maryland.

Charlie is equally inquisitive of my background and I spend a few minutes recapping the many things you have learned about my background by reading this book.

We chat, but we're flying the plane all the time too—our eyes scanning both the skies and instruments out of routine.

Washington Center switches us off to Indy Center. Indy Center clears us direct to the Bowling Green Fix and to join the LTOWN 6 RNAV STAR to Memphis International Airport.

LTOWN 6 is the name of the STAR associated with the LTOWN fix, a point defined by latitude and longitude coordinates. RNAV stands for "area navigation" and is a method of air navigation that allows an aircraft to fly from point to point. STAR is an acronym for "Standard Terminal Arrival Route" and is a published procedure describing specific instructions for descent, routing and communications for arrival to a specific runway at a specific airport.

Charlie obtains the Automatic Terminal Information (ATIS), computes landing performance data and transfers the information onto a landing performance card. ATIS is the continuous broadcast of essential information at busy airports, including weather, active runways, available approaches and other important information.

The weather is perfect.

It is CAVU, meaning that the ceiling and visibility is unrestricted. (CAVU is a pilot's favorite acronym.)

The Memphis ATIS information reads whiskey: time—03:55; winds—010 degrees at 5 knots; visibility—better than ten miles, few clouds at 16,000 feet; temperature—17 degrees Celsius; dew point—12 degrees Celsius; altimeter—29.96 inches; ILS parallel approaches landing 36L, 36C, 36R and 27. Read back all holding instructions and advise you have information Whiskey. In aviation, we use a phonetic code. 'A' is for Alpha, 'B' is for Bravo, 'C' is for Charlie, etc., and 'W' is for Whiskey. The flight is perfect.

So far.

Adjustments—and a Problem

Indy Center informs us to contact Memphis Center on 136.25. We check in with Memphis Center. On the primary flight display instrument, the projected descent arrow symbol appears. Like other pilots, I call this symbol the AOH, the Arrow of Happiness. If you are on a long, tiring flight and the projected descent arrow symbol appears, you become happy knowing that a descent to your destination will begin soon, thus the Arrow of Happiness. The beginning of the end.

However, the center issues us a route and speed change.

"Turn right 20 degrees and slow to .78 Mach. Maintain .78 Mach or less."

Jets fly at high speeds expressed in Mach numbers. Mach is the ratio of the speed of any object to the speed of sound. A jet flying at 2.0 Mach would be considered flying at twice the speed of sound.

"Roger. Right 20 degrees. Maintain .78 Mach or less."

I check the fuel, weather and all the jet's systems again, and then I start to brief Charlie on the Memphis LTOWN 6 RNAV STAR and the runway 36 Right approach. I load the ILS runway 36R approach into the Flight Management System primary flight plan and load the ILS runway 27 in the secondary flight plan. I start to brief Charlie on the particulars of the LTOWN 6 RNAV STAR.

After Bowling Green, we'll fly 240 degrees to the AXXEL Fix and plan on arriving there above flight level 240 and at an airspeed of 290 knots. Then, we will cross SPKER between 14,000 feet and flight level 230, turn to 226 degrees to cross at LTOWN between 10,000 and 16,000 feet. Then, we will slow down to be at DAPLE at 250 knots. Cross DASAC between 9,000 and 11,000 feet, cross CLARK above 8,000 feet and turn to 178 degrees, cross DIGLE above 6,000 feet and cross DINKE at 3,000 feet. After DINKE, expect radar vectors to HADAN for the visual approach backed up with the ILS approach to runway 36R. 36R LOC frequency is 111.35, the inbound course is 360 degrees, and the category one barometric decision height is 540 feet.

Runway 36R is 9,000 feet long and 150 feet wide with an approach light configuration system number two and a Vertical Approach Sight Indicator on the right side. The Minimum Sector Altitude for our sector is 2,500 feet. In the event we have to go around, the published Missed Approach Procedure for 36R is to fly 360 degrees, climb at 1,000 feet, and then turn to a heading of 070 degrees to intercept the Memphis VOR 117.5 040-degree radial. Then, proceed to OROCU and climb to 5,000 feet; enter the holding pattern at OROCU. If the landing goes as planned, I exit the runway at taxiway S3, make a right turn onto S, and enter spot number 10 entry point to proceed to parking spot 686 on the ramp.

"1340 cleared direct BWG, descend via the LTOWN 6 RNAV STAR, north transition, altimeter 29.96, resume normal speed, and contact Memphis Center 133.7."

The profile descent flight mode annunciator flashes, the autothrottles reduce to idle thrust speed setting and the autopilot pitches the nose down to start the descent. Passing through 18,000 feet, we reset our altimeters to 29.96, turn the seat-belt sign and the landing lights on, and ensure that everyone has fastened their seat belts and harnesses.

The in-range checklist is complete, the landing data and all aircraft systems have been checked—everything looks smooth and perfect.

Charlie contacts approach control and tells them we are descending via the LTOWN 6 arrival, north transition, we have ATIS info Whiskey, and we are parking in entry spot number ten. Approach control instructs us to turn left 20 degrees, descend to 3,000 feet and expect runway 27.

Runway 27—great.

Landing on 27 versus 36R will save us approximately four minutes of air time and two minutes of taxi time and about 500 pounds of fuel. Five hundred pounds of fuel equates to 75 gallons of fuel, which is a savings of approximately $450.

We comply with the new clearance.

Things are starting to get really busy.

Even though we had a brief discussion that we may land on runway 27, our mindset and aircraft set was programmed to land on runway 36R.

We have lots of changes to accomplish.

I reach down to the center console pedestal and change the LOC frequency to 108.9 and the LOC approach course to 270 degrees. I then reach forward to the main instrument panel and change the barometric category to 500 feet. Charlie retrieves the secondary flight plan information and activates it. He makes several other adjustments to the Flight Management System and acquires an audible in Morse code to verify that we have selected the correct LOC frequency for runway 27. The LOC frequency is audibled in Morse code so that a skilled listener can detect a series of on–off signals to correctly identify a particular LOC. We complete the approach checklist.

Approaching 10,000 feet during the descent, I slow to 250 knots, which is almost 290 miles per hour. As required by FAA law, the maximum speed permitted below 10,000 feet is 250 knots. Approaching 20 miles from runway 27, I slow to 210 knots.

"Slats extend," I say.

Charlie puts his left hand on the slats/flaps handle and extends the slats.

"Slats extended," Charlie responds.

Slats and flaps are electrically controlled by a computer and hydraulically operated by motors. Slats and flaps help increase lift generated by the wings by changing the overall shape of the wing. The additional lift helps support the weight of the jet needed for safe operation and control at slower jet airspeeds, such as when taking off or landing. We are on an extended right base leg to runway 27.

"Flaps 15."

Charlie extends the flaps to the 15-degree position.

"Flaps 15, set."

"1340, the field is at your one o'clock. Do you have the field in sight?" asks the tower.

On such a clear and perfect night, I had identified the Memphis aerodrome a few minutes earlier. However, I look at Charlie.

"Do you have the field?" I ask him.

"Yes."

"Tell approach we have the field."

"1340 has the field in sight," Charlie tells the tower.

"1340, you are cleared for the visual approach runway 27. Contact tower on 120.9."

"Cleared for the visual runway 27 and switching to the tower 120.9. Good evening, Memphis tower. 1340 nine miles out for runway 27."

"1340, cleared to land runway 27."

"Roger, cleared to land runway 27."

I slow the jet's airspeed to 170 knots.

"Flaps 20," I say.

Charlie selects flaps to 20.

But there's a problem.

The flaps do not extend to the 20-degree position; the indicator tells us they are not where they are supposed to be. Each wing is a complex system of movable parts and includes three single-slotted, Fowler-type flap sections.

"Charlie, cycle the slats/flaps handle."

He cycles the handle to the previous flaps 15 position and reselects the handle to the desired 20-degree position.

We are hoping that the cycling of the slats/flaps handle will be successful so that we can continue with our normal operations and land.

But it doesn't work.

"What do you think, Charlie?"

"We have to complete the flaps-stuck-at-less-than-20-degrees checklist."

"Here's what we are going to do," I say. At this stage of the game, decisions need to be made quickly. "We are going to abort the approach, split up the cockpit duties and try to fix the flight control problem."

We accomplish the go-around procedure. I increase the jet's pitch attitude and thrust power setting. Charlie retracts the slats/flaps and landing gear and engages the autopilot and flight management navigation system. Charlie contacts Memphis tower.

"Memphis Tower, this is 1340. We need to abort the approach due to a flight control problem."

"Roger, 1340. Fly runway heading to 3,000 feet and contact departure control on 122.9."

"Wilco 122.9."

"Wilco," as mentioned before, simply means that I have received your instructions and will comply.

"I have the airplane and the radios."

Normally, the non-flying pilot operates the radio while the other pilot is flying the airplane.

"You work the ECAM."

ECAM is the jet's electronic centralized aircraft monitoring system. With these two commands, the cockpit duties are divided. Charlie and I are now operating in our own worlds.

Earlier in the book, you may have wondered why pilots must gel to form a cohesive team. It's because the safety of flight depends on it. First, we must understand that it takes two or three pilots to operate a sophisticated jet airplane. With a two-pilot requirement during normal operations, one pilot (the flying pilot) flies the jet, and the other pilot (the non-flying pilot) navigates the jet and communicates with Air Traffic Control. Each pilot has other duties that they perform as well.

If an emergency or an abnormal situation should occur, it becomes more crucial to work as a team and trust each other. During an emergency, like the 2009 "Miracle on the Hudson" emergency with Sully Sullenberger, saving lives depends on working as a team and trusting each other.

Generally, during an emergency, one pilot flies the plane, navigates and communicates, while the other pilot executes and completes all normal and emergency checklist procedures. The cockpit duties are split up, and each pilot is working in his or her own world during the emergency. The pilots must put great trust in one another.

The flying pilot will update the non-flying pilot on the progress of the flight. The non-flying pilot will update the flying pilot on the aircraft conditions and the requirements and progress of all checklists that will need to be completed. The pilots will rejoin as a team before landing.

The pilots must work as a team and must trust each other. Survival is much more important than liking the other person. There is no time to like or dislike your co-worker; the safety of the flight depends on it.

There is an understanding that I will aviate, navigate, communicate and configure the jet's flight operations while Charlie executes and completes all the normal and abnormal checklist items. Charlie will update me on the aircraft conditions and the requirements and progress of all checklists he will need to accomplish. Conversely, I will update him on the progress of the flight. I prioritize my four goals in order:

1. Land the jet safely.

2. Operate the jet legally without violating any federal laws.

3. Continue to provide reliable service in order to deliver the packages to the customers.

4. Try to accomplish these tasks efficiently because I have a limited amount of fuel, which correlates directly to the amount of flight time remaining.

I check in with departure control.

"What is the problem and how can we be of assistance?" inquires departure control.

"We have a flap control problem; I am declaring an emergency. There are two souls on board, 12,000 pounds of fuel and no dangerous goods. We need 15 to 20 minutes to run some checklists."

"Roger. Understand you are declaring emergency. Fly the published missed approach procedure, hold over GOWRI, and let us know when you are ready for the approach."

"1340 will fly the published missed approach, hold over GOWRI and get back to you."

The published missed approach is a written, preplanned set of instructions associated with a particular runway approach directing the pilot to follow particular turns and climbs to a designated safe position in the airspace. GOWRI is a holding fix located at a safe position away from terrain and other aircraft.

We are in the Memphis International Airport airspace. Between 10 p.m. and 6 a.m., because it is used as a hub for FedEx and a sorting point for millions of pounds of cargo every night, Memphis becomes the busiest airport in the world. Approximately 200 planes will land, sometimes at intervals of only 45 seconds. Our position is a five-letter name called GROWI, located 17 miles from Memphis airport at 5,000 feet. Once we arrive at GOWRI, we will fly a race track pattern.

"Memphis departure, 1340 entered holding at 43 minutes past the hour at 5,000 feet."

"Roger, 1340. Keep us informed of your status. Expect 36L."

While Charlie is executing all the checklist items, I am reprogramming the flight management system and the flight control panel for an approach to runway 36L. Charlie completes the flight control malfunction checklist and provides me with a status report.

"The flaps are stuck at 15 degrees, the fuel consumption increases, the approach speed increases, the runway landing distance required for landing increases, and certain systems will be deactivated, like the auto-throttle system."

Charlie computes and completes a performance landing data card.

"You have the airplane." I give the aircraft control to Charlie. He is now flying the jet, which allows me to be a better resource manager. I brief our situation and then I brief the approach to runway 36L to Charlie.

After executing the in-range and approach checklist again, I contact Memphis approach.

"Memphis approach, 1340 is ready for the approach."

"1340, turn to a heading of 180 degrees and descend to 2,000 feet."

The clearance is acknowledged. Charlie departs the holding pattern, turns to the 180-degree heading and descends to 2,000 feet.

"1340, turn left to 090 degrees. The airport is at your ten o'clock position."

Charlie is doing a good job flying the jet. He turns the aircraft to the 90-degree heading, and I see runway 36L.

"Memphis approach, 1340 has the field in sight."

"You are cleared for the visual approach runway 36L. Contact tower on 120.9."

Charlie makes a turn to establish the final approach course, and I contact Memphis tower.

"1340, you are cleared to land runway 36L."

I acknowledge the clearance and turn to Charlie.

"I have the airplane."

Charlie was doing a great job flying the jet but as Captain, I am responsible for the safety of the jet and all souls on board. I want my hands and feet on the flight controls. I tell Charlie to extend the landing gear. I slow the aircraft to final approach speed. I disconnect the auto-throttles and autopilot, and I tell Charlie to execute the before-landing checklist.

Charlie checks that the landing lights are on, auto brakes are set, spoilers are armed, the landing gear is down and the flaps are set. Of course, I scan and verify that all those tasks are completed correctly. This jet has a radar altimeter system that measures the height above ground, and at 1,000 feet, the jet's cockpit computer calls out "1,000."

Looking outside toward the runway 36L, I notice the picture is different from what I normally see. Because of the flight control abnormality, we are landing with less than normal flaps, and we are flying at a faster approach speed. Therefore, I must maintain a higher-than-normal aircraft pitch attitude in order to fly a standard vertical flight path. To compensate for this illusion, I study the aircraft instruments and rely mostly on those instrument readings until I get within a few hundred feet above the ground. At five hundred feet above the ground, the jet's computer calls out "500."

At this elevation, it is mandatory that various performance factors be stabilized and not allowed to vary significantly. Charlie is monitoring my work. He is double-checking that the aircraft is figured correctly, the engine power setting is appropriate, the airspeed is appropriate, the vertical and lateral flight path is appropriate and that all briefings and checklists are accomplished.

He is satisfied with the results.

"Stable, cleared to land runway 36L."

I start my transition from looking mainly inside at the cockpit instruments to looking outside at the real world and the runway itself. I start increasing aileron inputs and rudder inputs to compensate for wind drift and to maintain runway alignment.

"100."

I make slight control and thrust inputs to maintain proper flight attitude and runway alignment.

"50."

I start transitioning my eyes from the target landing point to a point farther down the runway.

"40."

With my peripheral vision, I capture the ground rising. The nearness of the ground will help improve the aerodynamic efficiency of the jet.

"30."

I slowly pull back a little on the aircraft control yoke and a little on the thrust levers, just enough to decrease the rate of descent.

"20."

I am looking down the runway, slowly increasing the aircraft pitch attitude and slowly reducing the thrust power. I adjust the aileron and rudder inputs accordingly.

"10."

I maintain the landing pitch attitude while reducing the thrust power to idle. The main wheels, which are located more than 70 feet behind me, touch the runway surface. Releasing the aft yoke pressure, I lower the aircraft nose so that the nose wheel meets the runway surface.

The jet is no longer airborne.

I engage the reverse thrust; the spoilers deploy and the auto brakes engage.

The jet is slowing down.

I slow the jet to a taxi speed of around 15 knots (about 17 miles per hour) and exit the runway. I command Charlie to do the after-landing checklist, and he complies. "1340, contact ground control on 121.7," instructs Memphis tower. "Wilco. Ground control, 1340, clear of runway 36L on taxiway Mike 7."

"1340, cleared to taxi Mike, Zulu, Victor to the ramp."

We taxi to the gate, complete the shutdown checklist, and I debrief Charlie.

The aircraft mechanic approaches me.

"How's the aircraft? Any problems?"

If there were no mechanical problems to report, I sometimes jokingly respond, "Yeah, the attitude is all messed up on the captain's side. I didn't write it up. In fact, I'll take care of it myself."

No jokes this time. There was a flight control problem with the flaps, so I write up the problem in the aircraft logbook and debrief the mechanic.

Charlie and I hop on the flight crew bus, which will transport us to our flight operation center. Within the next four hours, the packages will be removed from all the arriving aircraft, re-sorted at the hub facility, and loaded back onto the appropriate departing aircraft.

On average, over 2 million packages weighing about 30 million pounds are offloaded from the fleet of FedEx planes in Memphis. About 20,000 workers and robots will remove the packages, scan each package with a bar-code label system, and re-sort the cargo through a package sorting matrix at a rate of 500,000 packages per hour.

Then, those packages will be reloaded onto the appropriate departing aircraft. The fleet of airplanes will deliver those packages to more than 220 countries and territories on six continents and every USA zip code. Within the next 24 to 48 hours, over 90 percent of the global economy will be serviced by FedEx.

The crew bus stops, and I say to the driver, "That was such a good ride, I'm coming back to get another one."

I get off the bus and walk into the flight operations crew room with over 500 pilots. Pilots are talking to pilots, telling good stories and not-so-good stories.

It always feels good to be on the ground, but particularly after you've had a challenging moment in the sky.

I believe in safety—live first. It is better to tell a bad, embarrassing story than to die and not be able to tell a story at all. As I said before, pilots can break any rule or law during an emergency to get the jet safely on the ground and save lives. I have safely landed the plane, and that is all that matters. The euphoria of conducting a safe, successful landing and the pilot chatter within the flight crew room was still bubbling up within me. Emotionally, I felt like a cool big-time pilot with a massive ego.

The "afterwards" would arrive. Those thoughts would continue to percolate: *Why did you do that? You should have done this! How come you decided to do it that way?* Those questions challenging my captain's pilot command decisions and actions would revisit me. Did I do everything right?

23

LAST FLIGHT

Fifi landed the plane.

During my 56th year, a reoccurring question entered my thoughts—*How much longer will I be doing this?* Many people choose to retire when they are very old or incapable of doing their job due to health issues. In the USA, early retirement age is 62, and the normal retirement age is 67 in order to receive Social Security. Airline pilots have a mandatory retirement age of 65. It was changed in the USA from age 60 to age 65 in 2007. Some people may have to retire at a certain age, like pilots, whereas some people will have a choice on when to retire. To retire before the age of 65 would be my choice to make, to retire at age 65 would be the federal government's choice to make. If a pilot loses his or her FAA pilot's license because of a violation or loses their FAA medical because of a disability such as cardiovascular conditions, blood pressure, cholesterol, et cetera, then the pilot may have to retire early.

You may desire to retire and struggle with when and how to retire. Some will have a choice and some will not. Once retired, what will you do? Where will you live? How will you live? How will you keep your brain sharp? Who will you socialize with? Will you have enough money? It is important to take your time in your transition to retirement life. Devise a plan, a two-year plan: one transition year prior to retirement and one transition year after retirement. For me there is no turning back; there are no redos.

One day, I was calculating the fun, money and time formula of my present life of an airline pilot. The results indicated that I was spending way too much time, having way too little fun. Commanding jets and making good money did not make up the differential. There is a point in one's life when time is more valuable than money. A point when the remaining time of your life is more important than flying jets around the world to make money. The calculation indicated I had reached that point. I still had this love of my job when I was half awake, but I did not enjoy it much when I was half asleep. Remember the "half awake, half asleep" poem? If I lose my love of flying when I am half awake, then I should retire. Another consideration is, if I no longer want the captain's responsibility, then I should retire. Well, before I get to that point, I decided to retire. The money reward was no longer worth the time reward. As I mentioned above, I may have to retire because of a loss of license or loss of medical. The decision to retire early was partially contributed to, *I want to go out on top, on my terms.*

What I'm Gonna Miss

I will miss the people and the jet. I will miss the pilots and their diverse flight personalities, our conversations and those great layover memories. Pilots congeal a special camaraderie within this unique group of professionals, and who I will miss this the most. Just flying jets is usually not enough to satisfy pilots in life; every pilot has another challenge, hobby or side gig going on in their lives. Pilots are a very interesting group of intellectual professionals.

I will also miss hand flying the jet, especially hand-flying the approach and landing of a wide-body, heavy jet. Many times, flying can be a walk in the park. There's nothing like clicking off the auto-throttles, the autopilot and the flight director to hand-fly a wide-body, heavy jet during the approach and landing. There is tremendous satisfaction in manipulating the controls of a large, sophisticated air machine to perform according to your wishes.

Usually, at least once per flight trip, I would jokingly say to the first officer during the approach to landing phase, "How's your blood pressure?" He would usually reply, "Okay" or something to that effect. At that point, I would disconnect the auto-throttles. Shortly after, I would disconnect the autopilot and ask, "How is it now?" Disconnecting the auto-throttles and autopilot triggered various responses ranging from "okay" to "it's rising." If the meteorological atmospheric conditions were favorable, then I would also disconnect the flight director as well.

Numerous first officers would nervously comment, "What are you doing?" By disconnecting these three sophisticated jet functions, I was reducing the automation capability of the jet and hand-flying the jet using raw data information. This required the utmost concentration and execution of my pilot skills. I will miss this type of hand-flying of the jet.

Yes, sometimes flying can be as easy as a walk in the park. This is especially true when there are no emergencies, no maintenance issues, no weather problems, no traffic delays, no physical or mental fatigue issues, and a whole slew of events that could or may happen. This I will not miss.

I will not miss 3:00 a.m. wakeup calls and the various flight schedules that affected my body's circadian rhythms. I will not miss flying through multiple time zones. I will not miss the extended duty nights, reroutes, diverts to another airport, and most trip revisions. The ongoing changing regulations, the CDLs, FCIFs, FOM, PHB, QRH and MEL changes. Then there's the paperwork: expense reports, incite reports, FOQA, ASAP and NASA reports. Those ongoing normal and abnormal flight operation procedure changes, and mandatory Phase One Emergency Memory procedure changes, I will not miss either.

Pilots can break any rule or law during an emergency to get the jet safely on the ground and save lives, just as Sully Sullenburger did on the NYC Hudson River. But then afterward you may have to answer the "Why did you," the "You should have" and "How comes" of your captain's pilot command decisions.

I will not miss all that is required to keep and maintain my job as mentioned in chapter 20, like the annual line checks, every six months check ride, every six months medical, and the numerous federal rules and regulations by which all pilots must abide. As previously mentioned, pilots are the most regulated professionals in the USA. Then there are the ever-changing work schedules, next month's trip pairings, deviating, dead-heading, and jump-seating. There are probably a few other things that I have already blocked out of my mind that I will not miss.

I will miss wearing the uniform, but I will not miss going to the cleaners, packing and unpacking. I will not miss studying for those rare emergencies that I hope I will never encounter—like an inflight engine fire.

I will miss all the personnel, the ramp loaders, ramp agents, mechanics, dispatchers, the weather man, the jump-seat personnel, corporate travel, and even screw—I mean crew—scheduling, the whole ALPA organization, and many other personnel that contribute to our company's flight operations. There were many good-hearted employees I have met throughout my career, and those I will especially miss.

What Am I Gonna Do?

Non-retirees question me, "What are you gonna do?" My response is, "Sleep from 10 p.m. to 6 a.m., whenever I choose, and give back." During the retirement transition year, the one year prior to retirement, I started to increase my involvement in philanthropy. This will help me stay busy, socialize and give back. Not working will provide additional time to my gardening, fishing and traveling hobbies. Instead of always reading and studying required pilot stuff, I will be able to expand my reading, researching and writing genres. More time will be available to produce pilot videos and write more books. When I look at my daily to-do list, a list that I compose the night before, I will now have the option to maybe just complete one of the to-do items on the list for the day. Switching to a routine sleep cycle, like from 10 p.m. to 6 a.m., will greatly improve my physical and mental health.

The Big Announcement

Initially, my goal was to retire at age 56, but I could not pull the lever after flying for over 30 years. It took me one full year of transition to retire before I made my big announcement: "Frank J. Donohue, AB-300 captain, seniority number 263 of approximately 4,800 pilots, will retire February 28, 2018.

My last flight was Saturday, February 17, 2018, from Baltimore, Maryland (BWI) to Memphis, Tennessee (MEM) in N744FD, an AB-300 jet. The trip started on Thursday, two days before, with a flight leg from MEM to BWI. After conferring with Derek, my first officer, that this trip would be my last trip at our company, we came to a mutual agreement that I would execute both the landings. The late afternoon landing in BWI was beautiful, enjoyable and perfect. After completing the 36-hour layover, my last layover, Saturday would be my last workday.

The early morning weather in BWI was gorgeous, but the weather in MEM was not so nice. My last takeoff was a beautiful experience; however, my last landing turned out different from I had expected.

This was the initial weather for MEM:

Pilot Raw data: KMEM 171355Z 34003 1/2SM BR OVC 005 20/19 A-2990, which means the 17th day of the month, 07:55 a.m. local time, wind 340° (west, northwest) at 3 knots, visibility 1/2 statue mile, mist clouds, overcast skies at 500 feet, temperature 20° Celsius, dew point 19° Celsius, and the barometric pressure is 29.90 in Hg.

The plan I had discussed with Derek was that I would fly an ILS approach, see the runway, kick off the autopilot and make my last landing manually. As we entered the airport environment, the weather report changed to:

1/2SM R36C/P6000FT FG BKN004

Notice the letter R in front of runway 36C. At airports (usually the big airports) that have Runway Visual Range (RVR) sensing equipment, the RVR is reported when the visibility is one mile or less. RVR is the measurement of the horizontal distance the pilot can expect to see a distinctive visual contrast, like the High-Intensity Runway Lights, on the runway. The letter "R" indicates RVR is being reported for runway 36C. The RVR is 6,000 feet, and the "P" means it is above the highest reported sensor. Also, fog is now present with the ceiling broken at 400 feet above ground.

As I mentioned, I was planning on flying an ILS approach, see the runway, kick off the autopilot and make my last landing manually, but now I was thinking about conducting a Coupled Autoland approach. All of a sudden, we received a special weather report:

Special 1/2SM R36C/3000V5000FT FG BKN003 14/14.

As mentioned earlier, special weather reports are issued when a significant change has occurred. In this weather report, the visibility has significantly deteriorated to 3,000 feet variable to 5,000 feet and the ceiling changed to 300 feet broken.

An Autoland is a specialized system that fully automates the landing procedure of the jet while the pilots monitor the process. The airport, the runway, the jet and the flight crew must be certified to conduct Autoland approaches. The next weather report read:

1/4SM R36C/1600FT FG OVC0003.

The RVR visibility was dropping from 3,000 to 1600 feet and the sky is now 300 feet overcast. The weather continued to get worse as we jetted closer to Memphis. With this report an Autoland approach to landing is recommended. If the visibility is reported at 1200 RVR or less, then an Autoland is mandatory.

Landing minimums is determined from the most restrictive of: the airport certified lowest landing minimums, the jet certified lowest landing minimum, and the crew (mainly the captain) authorized lowest landing minimum. The visibility landing minimums for MEM 36C, the AB-300 jet and I are the RVRs of 300, 300 and 300 feet (that equates to 75 meters for international airports). The three readings are for touchdown, midfield and rollout, located respectively along the landing runway.

Fifi Did My Last Landing

Derek speaks, "In range checklist complete weather is now: 1/4SM R36C/1400FT FG BKN002, the RVRs are dropping."

Although the RVR was still above the 1200 feet, the visibility that a mandatory Autoland must be conducted, I made a command decision that we would conduct an Autoland approach. Part of my thinking was, I did not want to execute a missed approach if the weather drops below landing minimums and then have to fly to another airport to land. The landing minimums are higher for a pilot executing a manual landing with the autopilot disconnected versus a pilot executing an Autoland with the autopilots engaged. My plans included landing in Memphis and taking a commercial flight home. This Autoland approach attempt may be my only chance to get in before the weather gets worse, and I will not be able to land in Memphis.

We set up for the Autoland procedure, as I briefed the procedure. All special procedures must be briefed. Go figure. I have made over 900 landings in the AB-300, but my last landing will not be made by me; it will be made by Fifi, the wide-body, heavy AB-300 jet. Fifi, with its sophisticated automation and autopilots engaged, will make the last landing for me.

Derek says, "The approach checklist is complete, the weather is now: 1/4SM R36C/M."

The "M" means the weather is measured at less than the reported sensor.

I command, "Slats/flaps 15'/0'" and he moves the handle. We are handed over to approach control." The ATC controller directs me to turn base and says, "36C RVR 1,200, 1200 and 1,000." I command, "Flaps 20." The visibility is so low that only the RVRs are reported to us. The controller gives us a turn to intercept final and says, "You are cleared for the 36C approach, RVR now 1,000/1,000/800." Flaps 20 is selected, Land mode is engaged, the second autopilot is engaged and the Autoland lite is tested. Autoland requires two working autopilots engaged. Derek says, "LOC Star."

I say, "Set runway heading."

He says, "Glide Slope star."

"Set missed approach attitude." We intercept and get the jet established on the final approach for 36C. I command, "Gear down, flaps 40, landing checklist." All of this the first officer does.

At 1,000 feet, Derek says, "Stable," confirming the jet is being flown within all the parameters required by law for the Autoland CAT III instrument approach. ATC says, "You are cleared to land, RVR now 800/800/600." Derek says, "Cleared to land." At 150 feet above minimums—the point at which the captain decides to land or go-around— Derek says, "Approaching alert height." If I see the approach lights I will say, "Approach lights"; however, I may only see the touchdown zone lights, and I am not required to see the runway to land.

REPEAT: I AM NOT REQUIRED TO SEE THE RUNWAY TO LAND DURING AN AUTOLAND APPROACH WITH AN ALERT HEIGHT! The only time I am required to see the runway to land during an Autoland procedure is if there is clutter on the runway, like snow- or ice-covered runways. If there is clutter on the runway, then I am required to see the runway by at least 50 feet above the runway in order for me to continue and land. Otherwise, I am not required to see the runway to land during and Autoland procedure.

Imagine you are on the fifth floor of a building looking at the ground and moving at a 150 miles per hour. At 150 miles per hour, at 50 feet above the runway, the captain must see the runway and decide if a safe landing can be accomplished or if a go-around must be executed. There is a great trust in the runway equipment, the airplane automation and pilot skills. If all or anything of the automation fails then the pilot will have to take over and fly the jet.

At the Alert Height, Derek says, "Minimums."

At 50 feet above the ground going almost 150 mph I must make a decision. I say, "Landing." The wide body Airbus A-300 automatically pitches the nose up, reduces the thrust levers, flares and lands the jet. My hands, feet and eyes are following the controls just like that first Cessna C-150 observation flight with my flight instructor performing the landing. Fifi landed the jet! I taxied Fifi to the gate, parked her and shut down her engines for the last time. Our divorce was final.

She and I would not be together anymore. She will not surround me and I would not be in her. We would not touch each other again. There is no unfinished emotional business between us. If Fifi is in the air with another pilot, I may look up at her, reminisce and crack an uncontrollable, pleasant smile. Memories of her and I in the air together may revisit me, but we will never be together again. Although I may embrace the past experience of Fifi with positive emotions, I am at peace with our permanent separation. I have accepted that I will no longer be consumed with those feeling of my old life with her, and I feel a sense of joy welcoming the oncoming changes of retirement life without her. We have accomplished emotional closure; this was an amicable divorce.

Today, most modern jets are equipped with Head-Up Display (HUD). A HUD is a see-through display of key flight instrument data in the cockpit. The HUD is positioned directly in the pilot's line of sight of their external forward vision. The HUD helps the pilot in the transition from controlling the plane from reference of internal aircraft instrument data, to controlling the aircraft from reference of external visual data. Military jet pilots have used HUDs for many years, and in recent years, civilian commercial pilots have adopted the use of this sophisticated technology.

I Tried to Sneak Out.

The best plans do not always work out, as mentioned above with the unplanned Autoland. One of my plans was to avoid the last flight car wash known as the "water salute." A water salute is a token of respect for ceremonial purposes to mark the retirement of a senior pilot and other notable events. When a pilot makes his final flight, the plane is honored with the water salute once it lands on the tarmac. An even number of fire trucks line up, and as the plane taxis between them, the truck's water cannons spray plumes of water like a wedding arch onto the plane. The plan to avoid this was successful—I was attempting to sneak out.

There is a retirement crew lounge "sendoff" ceremony, which included a scrumptious cake, a retirement package, pilot friends and family if requested, and several blustery speeches about me. As part of my sneak plan, I avoided this too. My plan was to sneak out unexpectedly, on a weekend when many others were not around, ten days before the end of the month. Usually, the fewest pilots are in the crew flight operations room on Saturday mornings. Loads of pilots and other non-pilot employees knew I was retiring at the end of the month. They did not know that February 18 would be my last flight. I was trying to sneak out, but the best plans do not always work out the way you want. Other than the unplanned Autoland, everything was going according to plan. Fifi landed the plane, I taxied in, parked the plane, shut down the engines and turned in the flight's paperwork. All I had to do is vacate the premises.

The chief pilot of all 4,800 pilots, Rob Disher, was speaking to a pilot new-hire class of 30 in the crew flight operations room. Rob is only five foot, six inches with a magnetic, attractive, boyish, smiley face. He always looked many years younger than his actual age. The first time Rob flew with me, he was in his 20s and could have easily passed for a teenage Romeo.

Years ago, in 1987, when I started flying jet airplanes, the cockpits required three crewmembers—a captain, a first officer and a second officer, also known as a flight engineer. The pilot industry is a small group of professionals. In 1987, there were only about 60,000 airline transport pilots in the USA. Today there are only around 160,000 active airline transport pilots in the USA. Many times as the flight engineer, I would say to the captain, "Be good to the flight engineer, because today's engineer could be tomorrow's chief pilot." This statement became a reality with Rob Disher and me.

Rob and I flew together on the B-727. Initially, he was a new hire during initial operating experience training on my flight that I commanded as a captain. We flew together several other times after he was fully checked out as a flight engineer on the B-727. During my 30-plus-year career, Rob climbed the ranks from B-727 Second Officer to chief pilot of all the pilots at our company. Our company has many chief pilots of various jet types, but there is only one grand chief pilot of all of them, and that is Rob. I never had a desire to become an airline flight instructor, chief pilot or any other pilot management position; I just wanted to fly the jet. *Be good to the flight engineer, because today's engineer could be tomorrow's chief pilot.* "Be nice to people on the way up because you'll meet them on your way down." –Wilson Mizner (featured in: Wilson Mizner Quotes). Rob was once my flight engineer and became my chief pilot.

Rob and a brand-new pilot new-hire class were positioned between the exit door and me. "Good morning, Rob." I saluted.

He responded, "Hi, Frank, are you on your way home?"

Without thinking, I spoke fast and subconsciously. "Yeah, I just finished my last flight," I responded.

"Your last flight for the month?" he inquired.

Always tell the truth, especially to the chief pilot. There are no cover-ups in aviation; the truth always emerges, eventually. Without reasoning, I blurted, "That was my last flight at FedEx."

Looking puzzled, Rob questioned, "No, you're kidding me! I didn't know. I must have missed the memo on the planned "water salute" and retirement party?"

I thought, *I tried to sneak out.* The Chief Pilot of all the 4,800 pilots leaned forward and gave me a big congratulations hug and said, "I will miss you."

This moment seemed like the scene near the end in the *Wizard of Oz* movie—the scene when the Scarecrow was giving Dorothy a great big sentimental hug, just before Dorothy was to return home to Kansas in a hot-air balloon. Dorothy was crying, and Frank the Pilot, a big-time cool American pilot with a massive ego, was starting to lose control. Frank had flown jets all over the world, flown in some of the worst weather, handled many abnormal and emergency flight events, landed and departed in the most terrible weather, executed many CAT III Autolands to minimums, flown fatigued, and many other pilot stuff. He has fought all forces to command the jet safely, legally, efficiently and reliably. The public, other employees and even some first officers at times, viewed him as godlike. Frank the Pilot is not godlike; he is human with human emotions. Trying not to choke up, as I was fighting to stop the tears from dripping out of my eyes, I begged Rob, "Don't make me cry!"

"Rob, I enjoyed flying with you years ago, and thank you for your much-appreciated chief pilot service."

Rob closed with, "Thank you, Frank, I will miss you."

Reflections

I scurried out the door, jumped on the crew bus, rode to the passenger terminal located on the other side of the airport, replaced the top half of my uniform with civilian clothing, entered the first airport bar and ordered a cold beer. Before I scooted out of the pilot crew room, I grabbed my retirement package from the pilot management administration office. Usually, this package is given to the retiring pilot during his retirement ceremony, but I was not going to attend that ritual, so I retrieved my mystery package.

My first thoughts were, *What did I just do?* Like a mother giving her baby up for adoption, I experienced emotions of relief, acceptance and gratitude while also feeling loss and regret. The decision to retire was made by me, 12 months ago and these 12 months were utilized to help me transition to today—retirement day. Maybe I was not prepared and I needed more transition time to retire. Doubts and second thoughts ping-ponged the edges of my brain waves.

The second cold beer arrived as I opened the package. In my hands, a prestigious pilot award plaque read: "*Captain Frank J. Donohue, #96846, Seniority #263 July 6, 1987 – February 28, 2018. Thank you on behalf of FedEx and Flying Tigers for over 30 years and 8,600 flight hours of impeccable service. Your dedication and commitment to the purple promise played a pivotal role in building the most successful transportation company worldwide. Congratulations on this very important milestone and may you always enjoy tailwinds.*" A welcoming, warm feeling within me triggered a glowing facial expression. Although I did not see my face, I knew I was smiling bigly for the whole world to see. I did it! I conquered all those challenges to complete an airline career. My seasoned massive ego had succumbed toward this euphoric feeling of gratitude, accomplishment and acceptance. My feelings were like Commander Neil Armstrong landing on the moon and returning home. He, like I, worked so hard to accomplish the ultimate goal and now we were headed home. These emotions stirred within me like a tornado, but a friendly tornado of wanted feelings, as I read the plaque again.

8,600 hours, I asked myself. Those 8,600 flight hours are misleading, because most of my flights were short flights, less than 90 minutes—there are over 6,000 landings attached to those flight hours. If those landings were attached to long international flights, then I would have racked up over 20,000 flight hours.

FedEx delivers over 6 million packages daily to over 240 countries and to every zip code in the United States. Packages are routinely delivered on time more than 98% of the time. Flying remains the safest form of transportation in the USA. I like to say I did my part to contribute to my company's success and that safety record.

Thank You

Retiring from my airline pilot career was a very important milestone for me. In that recognition, I proclaim, "*Thank you for giving me the opportunity in playing a pivotal role in building the most successful transportation company worldwide. Thank you to all the diverse professional pilots for great memories and your contributions to all those safe and legal flights. Thank you to all other personnel for your participation to the reliability and efficiency of the flight operations. I have enjoyed many blessings and tailwinds in my worldly flight career! And I am very thankful for that!*

24

FedEx Frank

Time becomes more valuable than money.

There is a time in one's life when time becomes more valuable than money. That time and my time has arrived. The cool big-time pilot with a massive ego has come to rest on planet Earth. That person no longer exists. A life time of experiences had transformed this person. This person is teeming with gratitude and humility. He is generous with his special gifts and talents in helping those in need. He has become a philanthropist. The long journey from there to here is filled with valuable information for the reader. To help you remember and to recommend to others, here is what happened.

Summary

At a young age, Frank discovered the use of ground transportation machines such as bikes, boats and cars, which enabled him to travel. His love for travel started at a young age. While traveling across the United States of America, he became curious about the life of a pilot. He enlists in the USAF as means to travel. While in England, Frank takes a discovery flight, gets hooked on flying, and makes plans to become a pilot. He describes his thoughts and emotions about flying a plane all by himself—his first solo flight. This major accomplishment forms an image of a cool, big-time pilot with a massive ego. This image comes and goes throughout his flight career.

Frank discusses the challenges of acquiring a private pilot's license. He reveals his thinking and emotions during the private pilot exam. The newly acquired pilot license is a license for him to learn and to develop into a seasoned pilot. Frank enrolls in college aviation classes, learns basic instrument flying and begins his journey toward a pilot career.

While trying to do almost anything to build up flight time, Frank gets himself into trouble. Frank leaves England and travels across the USA. He describes the beauty of California and flying. After serving in the USAF, Frank undertakes an aggressive college schedule and graduates from ERAU.

At 24 years old, four years after his first flight, he finally gets his first pilot job. He discusses the responsibility and the psychological effects of teaching college students to fly planes by themselves.

Frank explains how the banner-tow operation works and encounters his first pilot emergency—smoke in the cockpit. He leaves his first well-paying, stable job to find another job to help advance his career. Frank discusses the pilot experiences that mold him into an experienced captain pilot. He puts the reader into his cockpit seat during an almost career-ending emergency. Frank accepts another pilot job, his fourth within two years. He talks about flying passengers and a dangerous turbulent thunderstorm approach. He takes the reader behind the scenes of the airline pilot interview.

After six years in pursuit of his ultimate goal, Frank secures a pilot position at Flying Tigers. He discusses the history of the Flying Tigers and the Airline Pilots Association. Frank takes the reader with him on a fantastic journey around the world. He provides information on the largest airplane in the world, world travels and the experience of the most famous and dangerous Hong Kong checkerboard approach.

Frank gives the reader of view of the life of a pilot by discussing how plane crashes and major life changes can affect both work and personal life.

Frank becomes a jet pilot and provides a view into the mind of a first officer flying jets and flying for fun. He becomes a jet captain and details the responsibilities of an airline captain. Frank avoids a potential catastrophe with a landing gear problem on the B-727. The ongoing challenges a pilot endures in order to maintain flight status and keep his job are revealed. Frank almost gets fired from a sleeping incident.

The reader experiences the thoughts and emotions of the captain during a dangerous wind shear approach in a big, wide-body jet. A personal connection is made with the jet. The reader sits in the cockpit seat during a step-by-step story with Frank the pilot on the almost perfect flight. Finally, the reader joins Frank on his last flight, with a pre-planned exit strategy. His plans didn't always work out and sometimes the plane must land itself.

Dreams are important. Frank discusses his dreams of traveling, of becoming a pilot, of becoming an airline pilot, of a beautiful female flight instructor, of his solo students crashing into the ocean and of a nearly fatal choking incident. Years later, after retirement, nightmare dreams of failing a medical exam, failing a flight check ride, missing a trip causing employment termination, and a major flight emergency without a first officer onboard occur from time to time. Convincing nightmare dreams to transition to the awake life that Frank is retired, is a challenge, at times. Time has helped him overcome this.

These are some of Frank's one-liners weaved throughout the book:

- *Always remember and you'll never forget.*
- *Safety—live first! It is better to tell a bad, embarrassing story than to die and not be able to tell a story at all.*
- *Doing better than most but not as good as some.*
- *Learn from that mistake and don't make the same mistake twice.*
- *We make our money above planet Earth, and it is serious business.*
- *You know, you just can't pull over to a cloud and check the oil.*
- *When you get up there, don't forget to land.*
- *I have Yank and Bank school* (six-month flight simulator training school).
- *Today's second officer may be tomorrow's chief pilot.*
- *A cool big-time pilot with a massive ego.*
- *Enjoy the day, if not the night.*
- *Fly safely. Be safe and legal, then efficient and reliable.*
- *Going 600 mph.*
- *Always tell the truth.*
- *The attitude in the left seat is all screwed up.*
- *After now and before later.*

The Gouge. The inside information and secret sauce, known as "the gouge" is to provide valuable lessons learned with a few calls-to-action dotted here and there. There is so much to unpack here. These are "the gouge" Cliff Notes.

Be confident in yourself and invest in yourself. Go for it. Be proactive when advancing your career. Study to be prepared to be the best at your job. Set up a weekly or at least a monthly schedule to study. Work to improve on your weak skills while maintaining the strength of your strong skills. Learn from mentors. Keep a notebook and record your learnings from your mentors. Learn from mistakes others have made and from mistakes you have made.

When trying to learn something complicated, break it down into small pieces. Master the small pieces, and put all the pieces together. Make your own index cards, gouge list and checklist. Pilots have used checklists for years, and now doctors use checklists for surgery. Instructors should strive to be flexible and imaginative with their teaching techniques because students learn in different ways and at different rates.

One of the calls-to-action is to make a flight plan for life. Even if you do not want to be a pilot, make a plan. Compose short-term, medium-term and long-term goals for yourself. Develop a plan to achieve those goals and execute the plan. Devise a career plan: how to acquire that ultimate career position and how to keep that position. It is amazing the many diverse paths each pilot wannabe pursued to become a pilot. Each of us travels different paths in life. Have a backup plan. Also, develop a plan to maintain a healthy mental and physical lifestyle.

Do not let stress enter your work environment. Leave non-work issues at home, and learn to compartmentalize in order to perform the best at your work task. Just as pilots utilize their crew resource management skills, strive to get along with your co-workers. Don't let your ego get you into trouble. No one is above the law. When advancing your career, stay safe and legal. Admit when you are wrong, and always tell the truth.

Pilots: aim to be safe and legal. Always look for potential flight threats. Just when you think flying is as easy as a walk in the park, an emergency can occur. If something does not look or feel right, then execute a go-around, get out of there and go someplace else with more favorable conditions. If you feel uncomfortable with the flight situation, even if you are not the captain, speak up assertively. All that hard work to get that pilot job could get washed down the drain with one bad flight emergency. Pilots have died making an incorrect decision during pilot emergencies. There is always risk in aviation. Ignore your big ego and make good, safe pilot decisions. Do not make impulsive decisions; think before you act. Block out what others may think about you or the possible consequences of your actions, and land the plane safely. *It is better to tell a bad, embarrassing story, than to die and not be able to tell a story at all.*

Captains: customize your briefings and have a short backup statement to cover everything. My short backup statement is: *"At the minimum, in an emergency, we want to do the emergency checklist items, get the landing gear down, and land. Safety and legality are mandatory; our goal is also to be reliable and efficient, but it's optional."*

Flying is precious, delicate, valuable and unpredictable—savor each flight because one day it may be your last. Commanding airplanes in the atmosphere above planet Earth is a special privilege. Enjoy every moment of flight because you do not know when your last moment of flying will be.

Passengers: wear your seat belt in flight, thank the pilots for their expert pilot skills and critical decision-making skills, and for getting you to your destination safely.

My first taste of pilot camaraderie occurred at ERAU with 50 other flight instructors. At Midnight Express, a bond formed within the small ten-pilot group. There is widespread pilot camaraderie at Atlantic Southeast Airlines, but my time there was short-lived. With only a hundred days of employment, my pilot camaraderie experience was limited at ASA. The strongest, most-memorable pilot camaraderie was formed at Flying Tigers, especially during those ten-day trips around the world. My most widespread and long-lasting pilot camaraderie bond formed through my 30-year flight career at FedEx.

There is life after a flight career. I have joined a secretive male pilot club. The club started a long-time ago as an aviator's drinking club and has spread throughout the USA and other countries. Members must be invited to join, and they join for life. The members are boisterous and consist of all kinds of pilots: private, commercial, airline, civilian, military and freight pilots, as well as a few astronauts. The club has no constitution, by-laws, dues, assessments or club officers. There is no business or sale conducted at these gatherings, just pilots talking pilot talk to other pilots. A new pilot camaraderie is forming for me and growing in strength. This new group of pilot friends call me FedEx Frank, my fifth call sign. From Frank the Yank, to Frank the pilot, to Seagull, to Fast Frank and now FedEx Frank. New pilot stories from these pilots are developing.

Last Words

Pilots have a unique skill set that might prove valuable. It's in that spirit that I share these reflections on a host of pilot stories in hopes that it helps provide the reader with a view into the mind and emotions of an experienced pilot. A pilot encounters many emotional swings during his career, similar to the emotional swings pregnant women encounter with their elevated hormones. During normal, abnormal and emergency flight operations, there is a tremendous amount of thinking going on, and it is after the fact, when most pilots reflect on what has happened, that emotions kick in. These emotions affect the personal and family life of a pilot.

These are the questions I attempted to answer: What goes on in the cockpit? What is the human nature of pilot errors? How does the pilot's job affect the passengers? How do pilot mistakes affect passengers' safety? Throughout my career, I tried my best but I have made mistakes, and you have read what has happened. Flying with the mindset of safety, legality, efficiency and reliability are entwined into the fabric of numerous pilot stories throughout this read. The laws of aviation, and how maintenance, weather, human error, federal rules and regulations, and medical health are factors affecting pilot operations were discussed. Throughout my pilot career, I have learned to respect these laws.

My vision is to provide some details of my career as a pilot and put the reader in my pilot's seat to experience what Frank the Pilot was thinking and feeling. This is an opportunity for an experienced pilot to share some lessons and suggest how they might apply to the lives of others. It's my hope that this book enlightened the reader on what I accomplished, who I am, and how the lessons I learned as a pilot might help you improve your life.

The multiple interesting pilot stories attempted to transport you and evoke emotion by revealing what happened, where and when it happened; who was involved; why it happened, and most importantly, how it affected Frank the Pilot. There are many more pilot stories that are not included in this book, but these stories were presented to you to provide you with a window into the mind and emotions of an airline pilot. The gouge is provided for your benefit. My hopes are to leave you with a sense of longing for more.

One of the goals of this book is to inspire and motivate people to pursue their dream career. Many of the lessons of how I became a pilot can help others in the pursuit of their ultimate career position. Pilots are an elite group of professionals. When equipment malfunctions occur or when the visibility is near zero, it takes a certain toughness and point of view to keep things together and maintain control. Flying remains the safest form of transportation in the USA. Flying for a living is a cool, elite and prestigious professional career. Even though becoming a pilot and maintaining pilot status is very hard work, an airline career was great for me, and I recommend it to you.

I have arrived at that point when time has become more valuable than money. Here, I leave you with these last words.

Pilots make their money above planet Earth and it is serious business. If something goes wrong up there, the pilot cannot just pull over to a cloud and check the oil. At the minimum, in an emergency, pilots should do the emergency checklist items, get the landing gear down, and land. Safety and legality are mandatory. We have other goals, like to operate reliably and efficiently, but it's optional!

Safety—live first!

It is better to tell a bad, embarrassing story then to die and not be able to tell a story at all!

Fly safely!

Enjoy the day, if not the night!

In the works: Frank the Pilot's non-pilot stories with people while practicing philanthropy.

BONUS

FREE DOWNLOAD

TEN HEALTHY TIPS

PDF/POSTER

Visit

www.FrankJDonohue.com/tenhealthytips

to download the bonus

Ten Healthy Tips book

Acknowledgments

I like to thank Steven W. Rodgers for his excellent help in editing and shaping the finished product. I'd also like to thank Adrian, Dane and John Low of Ebook Launch, as well as their helpers Darya and Alisha, for their expertise in graphic book design, proofreading and book formatting. To a very successful author Wes Oleszewski, thank you for writing the foreword. Matt Sudik rose to the occasion when I needed a side-by-side photo of a Cessna C-150 plane parked next to a Tesla 3 car. Thank you, Matt, for flying the C-150 airplane to Hampton Roads Executive Airport for the photo shoot. To the over 1,000 pilots I have flown with, who have shaped my pilot personality and influenced the pilot I have become, I thank you for those safe flights and experiences. I thank my mother and father for having and raising me, my loving wife and God for giving me the precious opportunity to be a father. To my sons, who have inspired me to write this book, I wish the best of all good things to come to you in this earthly life and the life after.

Website- www.frankjdonohue.com

Bibliography

1. David McCullough, *The Wright Brothers* (New York: Simon and Schuster, 2015).
2. "Aircraft Data and History," *Airliners*. Last modified March 5, 2008. http://.airliners.net/aircraft-data/stats.html. Dec 15, 2011.
3. Marsh, Harry. *Borough of St. Edmundsbury: Official Guide*. Norwich: St. Edmundsbury Borough Council, 1976.
4. See note 2 above.
5. "Space Shuttle Missions," *NASA*. http://.nasa.gov/mission-pages/shuttle/launch.html (accessed Jan. 3, 2012).
6. https://www.goodreads.com/quotes/127360-if-we-all-threw-our-problems-in-a-pile-and).
7. McCullough, David, *The Wright Brothers* Simon and Schuster, 2015 (page 10).
8. See note 2 above.
9. "Glaze and Black Ice," *Weather Online*. http:/www.weatheronline.co.uk/reports/wxfacts/
1. Glaze-and-Black-Ice.html (accessed March 29, 2012).
10. https://oldcc.gov/project/mcclellan-air-force-base-colorado-previously-single-largest-industrial-facility-northern) (accessed June 2, 2021).
11. Https://www.afcec.af.mil/Home/BRAC/McClellan-AFB/History/ (accessed June 2, 2021).
12. Hugh Ross, *Why the Universe is the Way it is* (Grand Rapids: Baker Books, 2010) 507-508
13. Ibid. 48.

14. "The Embry-Riddle Story," *Embry-Riddle Aeronautical University*. http://erau.edu/about/ story.html (accessed March 21, 2013).

15. 12. Dunn, Marcia "Challenger: 25 Years Later, a Still Painful Wound," *The Associated Press*. 2011. http://community.statesmanjournal.com/blogs/science/2011/01/28/challenger-25-years-later-a-still-painful-wound/.html.

16. Ibid.

2. 17 "NTSB Identification: MIA85LKG01" *National Transportation Safety Board*. NTSB microfiche number 29830. http://ntsb.gov/aviationquery/brief.aspx?ev_id= 20001214X36273&key= 1.html (accessed March 20, 2013).

17. See note 2 above.

18. Wood, Charles. "The Instrument Landing System," *Navflight*, 2008. http://navfltsm.addr.com./ils.htm.

19. See note 2 above.

20. *Flying Tigers 1945–1989*, Lost Angeles: Ashbrook and Wacker, 1989.

21. "History of Flying Tiger Aircraft," *Flying Tiger Line Pilots Association*. http://.flyingtigerline.org/history.html (accessed March 21, 2012)

22. "A History of Pride: 80 Years of Pilots Putting Safety and Security First," *Air Line Pilots Association, International*, 2011, 7, http://cf.alpa.org/internet/accomplishments/safety/1930.html

23. Hopkins, George. *Flying the Line*. Washington D.C.: The Air Line Pilots Association, International, 1982.

24. "Code of Ethics," *Air Line Pilots Association, International*. http://alpa.org/ethics/WhoWeAre/CodeofEthics/tabid/2262/Default.aspx.html (accessed January 08, 2022)

25. Ibid.

26. Dominick A Pisano and F. Robert Van Der Linden, *Charles Lindbergh and the Spirit of St. Louis* (New York: Harry N. Abrams Inc., 2002) 66-69.

27. See not 2 above.

28. "NSTB Investigation: AAR-89-04, NTIS: PB89-910406," *National Transportation Safety Board.* http://ntsb.gov/investigations/reports_aviation.html

29. https://www.google.com/search?client=firefox-b-1-d&q=what+is+crew+resource+management (accessed June 21, 2021)

30. "Frederick W. Smith," *Academy of Achievement.* Last modified January 9, 2008. http://achievement.org/autodoc/page/smi0bio-1.html.

31. Greene, Meg "Fred Smith 1944-Biograhy*," Reference for Business.* http://referenceforbusiness.com/biography/S-Z/Smith-Fred-1944.html (accessed April 4, 2012).

32. https://calaero.edu/propeller-versus-jet-propulsion/ California Aeronautical University (accessed June 22, 2021)

33. See note 2 above.

34. "The Labor Movement in America," *Social Studies Help Center.* Last modified March 22, 2013.http://socialstudieshelp.com/Eco_Unionization.htm

35. Ibid.

36. "FedEx Pilot History*," ALPA FedEx MEC.* http://crewroom.alpa.org/fdx/DesktopModules/ViewDocumentaspx?DocumentID=19085.html (accessed July 1, 2012)

3. This material is used with the permission of ALPA FedEx MEC secretary-treasurer.

37. U.S. Department of Federal Aviation Administration. *Electronic Code of the Federal Aviation Regulations.* Washington DC: US Government Printing Office, 2012. http://eecfr.gov/cgr-bin/text.html.

38. Ibid.

39. Ibid.

40. See note 2 above.

41. https://www.vaisala.com/sites/default/files/documents/Windshear-white-paper-300609-Lowres.pdf (accessed June 7, 2021).

About The Author

Frank J. Donohue, born in New York, is an American pilot, author, publisher and video producer. He earned his bachelor's degree and several pilot licenses at Embry-Riddle Aeronautical University after serving one tour of duty in the United States Air Force. Frank holds the Airline Transport Pilot license, Flight Instructor license, Advanced and Instrument Ground Instructor licenses, Flight Engineer License, Aircraft Dispatcher license and Remote Pilot Certificate. With over 36 years of flying experience, Frank received a prestigious pilot award for over 30 years of impeccable service for a very distinguished career of flying excellence with FedEx in 2018.

Frank is the author of *School and Schooled*, #1 Bestselling author of *Ten Healthy Tips* and author of *From Hate to Love*. Frank is the owner and creator of NOT-Y a pilot video channel featuring pilot flight and non-flight stories. Frank lives in Virginia Beach with his wife. They have two grown children. He enjoys traveling, gardening, fishing and helping people through various philanthropic organizations.

Author's Note

Frank the Pilot was written, designed, produced and published by its author to the same high standards as the mainstream publishing industry. It is really hard to put a good book together. I invite you to post an honest and objective review of this book in the online bookstore of your choice. Your comments will help improve the quality of what good writers write and what good readers read. Thank you for your time and service. You can contact Frank J. Donohue on FB, LinkedIn, Twitter and Instagram and visit his websites:www.frankjdonohue.com, and www.not-y.com.

End of book

"You just can't pull over to a cloud and check the oil..."

Fasten your seat belt and soar around the globe—with a view from the cockpit...

Captain Frank Donohue takes readers on a remarkable, behind-the-scenes journey of the making of an airline pilot—revealing the ups and downs of each flight. He shares the one thing that sparked his interest in becoming a pilot, the challenge of obtaining a license, and the career path that nearly took a nosedive. Now, with over three decades of flying experience, Frank gives others the opportunity to see the world from the cockpit—and a guide to life in the skies.

Whether you're a pilot, aspiring to become one...or prefer your passenger status, Frank gives a vivid firsthand account of the *not*-so-glamorous side of flying. Pilots must make quick, intense decisions, and Frank shares impressive details of the time he faced a mechanical emergency, circumnavigating the globe, and a hair-raising wind-shear landing. Each story gives readers a unique perspective—and an adventure one can only witness while *flying* with Frank.

I began to feel the increased heart rate and sweaty palms each time he describes a scenario...great book and stories about "flying the line." —Robert Fogelsanger, FedEx B-777 First Officer

To the public, it gracefully translates the aviation lingo into an idiom, which makes you understand the world of flying and the reasoning behind pilots' decisions. —Captain Joey Uliana, Pilot

Frank J. Donohue is a retired airline captain, with 36 years' flight experience, 7 FAA licenses, an ERAU BS Aeronautical Science degree, and author of four books. Frank and his wife live in Virginia Beach. They have two grown children. *Getting there was so hard; staying there was harder.*

Memoir/Self Help
Not-Y Publishing

Soft cover $19.91